CRISES IN THE COCKPIT

CRISES IN THE COCKPIT

Edited by Norbert Slepyan

Foreword by Edward G. Tripp

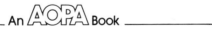

An AOPA Book

AN ELEANOR FRIEDE BOOK

Macmillan Publishing Company · New York

Collier Macmillan Publishers · London

Macmillan Publishing Company
866 Third Avenue, New York, N.Y. 10022
Collier Macmillan Canada, Inc.

Library of Congress Cataloging in Publication Data
Main entry under title:
Crises in the cockpit.
''An AOPA book.''
''An Eleanor Friede book.''
Includes index.
1. Airplanes—Piloting.
I. Slepyan, Norbert.
TL710.C75   1986   629.132′5214   85-19844
ISBN 0-02-611500-X

Macmillan books are available at special discounts for bulk purchases
for sales promotions, premiums, fund-raising, or educational use.
For details, contact:
Special Sales Director
Macmillan Publishing Company
866 Third Avenue
New York, N.Y. 10022

10 9 8 7 6 5 4 3 2 1
Designed by Jack Meserole

Printed in the United States of America

CONTENTS

ACKNOWLEDGMENTS

From the pages of *AOPA Pilot*, the following contributors are acknowledged with thanks:

Frank P. Bacci
T. L. Barber
David Bielefeld
W. G. Bradley
Terrence A. Brock
Robert Christian
Harlan R. Davis
John V. Dean
Tom Eggleston
Robert W. Ehrlich
Chuck Filippi
Ken Gardner
A. C. Grimes
Robert Harrison
Thomas A. Horne
Tom Jones

Mark M. Lacagnina
Burnard McHone
Paul A. Mickey
J. Jefferson Miller
Larry Ostby
John C. Pickels
Jeff Richmond
Roger Rozelle
Jerry D. Sanders
Mary F. Silitch
Dennis L. Stockdale
Robert T. Styer
Steve Widmer
David G. Wood
Rogers H. Wright

FOREWORD

Pilots are divided or segregated in an almost infinite number of ways. Pilots themselves are frequently responsible, separating themselves from others based on a self-constructed image of worth or importance. Their definitions usually bestow some special place or value on their activities and consign all others to some inferior plateau of the pecking order. There are pleasure pilots and those who fly for a paycheck; tail dragger pilots and spam can drivers; pilots of single-engine aircraft and multi-engine ones, or piston engine versus turbine.

Most of us, however, find the breadth and variety of uses and types of aircraft fascinating and dream that eventually we can experience all forms of flight.

There is one crucial distinction among pilots, however, and that is what this book is all about. That distinction is between those who think they know it all, and those who think there will always be more to learn, that each flight is a new adventure and experience to add to their store of information and a building block in their skill.

There is a surprising stock of aviation how-to books. Most are eagerly devoured by the learners—who range in experience from those who want to learn to fly to those with tens of thousands of hours and the humility gained by experience that leads them to learn more.

Some of these books are classics, read and reread by pilots of all kinds for the wisdom they contain. Far too many, however, are not worth the time it takes to read them; they add nothing to our body of knowledge. Many employ dry theory unleavened by experience or postulate rote practice not tested in the dynamic circumstances of flight.

Quite a few books on the currently available list are compilations of, or merely reprints of, magazine articles. That is not to say that some are not of value, even if they serve only to gather together interesting or useful articles scattered through years of magazines.

Crises in the Cockpit began as just such a publishing exercise. It was intended to combine the real-life experiences, the successful decisions made and actions taken in real-life emergencies and the lessons to be drawn for all pilots, from the popular "Never Again" series that has appeared in *AOPA Pilot* for dozens of years.

Had we done so, the book would have had value and would have successfully responded to the requests of many pilots to locate the hundreds of experiences in one convenient book.

However, there was considerably more real-time and real-life experience to be gained from *AOPA Pilot* beyond "Never Again"—not all resulting in a successful conclusion—that fit the objective of sharing the trials of pilots in crisis in hope that others may avoid similar ones in the future.

The original material has been edited, expanded, and organized to provide both the general principles and the real-life situations in logical sequence and to enhance the learning value.

Crises in the Cockpit, then, is not merely an opportunity for vicarious sharing of others' experiences, but an exercise in crisis prevention based on the realities of human factors, the dynamics of flight, and the ever changing dynamics of the elements.

The product you hold is the work of many people, most especially those pilots whose adventures and misadventures form its core. The editor, Norbert Slepyan, offers the special blend of a professional book editor with many years of magazine experience. He is an experienced pilot and a thoughtful man who has reflected long about flying and the value of sharing the lessons of individuals with fellow airmen.

It is intended to offer a good read initially, yet—more importantly—a resource and reference for continued use.

Edward G. Tripp
Senior Vice President
Aircraft Owners and Pilots Association
Frederick, Maryland

Part One
VISIBILITY LIMITED

1
Going Blind

You enter another world. What lies outside your cockpit offers no safety. This contourless world is only the deep gray of
cloud, the blank whiteness of fog, or the blackness of night. If
you are not up to handling it, being here is like going blind.
Going to your instruments may save the day, but not always.
Even if the obscuration is only partial, what it hides may be
towers, hills, or other hard realities masked by illusions. Especially near the ground, the crises posed by limited visibility are
too many to be resolved by one simple cure. And what if not
even that cure is available to you?

Take inadvertently entering cloud, a dominant cause of accidents. If you are IFR rated, proficient, and equipped, you have
much to do, but the odds are reasonable that you will survive.
Otherwise, you are in trouble. You must scamper out of the murk,
but how much instrument skill do you have? Can you keep your
head clear and your self-control intact? Can you turn and backtrack without careening downward? Do you have the room to do
so? What if the cloud or fog has curled behind you, locking you
into dark, wet uncertainties? How long can you hold the plane
if pressured by turbulence, precipitation, inadequate instrumen-
tation, the shocks of disorientation? Ultimately, how can you get
down safely—anywhere?

Every year, thousands of pilots—VFR and IFR—go blind with
their eyes wide open. They gamble on weather conditions that
are beyond their training, experience, or equipment. It is a losing game. One study by the National Transportation Safety Board
for a sample period 1964–72 showed that in four out of every

3

ten fatal accidents, the weather was a causal factor. Low ceilings, fog, and rain were most frequently cited. The NTSB said that overconfidence could also have been a major ingredient, in that the pilot had flown enough to feel secure in his or her abilities but did not have the background to appreciate or handle the dangers of adverse weather. The data showed that a majority of the pilots had had up to twenty hours of simulated instrument time but no experience in actual IFR conditions. Has the situation improved since then? No. Since 1975, approximately 40 percent of all fatal general aviation accidents have involved adverse weather.

This chapter is about going into blinding and near-blinding conditions, situations that can create crises in *any* cockpit, for they have killed, injured, and terrified many of the IFR-rated, who learned too late that the instrument ticket in itself is not invulnerable armor. We shall discuss how to avoid these hazards and how to take action should they confront you.

"If I Can't . . ."

How does such a confrontation happen? It can begin with clouded thinking on the ground:

• A low-pressure center was located in Canada. A warm front radiating out of it extended through western New York, central Pennsylvania, western Maryland, and central West Virginia. A cold front followed only 100 miles or so to the west. The system was moving eastward very slowly. Airmets for IFR conditions were in effect all over the area.

The pilot was an attorney, age forty-five, with a private certificate and 400 total hours, all in type—Cessna 182. His route would take him from Gaithersburg, Maryland, to Wilkes-Barre/Scranton Airport, in northeast Pennsylvania.

Before his flight, he telephoned the Washington, D.C., Flight

Service Station for weather information twice, just after midnight and at 7:20 A.M. During the second call, he learned that the current Wilkes-Barre weather was 1,500 scattered, measured ceiling 2,000 overcast, visibility 12 miles. The forecast for the rest of the day at Wilkes-Barre called for 1,000 scattered, ceiling 5,000 overcast, visibility 4 in fog and haze, with a chance of 800 overcast, visibility 1 mile in rain showers or thunderstorms. Based on the current and forecast conditions for his route, the pilot could expect to encounter a layer of scattered to variable to broken clouds at 1,000 to 2,000 feet and an overcast layer at 5,000. Visibilities en route were forecast to have a chance of dropping to 2 to 4 miles in rain showers, fog, and haze.

The briefing transcript records the second briefer as saying, "Not really good for any VFR; conditions right now are marginal VFR, as you can see, all the way up there; but I mean you can expect these conditions to be lowering and raising throughout the day with IFR conditions, uh, quite frequent."

Then the following conversation took place:

PILOT: Do you have, uh *[pause, with no audible sound]*, uh, Scranton?

BRIEFER: What the tops of the mountains are?

PILOT: Yeah, what's the height of the . . .

BRIEFER: Well, some of those mountains go up to, uh, 4, uh, 4,000 feet.

PILOT: They would be obscured.

BRIEFER: Right. They would be obscured; see, you, you'd run in with that situation.

PILOT: Okay, uh, fine.

BRIEFER: Uh, it's very marginal, and 'course with this activity moving in, you would expect it to go IFR at the airport some time, you know.

PILOT: Yeah.

BRIEFER: At times, be up and down, because this, uh, these storms, uh, you know, associated with the front move along.

PILOT: Mmmm.

BRIEFER: The front's moving ever so slowly, as you can see.

PILOT: Yeah. (Yeah. If I can't, I can't.) *[This portion of the recording is not entirely clear, but this represents the best interpretation possible under the circumstances.]* Okay, that's what I need. Nine-Two-Three-Seven-Golf.

BRIEFER: Okay, sir.

PILOT: Thank you.

BRIEFER: Yes, sir. You're welcome.

The pilot departed Gaithersburg at about 10 A.M. in VFR conditions, and, at 11:48 A.M., made initial radio contact with a controller on duty at Wilkes-Barre Approach Control. He said that he was at 6,500 feet, on top of a cloud layer, and wanted to land at Wilkes-Barre. He also told Approach that he was "approximately" over the airport at the time of the first transmission. Beginning at 11:50 A.M., this conversation took place:

APPROACH CONTROL: Nine-Two-Three-Seven-Golf, Wilkes-Barre weather measured 1,300 broken, 2,500 overcast, visibility 5 with fog; we're landing Runway 22. What are your intentions?

37G: Uh, I'd like to come in.

APC: Are you IFR rated?

37G: The plane is, I am not.

APC: Are you declaring an emergency?

37G: No, I'm not.

APC: Okay, uh, the weather is VFR at the field a little. With that overcast, if you can't find a hole, you're gonna have to get down some way.

37G: I can find a hole, if you can give me vectors.

APC: Okay, Three-Seven-Golf, what kind of vectors do you wish from me?

37G: Uh, Three-Seven-Golf, uh, I'd like to make a straight-in approach to Runway 22. I'm not sure of the height of any of your mountains. Are they obscured?

APC: Affirmative. All the mountains surrounding the field are obscured.

37G: I'm circling your field now. I can see patches now and then. Can I come straight down over the field?

APC: . . . if you can descend in VFR conditions through a hole, there's no problem there to come down and inbound to the airport.

The pilot acknowledged another transmission and was advised that ridges to the southeast and east were visible through the haze, but those northwest to northeast of the field were obscured. After 11:55 A.M., no further transmissions from the Cessna were received.

The wreckage of the Cessna was found the next day in rugged terrain at an elevation of 1,966 feet above sea level. The pilot had been killed on impact. The NTSB attributed the crash to "continued flight into adverse weather conditions" and "improper in-flight decisions or planning" as the probable causes, with low ceiling and fog contributing factors.

The cause-and-effect pattern is familiar: The weather briefer tried to discourage the pilot from challenging the marginal VFR conditions; the pilot seemed to understand the message but went anyway; the non-IFR pilot was caught by cloud and hoped somehow to find a visual way down; ignorant about the terrain below, he needed a controller to pass a miracle and guide him to his destination; apparently, the pilot had either no alternate plan or, by then, too little presence of mind (or fuel?) to seek a better field. His best move would have been to cancel the flight, but even as he said, "If I can't, I can't," a brief for daring the odds apparently was being too forcefully argued in his mind, against better judgment.

Causes in Point

Undoubtedly, many VFR pilots fly for years in marginal, sometimes IFR, conditions and get away with it. Each time, the notion that "I know I can make it" is crazily reinforced. How to judge? What may be adverse weather for one pilot may be workable for another, depending on skill, attitude, and experience. A pilot can be noninstrument rated and survive in marginal VFR—if he has maintained solid proficiency, has planned his flight meticulously, and has a thorough knowledge of the area and weather on his route. But such a careful pilot also knows that there is a point where "marginal" VFR becomes adverse or dangerous VFR. Such a pilot stays clear of that point.

The continuum of weather phenomena ranges in difficulty from light rain with 10-mile visibility through a multitude of increasingly taxing conditions. At the severe end of the range are conditions that no pilot without special equipment and training could expect to manage. This would include thunderstorms, icing, and extremely low ceilings and visibilities. Other weather, such as freezing rain or severe turbulence, may make continued flight impossible for even highly skilled pilots flying well-endowed aircraft. Where you safely fit in this continuum will be dictated by your ability and level of experience. Pilots who are not instrument rated are truly qualified to fly in a narrow range at the modest end of the scale. Furthermore, an instrument pilot's being legal in tackling severe weather does not mean that he ought to do so, just because such conditions happen to lie along his route. Every year, accidents occur that could be labeled "continued *IFR* into adverse weather conditions" but are described instead as "attempted operation beyond experience or ability level."

Doom at the Top

Within the skull, protected by the strongest, densest bone in the body, is a remarkable set of organs. Though commonly called the inner ear, these organs have nothing to do with hearing; they are neurological receptors that help us to sense our body position and maintain our balance. They inform us about gravitational forces and keep us oriented as we move about. In conjunction with our eyes and the sensing nerves in our limbs, muscles, and joints, they are a miraculous product of evolution—and they can kill us. Many pilots have succumbed to false signals and commands from this flawed marvel, responding to false inner ear signals to escape dangers that did not exist. Out of one year's 761 fatal general aviation accidents, 88 were attributed to the effects of *spatial disorientation.*

The canals that comprise the inertia-perceiving elements of the inner ear detect only *changes* in one's position. Assume that you are flying in cloud and you initiate a turn to the left. The canals of the inner ear contain fluid. When your body or head is repositioned, the fluid circulates through the canals and passes over tiny hairlike cells, called *cilia.* This sparks transmissions to the brain, reporting your angular movement in space. The turn you have started is sensed as the fluid moves through the appropriate canal. But once you are *stabilized* in the turn, the fluid becomes stationary. If you are not flying by your instruments, you can be misled into believing you are flying level.

Now let us say that you have overshot your turn, have noticed your error, and have attempted to return to level flight. As you do, the fluid moves again, and another change is sensed. But the fluid keeps moving and so creates the "seat-of-the-pants" impression that you are banking past level into a right turn. If you believe this signal, you can easily fall behind and overcontrol the airplane, piling illusion upon illusion and reversal upon reversal, despairing of being able to regain level flight, until you overcontrol the craft out of control. You need a solid visual reference to tell you where level is—a horizon, natural or artificial.

The semicircular canals also have a high threshold of excitation. Small movements, like a slow, shallow bank, may go undetected, so that the airplane may gradually turn unnoticed far from the intended heading. Inattentive instrument pilots tend to stray because they do not adequately monitor the directional gyro, attitude indicator, and turn-and-bank. The best defense against disorientation generally is reliance on the gauges.

Knowing Vertigo

The semicircular canals also cause *vertigo,* which is the result of overstimulation within all three canals by sudden movement. A classic cause of vertigo is a pilot's tilting his head, bending over, or leaning to one side at the same time that the airplane turns. He may have a swimming sensation or feel that he and the airplane are tumbling backward or sideways. Not only will he probably be dizzy but he may be nauseous and may even vomit. His eye muscles may oscillate involuntarily (a condition called *nystagmus*) due to elevated levels of electrical activity through the nerves connecting the eyes and inner ear. This condition can extend to the vagus nerve, near the inner ear, which relays the electrical firing to the stomach, hence nausea. To all intents and purposes, a pilot hit by vertigo is incapacitated, and an episode can last from forty-five seconds to two minutes.

Vertigo can overwhelm a pilot in cloud, in darkness, or even in the clear, and especially during departure and approach. For prevention, anticipate its onset and avoid making head and body movements during turns. If, in any flight regime, you must make a substantial movement—to switch tanks, crank a landing gear, reach behind you, or pick something off the floor—do not do it abruptly, and take your hands and feet off the controls (assuming the airplane is trimmed). Refer back to the instruments, and if you feel dizzy or disoriented, do not react violently.

Seeing nothing while we are in midair and in the dark can confuse our sense of up and down. Our gravity-perceiving receptors are located in small chambers beneath the semicircular canals. Sensitive membranes line these chambers, and resting on the membranes are small calciferous stones, called *otoliths*. The otoliths are free to move; their location is normally dictated by gravity. This system works fine until we fly an airplane without outside visual cues. For instance, the acceleration that occurs on takeoff rolls the otoliths backward, which creates the illusion of a pitch upward. Pilots deceived by such a signal and attempting to correct have dived into the ground. The actions of the otoliths can disorient you, particularly if they are supported by conflicting visual cues like a sloping cloud layer or, at night, ground lights merging with a background of stars. As your orientation and visual impulses clash, your body can mistakenly try to correct by leaning to the side.

Spatial disorientation is a normal physiological reaction; encounters with simple disorientation are no major concern, *if you are prepared for them.* Vertigo, however, is much more dangerous for every pilot. For the VFR-only pilot, the most prudent way of avoiding all spatial disorientation is to beware of below-VFR visibilities. This also applies to instrument pilots who neglect their responsibility to stay current and practiced. Try to get some experience of vertigo at least once, *under controlled, supervised conditions,* to be aware of the sensations. The FAA can arrange it.

Night Flight

Because things look different at night, flight after sunset can create cockpit crises. Pilots generally are unfamiliar with nighttime illusions, yet many flights are extended carelessly into darkness: A delayed takeoff, an unforeseen headwind, a deviation due to weather, or an unscheduled pit stop can leave you barreling into the dusk, tired and eager to get home, unprepared for the questions posed by the gloom. If you are heading for an unfamiliar airport, the answers may be even more elusive.

The physiology of night vision is complex. It is essential to know that it takes time for the rods-and-cones mechanism of the eyeball to adjust to reduced light—at least thirty minutes at best—and that night vision can be dimmed by the lights of a city, the strobes from a nearby parked airplane, or a lighted match or flashlight. Bright lights cause the rods, which do the heavy night work, to lose some function, so turn the panel lights up no more than you need, and turn on the dome light. (You may have to use a flashlight or maplight to read Sectionals, for a red glow obliterates red lines.)

Do not smoke. The rods and cones are extremely sensitive to a lack of oxygen, and smoking impairs oxygen transport. Even three cigarettes per day reduces the oxygen going to the rods and cones to the amount available at 8,000 feet, and if you smoke at 10,000 feet, the oxygen will be that at 14,000.

Another impairment to night vision is a spot, at the back of the eye, that is devoid of light receptors. However, by scanning across what you want to see, the image will fall into light-sensitive cells, and the total picture will be transmitted to the brain. Also, by focusing alternately inside and outside the cockpit— "see and avoid" is your responsibility at night, too—you will exercise the muscles that change the shape of the lens and prevent your eyes from fixating yet not focusing.

When night flying is even a possibility, your preflight planning, weather briefing, and aircraft check should be as thorough as you can make them. Your charts should be current, with salient frequencies, peaks, landmarks, and courses marked for rapid recognition. Learn all you can about cloud conditions, including scattered clouds and layers. Clouds are difficult to see at night, and it is easy to discover yourself on top of anything from a fog bank to mounting cumulus, with no visual path to the ground. Check out the conditions along your route and at any airport you expect to use, including relevant Notams, and have in mind at least one well-lighted airport—within the night fuel-requirement range—as an alternative. At night, equipment glitches can be deadly, so be uncompromising in your preflight. Be intolerant of any inoperative lights. Check the fuel not only for quantity— be topped—but quality, purging all water from the gas and system. Clean the windscreen of mist and glare-enhancing substances, such as insect remains and dirt.

A flashlight can be invaluable not only in the cockpit but outside. When the taxi light mysteriously dies, a strong, hand-held beam to guide you on badly lit taxiways and around parked airplanes can be a lifesaver. A backup flashlight is essential— don't pretend that you can easily fly and change cells or bulbs without an autopilot. A good combination is a small light for cockpit chores and a larger one for preflighting and outside guidance. Before taking off, set up a firm support to fix the beam on your kneeboard and/or panel.

Slow and Sure

Nighttime sensory illusions can be difficult to diagnose. During taxi, nearby visual references suggest that the airplane is moving superslowly. This, combined with meager hints of how close your wingtips are to objects, calls for purposely taxiing more slowly than by day. Roll no faster than walking speed. Before turning, slow the airplane, then accelerate slightly as you turn; be sure you see what you are turning toward. Observe holding lines. Before turning onto the active, check the DG for the correct runway heading. *Always* regard the approach path for traffic, and don't assume that a landing light will give you warning. *Scan* for nav lights or other hints that a darkened aircraft may be coming in, and be doubly considerate in giving an approaching plane the right of way—you may be virtually invisible to him. Monitor the proper frequency, but keep in mind that inconsiderate pilots don't report their location in the pattern and radioless pilots can't.

Night takeoffs and landings require precision, for they are accompanied by speed and altitude illusions. For example, during takeoff and approach, when the nose is raised, the landing light suggests you are high; when pointed down, it does the opposite. When you change pitch, check the altimeter.

You should know from experience what the normal climbout attitudes look like on your attitude and airspeed indicators (AI and ASI) and the VSI. At night, refer to them diligently. Also monitor the DG and ball to maintain heading. These references are critical when blackness or lights (including bright stars) depict a horizon that really isn't there.

Landing in the Dark

In the pattern, if the right wing is low and outside references are lacking, from the left seat you may believe you are higher than you are, because the bank angle creates a false horizon. This is common on leveling from a downwind-to-base turn, or in a right-hand pattern. Again, check the attitude and turn-and-bank indicators, backed by the airspeed indicator, altimeter, and vertical speed indicator. Avoid long, straight-in approaches, especially over hilly or tree-covered terrain. It is dangerously easy to approach the parallel runway lights without noticing that the threshold end is obscured by a hill or stand of trees. Check the Sectional or airport chart for a road running by the approach end, for it could be flanked by telephone wires.

Glideslopes guided by visual approach slope indicator (VASI) lights also require special care. Stay slightly on the high side (white over white), for the shallow VASI approach angle (2.5 to 4 degrees) requires a power-on, flat, or nose-high descent. At night, VASI is visible from far away, but the reds tend to blur into yellow, especially in haze, with the bars showing their true colors only relatively close to the runway. When approaching a strange airport, fly a normal pattern and use VASI as an aid on short final. Even with VASI, as touchdown nears, the runway lights can suggest that the pavement is higher than it is, particularly if the runway is wide. To avoid a high flare/sink into the "black hole" between the lights, scan the sides.

A landing light can create almost hypnotic illusions. You can fixate on the circle of light on the pavement so that you try to land on it and hit nosewheel-first. Similarly, as you begin to flare, the circle lengthens and appears to move away. Do not chase the light. The runway lights indicate the location and height of the surface and must be integral to your scan. Continually cross-check the runway and the lights (peripherally), glancing up and down the runway. As you flare, don't rush the touchdown; reduce power and *allow* a gentle contact.

To land without airborne lights, fly a higher-than-normal pattern and use the runway for essential guidance. Carry some power and descend at a slightly shallower angle than normal, to be almost flat over the threshold. The wingtip lights will then cause the pavement to glow red and green, signaling time for the flare and final power reduction.

Because groundspeed clues are sparse and deceptive at night, make sure that you are on the correct airspeeds throughout the approach, and be wary of the wind. At a nontower airport, you may not be able to get a report or see a windsock. If so, check with the nearest tower or ATIS to get some idea of the area's wind direction and speed. Watch out for hills that may cause wind roiling or shearing (sudden direction and/or speed changes) that could affect your ground and air speeds and crosswind corrections.

Strange Shapes and Lights

Crabbing on final also creates illusions. If you are crabbing left, the approach and runway lights appearing right of center on the windscreen suggest greater height; vice versa on a right crab. A long or narrow runway implies that you are high; vice versa for short or wide. Upsloping and downsloping runways have similar effects. Study the airport diagram and the *Airport/ Facility Directory* for runway dimensions, the wind indicator location, and conditions that could affect your perceptions or aircraft handling on approach.

The night sky also creates confusion during cruise. Any noticeable change in your airplane's noise level calls for an immediate check of the ASI, altitude indicator, and altimeter for an inadvertent descent or climb. If the airplane slows, the noise falls off; acceleration brings a louder engine and rush of air. You may be tempted to see a line of lights (say, a road) slightly perpendicular to your flight path as a horizon, as a gentle bank will demonstrate. Similarly, city lights, scattered rural lights, stars (the planet Venus is seductive), even other airplanes can inspire false impressions about your altitude, attitude, and position, as can lights rimming lake and ocean beaches. It is easy to make snap judgments about whether lights are above, below, or level with you. More pilots than will admit it have taken evasive action on seeing stars or farmhouses, and others have been jolted by near misses when a star or house suddenly became an airplane. Finding an airport within a sea of city or town lights can be a suspense thriller in itself. The best detection device is frequent night training.

Partial Self-Blinding

Low-altitude flying in marginal VFR is dangerous, often barely legal, and engaged in by enough pilots to make it a major cause of accidents. Scud-running is often practiced beneath the law, for conditions that hover at a 1,200-foot ceiling, 1-mile visibility, and "just enough room" clear of clouds are as likely to go below that as remain that. Many pilots dart like outlaws among the puffs and hillsides, determined to get away with it one more time. Others blunder on, hoping to stretch legality to the last strand. Pilot Robert Christian tells about being pressed down while gamely pressing on:

My first mistake was in the planning. Or lack of it. You shouldn't take lightly something as consistent as nightfall, especially in unfamiliar mountain terrain. My second mistake concerned the weather.

On a clear day in August, my wife and I took off from Fitchburg, Massachusetts, for Piseco Airport, near Piseco Lake, in the Adirondack Mountains of upstate New York. I pointed the nose of the Skyhawk northwestward with some misgivings. The area forecast called for scattered thunderstorms moving eastward across New York state. However, they were not due to reach the Adirondacks until later. With that microgram of encouragement, I decided to play aerial Russian roulette.

As we sliced through the blue Massachusetts sky, I began to relax. It was a beautiful day, and the horizon looked promising. I had a hunch that we would find clear weather in the mountains, too. We intersected the southwest corner of Vermont, and I could see clouds on the horizon. They did not look menacing, but my nervousness returned. By the time we crossed the Vermont–New York border, there was an overcast above us and scattered clouds below. Ground features were blending together, for night would soon be falling. We could still turn back, for the weather was good behind us, but we didn't, and that was mistake number three. I reasoned that we were only about a half hour from Piseco. If the weather held, even at its present quality, we should have no trouble making the airport, though darkness would be minutes away when we arrived. I could see worry on Sheree's face.

Everything might have been fine if I had known the area, but I did not. At the Cambridge VOR, I headed outbound on a radial that would take us to Piseco Airport. We were soon in the mountains, and the weather was looking less than pretty. The overcast was lower now and had taken on a threatening quality. Below us, the scattered clouds hung about the rapidly darkening landscape. The CDI bobbed uncertainly as we progressed farther from the VOR. My palms were moist with sweat.

I was trying to keep track on the Sectional of how far we had come into the mountains, but I wasn't having much luck. I estimated that we had one more ridge of hills to cross before we would reach Piseco Lake and the airport. The overcast had dropped and was covering the peaks with a blackness that defied approach. Lower clouds rolled ominously down the valleys. I was about to make another and by now routine decision to seek a way through, when rain lightly hit the windshield.

I looked at Sheree, who looked questioningly at me. "Okay," I said, "it's back we go. We'll take a rain check on this vacation." As I put the Skyhawk into a 180, relief washed over me. I was confident about the weather we had passed through and felt we could make it out of the mountains before total darkness fell. As I brought the plane around, the rain suddenly hit the windshield in torrents; we could see nothing through it. I tried looking out the side window, but the propwash and the plane's airspeed were causing rivers to flow across it. We were nearly blind, with mountains close around us.

My first impulse was to go to the instruments and start a steep climb, but that thought scared me so badly that I immediately pigeonholed it. At least I was starting to be honest with myself. I knew that my instrument skill was rudimentary and that relying on it in this soup was likely to mean our deaths. But if worse came to . . .

Instead of climbing, I chose an opposite course of action. I cut the throttle back to reduce our airspeed and the force of the propwash. The merciless pounding against the windshield slackened almost immediately, and visibility returned. We were a couple of hundred feet above the ground, and the clouds seemed to be boiling around and above us, as if in a time-lapse filmstrip.

The dropping overcast now covered the peaks between us and home. The only remaining choice other than instruments or an attempted landing was to follow the valleys out. But which valleys led out? I was thoroughly lost and could not even guess where we might be located on the Sectional. I dreaded following a valley deeper into the mountains or into a box canyon. Yet making an emergency landing in this terrain was no more appealing. We were on one side of a relatively wide valley. There was nothing but trees beneath us, but on the other side, I thought I could see a clear area. Ahead and to our left, the mountains opened into a narrower valley, which ran in an easterly direction. In the present state of affairs, it looked promising, so I headed for it, keeping the clearing in mind, in case we had to backtrack.

We were not far into the valley, when it began to narrow further. Soon the hills squeezed in uncomfortably close on either side, and the clouds hung lower on their slopes. We were flying near the cloud bases, and the ride was very rough. Yet I hesitated to descend. As it was, we were only about 200 feet AGL, and, owing to the fact that the hills sloped in toward each other, I wondered if we would have enough room at our altitude to turn around if it became necessary. That uncertainty kept me going ahead until the decision was taken out of my hands.

The valley meandered in harmony with its small river, and, as we rounded a bend, before us appeared a black wall of cloud that extended all the way to the ground and from one hillside to the other. Frantically I banked the Skyhawk sharply and brought it around in a tight 180. The nose rose into the cloud, and instantly we were in zero visibility. A moment later, the plane stalled!

As we plummeted out of the cloud, I heard Sheree's scream catch in her throat and exit in a strangled whisper: "We're going to die!"

I crammed the throttle all the way home and nosed down toward the oncoming trees. Seconds before we would have become scrap metal, I pulled up to level flight. We were headed away from the wall of cloud!

That amazed me. Now I played my last card: I headed for the wide valley and what had seemed from afar to be a clear area. I anticipated flipping the plane while landing in a marsh or other soft ground, but at least we might survive. As we approached the clearing, something long and shiny appeared in the middle of it, though darkness was but minutes away. Then a roof showed to the left, and farther left still, a lake—which had been obscured at our low height by trees and clouds. We neared it at treetop level; then, before us was a long, wet asphalt strip with the numbers 22 at the closest end: Piseco Airport!

Waiting at the tiedown to be picked up, I basked in the feeling of being alive. We were where I had planned to take us, but that was all I could say for my planning. A good plan always leaves at least one way out—and a way out must be more than wishful thinking.

My second mistake had been to take the weather report lightly. Now I was a born-again pessimist, who would expect the weather to be worse than forecast. And I would never again count on the weather behind me to remain stationary, lest I find myself making a 180 into marginal or zero-zero conditions. Failing to heed these principles, I had made a third mistake by not "bailing out" while I could. Long before we had entered the mountains, I *knew* a U-turn was called for.

There is a fairy-tale quality to the *outcome* of this account: The pilot stumbled onto his airport. The odds are not high for that happening, once a pilot has boxed himself in as badly as did Mr. Christian, the newly raised skeptic. He was realistic about one thing—his inability to sustain himself on instruments. Yet that made his choice to press on even worse, for, as he admits, he was knowingly leaving himself no sure out.

Navigation among hills, valleys, and masses of cloud can be reduced to exploring what is just past the next slope—if you can see that far. Pilotage helps little when valleys and streams look alike and one doesn't have time to pore over a chart. Roads and tracks are more reliable, but they get lost beneath tunnels, behind rises, in clouds and haze. Furthermore, at low altitude in such terrain, VOR signals lose their authority, and the pilot has little time to be twiddling knobs and reading cross-bearings. A major rule of the dubious craft of scud-running is to have your course marked out clearly, with easily readable, standout checkpoints indicated at close intervals; and if you lose your way, accept that you've lost your little game and turn back. Head for survival. Some pilots, however, fear turning back when pressed by scud. Seeing ground points behind them swallowed by the murk, they assume that that way spells no relief. Especially since they can still see the ground ahead as they fly, they hope that the low ceilings and visibility won't last forever. But what's ahead can also disappear.

Turning back to better climes, keep the wind direction in mind, so that you can compensate for drift. In windless air, a standard-rate 180 would not put you on the track you have been flying. If the terrain and cloud allow, turn not first to the reciprocal but about 210 degrees and then back 30 to that track. When low and evasive, do not *fixate* on a chart—fly the plane.

Punch Bunk

Scud-running among the slopes is particularly hazardous, but it can also be horrifying above the flatlands. Pilot Burnard McHone's story illustrates how crises can spring up virtually anywhere in our high-tech environment:

It started with a trip I had planned from Moline, Illinois, to Lakeland, Florida. For several months, I had planned the flight as thoroughly as an instrument student should. For three days before preparing my VFR flight plan, I had kept up with the weather. Just before taking off, I checked with the Cedar Rapids, Iowa, FSS. Assured of nothing worse than low ceilings, two friends and I departed under a 3,000-foot ceiling.

The first half of the flight was uneventful, in 5-mile visibility with light haze. We set down at Shelbyville, Tennessee, for refueling. There, I found the line to Nashville Flight Service busy. As I looked out at the weather, I began to fear a delay. Soon a Cherokee Six from the south landed. The pilot motioned for a telephone and somewhat nervously began to lay out charts in every direction. I asked him about the weather he had just encountered. "Not bad," he said, like someone quickly trying to forget a surprise he had just survived.

The predictions from Flight Service were uncertain. "Wait a minute," the voice said, "I've got something coming up now." The briefer then told me that although my route to Florida would be marginal VFR in spots, especially around Columbus, Georgia, it looked pretty good. But there was uncertainty in the report. He had said something about "punching through." I grasped at the phrase: "Yeah," I said, "it looks like I might have to punch through around Columbus, but other than that, it looks okay, right?"

I hesitated slightly after hanging up. What *was* the weather like? A look outside showed nothing I had not already seen. Did he say thunderstorms? No. But he did say that I could punch through. Florida sunshine beckoned. I saw myself courageously flying under dark ceilings and then basking in yellows, blues, and white, impressing my passengers.

After takeoff, we climbed to 3,000 feet on a southeasterly heading and soon were passing the second VOR check. I turned to my next heading, studied the charts briefly, then searched the horizon. I did not like what I saw. Ahead, the ceiling was lowering from perhaps 3,500 to 2,500 feet, hidden below my present altitude. I trimmed down slightly and looked at the chart again, recalling an instructor's advice to keep track of nearby airports, just in case, and to pick a field with a VOR close by and remember the frequency. I scanned the airports west of my position and casually noted Tuskegee, Alabama.

When I looked up again, just ahead, too close already, was a definite weather change. At my present altitude, I was not going to make it under the new ceiling. I trimmed down farther and checked my altimeter—1,600 and still dropping. The needle seemed to resist leveling out. Suddenly there were little gray clouds ahead, but with neat spaces between them. A reprieve, temporary perhaps, but at least I could weave through them. I banked left and headed for open space, but a cloud swallowed me. Light rain started to pepper the windshield. I tried to make a joke to the passengers without looking away. It didn't work. Now we were in the clear again. A hard bank to the right to avoid some more clouds (now much denser), and I was in it again, up to my wingtips. The indicated altitude was 1,000—where was my altitude going? Fly the airplane, I reminded myself.

I remembered something else: *towers!* I grabbed the chart again and searched for Columbus. Wrong side, dammit! I fumbled a bit, found the frequency and waited for the DME to read out. All ground references were gone. I was enmeshed in rapidly worsening weather. Rain poured down, deafening everyone as it washed around the cabin. Glancing down at the map, I spotted the towers. A twin group, then some more. Where were they—a mile away, 20 miles? There was a twin group, maybe just a few minutes away. As calmly as I could, I told my passengers not to worry: I had expected this. We would be punching through soon.

The minutes advanced, and we didn't. Instead, the weather grew progressively worse. I confirmed the local elevations and dropped even farther. We were scooting in and out of countless small clouds that melted into a thick mist. I caught sight of some ground and then a blue form that seemed not to rise from the ground but to fall away from the clouds. It was not more than 3,000 feet away at one o'clock. I caught sight of a low hill dangerously near. I thought for only a split second, then banked even more steeply to the north, slowly coming about.

I waited for the sounds of rending metal, a quick snap, air rushing about. If only I could keep control. After a few seconds, I glimpsed a brown field below. Thank God I was still flying. I quickly leveled out and dialed the Tuskegee DME frequency. The light blinked on, then off, then on again. I heard a deep rumble. The rain's intensity increased. What was that airport again? What did it look like? I centered the needle to 240 degrees and descended still more until I caught sight of the ground.

I had forgotten about my passengers. "I'm setting down in Tuskegee," I choked out, my throat dry. "There's a road!" my right-seat passenger said. "Should it be there?" "Yes, it should be there. It leads right by the airport—Moton Field." In just a few minutes, I passed over the terminal at 300 feet and was soon on a close final.

Inside the office briefing room, I stood alone by a window, looking at the field. The rain still had that deceptively safe look you get from a port in the storm. It came to me as suddenly as the towers had appeared: I was thinking of combinations of 500 above, 1,000 below, and 2,000 horizontal, or was it 500 below, 1,000 above, and 2,000 horizontal? I determined to fix those numbers in my mind, but what I was really pondering was the true meaning of *visual flight rules*. Personal safety—that's what the law is all about. And I thought about *someone* out there, maybe at that very moment, who still did not understand.

Uncontrollable Towers

Pilots who fly below 2,000 feet AGL are candidates for collisions with intruders that "shouldn't be there" but are. One example:

A Cessna departed a Pennsylvania airport with its 1,242-hour pilot and two passengers. No weather briefing had been obtained. At the time, it was marginal VFR, with ceilings below 1,000 and visibility 1 mile in rain and fog. Fourteen minutes into the flight, the airplane struck the upper static cable between two powerline transmission towers. The initial impact tore the left wing from the fuselage, but the aircraft traveled another 700 feet before crashing in an open field. The airplane was destroyed, and the three occupants were fatally injured. Witnesses at the crash site reported that fog obscured the towers, one of which rose 94 feet AGL and the other 162. The electric lines could not be seen at all.

High-power transmission lines are nearly invisible against terrain features. When exposed to weather, they become too dull to reflect light. In other cases, the wire has low reflective characteristics and is often combined with towers constructed to blend harmoniously into the surroundings. Cables sag so that it is hard to judge their height. Flying under them is dangerous; and thin cables are often run *above* them for lightning protection. While these upper cables are very small in diameter, they are strong.

The towers that support powerlines usually can be seen but vary in height, so that in overflying one you may not clear the next. If you must fly over a powerline while low, it is safest to top a specific tower. Guy wires end more flights than towers; they may stretch 2,000 feet and more beyond the tower bases. Airports seem to attract such towers, and special procedures may be set for safety, as Notams or a local FBO may point out. Pilots also collide with smokestacks, derricks, and similar hazards which can be masked by haze, pollution, glare, or even sunglasses worn in dull light.

Obstructions are a major nighttime problem, particularly in urban areas, where the number and variety of lights may disguise warning beacons.

Terrain that is useful for VFR navigation—peaks, rivers, shorelines, railways, and highways—attracts tall structures. Tall towers and cables may lurk even where there is little sign of civilization. Narrow valleys deserve special care because of unmarked wires that may be strung across them. Flight planning and position tracking should include checks for obstructions that appear on the charts; note them carefully on approach plates.

Keeping Slow When Low

Low-altitude flying should be at the slow end of cruise to make decision making and hazard avoidance easier. Slow flight is made more secure by deflecting the flaps a notch or two; this lowers the stall speed and may pitch the plane downward for better vision. In low flight, groundspeed clues can mislead. The ground seems to rush by faster, tempting a pullback on the throttle and/or yoke. In slowing, decide upon a minimum safe speed above stall and stay above it. That is particularly crucial while making turns.

Altitude care is also critical during any turn, especially a prolonged low-speed 180. Keep your turns coordinated and shallow. At low altitude, the wind can be tricky, as can the visibility through a rain-streaked windscreen—conditions conducive to optical illusions. As you turn even through a small arc, the bank angle, a restricted view, rising terrain, or a partially shrouded landform can imply a descent, leading to cross-controlled pulling on the yoke and a stall/spin. Avoid sudden or violent evasive maneuvers. In low visibility, keep your landing light and nav lights on—except when actually in fog or cloud—and stay to the right side of natural flight paths like valleys, highways, rivers, and rail lines.

When conditions are pressing like a vise, a precautionary landing can be like a liferaft. Airports, even abandoned ones, are best, of course, but if you are slithering through scud, look realistically at likely open fields. Unspoiled by concrete runways, the old barnstormers welcomed soft fields when in trouble. Try to drag the field at least once to detect ditches, hidden water, or other snags.

Manage low approaches so as to have room and time to stabilize your descent, airspeed, and wind corrections—meaning wide downwind and base legs and no steep turns. Note the terrain for conditions that might produce sharp updrafts or downdrafts.

The Ultimate Low-Level Threat

The most common cause of pilots going blind without losing their eyesight is fog. Its variability and production of illusions can be bewildering, as pilot Larry Ostby relates:

It sure is dark, with just a dim moon occasionally trying to poke through a high cloud layer. This flight from Minot, North Dakota, home to northeastern Montana in our small Grumman should be pleasant.

The hourly sequence shows our departure weather at Minot to be 8,000 scattered, 12,000 overcast; Williston, 110 miles to our west, reports 5,000 scattered, 8,000 broken, with a rain shower ending at thirty-five minutes past the hour; and Glasgow, the next reporting station, 100 miles west of our destination, reported 20,000 thin scattered. The weather is not as expected, but is still very good. No fronts, light and variable winds, no thunderstorms, nothing significant, our briefer has said.

One hour and twenty minutes over familiar territory should put us on the runway at home. I'm able to relax as the Grumman seems to sense its destination. . . .

There are the lights of Williston—but it seems unusual that the runway lights are not on. The energy crunch must be affecting everyone these days. Thirty-five miles to go, and our destination's beacon is now clearly in sight. Another aircraft passes below, heading in the opposite direction. The lights of two 900-foot TV towers wink off to the left. Just a few minutes more. Wait, what's that? Looks like fog forming in the low spots ahead. A few wisps are hanging in some of the coulees of the rolling prairie ahead of us, but none in the Missouri Valley off to our left.

Only 10 miles to go; we should make it home okay. Could turn back, but our destination is now the closest airport, and it sure would be nice to get home. The sighting of fog does bring me upright in the seat. I don't like the idea of fog, but so far this is quite scattered. The runway lights are in sight, and the airport beacon at Plentywood, 45 miles to the north, is flashing reassuringly.

Start the descent down to pattern altitude; landing check complete; down the final approach at 80. Looks like we will make it, but it will be close—fog is now visible to our left in the river valley. No fog below or ahead to the runway, but it appears that the city lights on the far edge of town on our left are being obscured in mist.

One minute to touchdown. I glance nervously off the right wingtip to make sure the neighboring airport beacon is still visible. If the cockpit mood was relaxed a few minutes ago, the situation has changed. All sorts of thoughts are racing through my mind, but surely we won't be doing anything but landing straight ahead in seconds, will we?

I shift my glance back from the right. The runway lights have just vanished, along with those of the city! They've disappeared in the seconds it took to glance out the side window. So this is why they teach about the 180-degree turn. But we're getting low—still not in the fog, but higher wisps are now visible in the dim light ahead.

Up we go: full throttle, flaps up. The glow from the nav lights now begins to blink as we fly in and out of the tops of the billowing mist, which minutes before had seemed to be only harmless streaks of vapor. Stay on the gauges. Up and around we go. Still in cloud, I twirl on the OBS and center the needle. It seems to take forever. And why isn't the ADF pointing where it should?

We're heading back to Williston, retreating 35 miles, and we are now finally above a complete blanket of fog at 4,500 feet. That ADF needle should be pointing straight ahead! Testing it yields only silence and no needle response. Good old KEYZ has left the air.

The friendly lights on those 900-foot TV towers we passed 20 minutes ago are now covered. The top light of one tower is barely visible in the mist. That landmark means 15 miles to Williston.

We need help. How do we get those runway lights at Williston turned on? Let's try to raise someone on Unicom. I get no response on 122.8, but I try again. Nothing. I've told Minot Flight Service of our predicament; better call them again for help.

How much fuel remaining? We should be able to reach one of the airports between Williston and Minot or even Minot itself, but it will be close. The FSS calls back to say that they have asked the Weather Bureau to turn on the runway lights. That sounds good, as the city lights are in sight, with no fog ahead yet. I know exactly where those runway lights should be, they're not yet on, so I make one more plea. Well, I can't waste time. I'll make the approach and use the landing light to find the runway. The fog is racing right behind us.

On come the lights, but are they dim! This must be lowest possible intensity. I am lined up with the runway and am still barely able to see them. I hope we don't have a replay of our last landing attempt.

Seconds later, the wheels squeak on the runway.

What they say about the domino effect and trouble is true: Many things probably will happen to make a bad spot worse. So, I will never again take a weather briefing for granted—I will probe for all the available data, however seemingly insignificant. In this case, the temperature-dewpoint spread would have been a crucial clue, and the report of rain showers in our flight path should have led me to ask. Fog can form extremely fast: The area within the airport boundaries must have gone from clear to a 500-foot-thick fog layer in two minutes.

Chaos through Stability

Fog is produced by an air mass cooling to its dewpoint or by moisture being added to the air near the ground. The dewpoint is the temperature to which the air must be cooled to achieve water vapor saturation. When the spread between the ambient temperature and the dewpoint temperature is 5 degrees or less and decreasing, expect fog. *Smog* is a combination of water vapor and smoke or industrial pollutants; fog quickly forms upon such particles.

Fog is a stable-air phenomenon. Cool, foggy air can linger for days, and warm air aloft can trap a fog layer beneath it in a temperature inversion, until improvement arrives with a new weather system. As you ponder your weather briefing data, keep in mind how various kinds of fog develop:

• *Radiation* fog results from the nighttime cooling of the ground lowering the air temperature to the dewpoint. High relative humidity helps the process along. Radiation fog reaches its maximum development on clear nights with light winds—otherwise fine flying weather except that cloudlessness allows more heat radiation from the earth, and a light wind spreads the cooling and deepens the fog.

• *Advection* fog forms when moist, warm air flows over a cool surface. This often happens along our west coast, where Arctic currents are overridden by warm, westerly flows, which carry the fog onto coastal areas.

• *Upslope* fog is caused by stable air moving up mountains and valleys and being cooled adiabatically. It most often appears on the Rockies' eastern slopes, aided by moist winds from the Gulf of Mexico, and along the eastern side of the Appalachians, when winds come off the Atlantic.

• *Frontal* fog occurs most frequently when a warm front overrides a cold air mass. The precipitation falling through the frontal zone into cooler air evaporates and saturates the air to form what is at times called *precipitation* fog. Though usually associated with winter warm fronts, it can occur in a slow-moving, cold, stationary, or occluded front. Frontal fog can portend turbulence, thunderstorms, or icing.

• *Steam* fog appears when cold air lies over a warmer, water surface, like lakes and streams in autumn, and when the water vapor cools sufficiently.

• *Ice* fog is associated with temperatures of 25 degrees or less and can occur in Arctic areas where water vapor passes directly into ice crystals. Fog can condense around suspended automobile or aircraft exhaust particles.

Down but Not Across

Fog may allow good visibility straight down, leading you to believe that you can make a visual landing after spotting the airport, but it can also restrict slant-range visibility to zero. As a result, ILS minimums indicate the visibility needed at decision height *to continue lower,* but there is no guarantee that the viewing range won't close. Fog can lie in layers of different densities, and it moves with the wind. What you can see on short final can disappear before you reach the touchdown zone, whereupon you must fly a missed approach or go around. In fact, it could be better to go elsewhere, to clearer conditions. Consider fog spread in your flight planning.

Even for experts, estimating the depth of fog and visibility in it is difficult, which makes it even sillier that some pilots attempt takeoffs into fog in the expectation (read *hope*) of improvement. Private-pilot IFR regulations permit zero-zero departures, but in this case, he who lives solely by the book—forgetting common sense—may end up regretting it. Similarly, eager noninstrument pilots attempt sneaking up through a supposedly thin layer, but the grayness goes on and on as they get farther from the field, until they are at the mercy of their negligible instrument skills.

To get the most out of fog reports, you must know the terminology. Be sure to check your destination's hourly sequence reports for indications of *obscuration*. A "partial obscuration" of the sky due to fog can mean many things. The sky can be from one-tenth to nine-tenths obscured, so check the remarks section, which may say something like "F3," meaning that fog was obscuring three-tenths of the sky.

If the sky is totally obscured, the report will provide an indefinite ceiling. This item can be deceptive, for it does not describe a ceiling as such but how high into the fog an observer on the ground estimated he could see. A pilot approaching an airport with an "indefinite ceiling 500 feet, sky obscured" would not break cleanly out of a fog layer at 500 feet but would face poor horizontal visibility to the ground. To avoid such a surprise, ask the weather briefer to explain the fog report in detail, then use your own good judgment and either choose an alternate airport and plan of action or, if more practical, cancel.

No one willingly gives up his vital senses, yet, as we have seen, under the guise of shrewd or daring or prayerful judgments, pilots point their airplanes into the blind, betting on blind odds. As aviation has evolved, however, there have grown with it a craft and a technology that have opened the clouds and the blackness of night to the pilot willing to learn to use them. Even for the VFR blunderer, this IFR asset is available, in highly limited form, as an escape device. But, as the next chapter will discuss, with the benefits have come crises that can oppress the instrument captain's cockpit, if he lacks the craft to overcome them.

2
Power plus Attitude

You have gone into the blind. Perhaps you intend to be in the soup, perhaps not. If you are not instrument rated, you have a major problem on your hands. If you are so rated, you still have many tasks to deal with and could meet with some of several kinds of cockpit crises that are part of IFR territory. If the soup is lumpy with menacing conditions and your proficiency and experience are not up to them, what you confront may not be significantly less dangerous than those a pilot without the instrument ticket may face. In any case, this chapter is meant for you. It is not a capsule course in instrument flying, but it will address some key situations that bedevil cloud flying.

Stumbling into IFR

Let's consider first the non-IFR pilot who lets himself become trapped in cloud or total darkness. He may be able to beat the crisis if he can bring to bear on it the power he has available to him—the airplane itself. If he has a *workable* knowledge of basic instrument flying and can apply a disciplined, "cool" attitude to the emergency, he can use that power to survive. It is a basic adage of flying that power plus attitude equals performance. That generally defines how airplanes fly. It also can describe the essentials of how they are flown by those at the controls.

How an airplane performs is governed by changes in thrust, pitch, bank, and yaw. In reasonably untroubled air, and with the power and attitude kept constant, an airplane will fly straight and level, or climb, descend, or turn with little additional control input. This relative stability allows an airplane trimmed for a desired airspeed to continue mostly "hands-off." Heading and pitch deviations can usually be countered with light pressures on the pedals or the yoke. That applies in cloud and out, but the pilot must be able to correct as necessary. If he lacks an external horizon, he can fly by the artificial horizon on the instrument panel. He can direct the plane IFR—if he knows what to look at on the panel and trusts what he sees. Otherwise, he can easily let "body clues" disorient him.

The proficient instrument pilot continually and rapidly scans the relevant instruments, applying light control pressures to make corrections and maintain the desired attitude, airspeed, and power. Power plus attitude equals performance. The crucial thing is to know what performance you want and, therefore, what you want the instruments to show you. That is obtained nonviolently and methodically.

If you lose your outside horizon, even sporadically, concentrate immediately on the instruments, particularly the attitude indicator or artificial horizon (AI), no matter what your "seat-of-the-pants" senses may tell you. Your eyes should return constantly to the AI as you scan the other gauges. For bank indications it is helpful to read the pointer at the top of the instrument. Its message is clear. An airplane does not turn from a heading unless it is banking. With the airplane in stable flight, the directional gyro is essential for monitoring heading control. However, using the DG alone to maintain heading is as inefficient as chasing the airspeed indicator (ASI) and altimeter needles to establish level pitch. The AI is the surest tool for keeping in charge of the airplane's pitch and bank status.

The Spiral Dive

The most common way that inexperienced pilots lose their airplanes in cloud is by putting or allowing them to fall into a spiral dive to the ground. Experience has shown that VFR pilots surprised in IFR tend to take a while to digest and acclimate themselves to the situation. Panic can set in before the pilot can reestablish control over himself and the aircraft, leading to disorientation and perhaps vertigo, with the victim wrongly manipulating the controls. In such a state the pilot may not realize that he has put the plane into a dive (or a speed-decaying climb). Failing to use the instruments, he does not notice what is happening to the airplane. The longer a spiral dive is allowed to develop, the harder the recovery. Your first move on stumbling into cloud, therefore, is to go to the panel; ignore your body clues and check the AI and turn-and-bank indicator.

On the AI, a spiral dive is indicated by a wing and the nose being low. On the turn-and-bank, the needle will be to the side. It is important to check the turn-and-bank or turn coordinator, in case the gyro governing the AI has tumbled. (On the rest of the panel, the altimeter will be spinning down, the airspeed needle will be moving toward the red line, the VSI will point downward. Outside, the sounds of the engine and passing air will be louder. Don't wait for all these confirmations.) The instant you recognize that you are in a spiral dive, reduce power all the way. *Don't try to pull out yet; don't pull back on the wheel.* Level the wings. If the AI or turn-and-bank, or both, indicate, say, that the left wing is low, press right rudder firmly and also apply right aileron until the pointers are straight up. Don't overcontrol so that you blunder into an opposite bank.

Then *draw*—don't yank—back on the yoke. Your airplane isn't a dive bomber, and violent action can break the airframe. You should feel some force pressing you down, but not too much. Hold the wings level and keep the power back until you see by the altimeter that the descent has virtually stopped, then deliberately and smoothly bring in power to establish level flight at cruise airspeed. Use the AI as your first reference, keeping the nose dot on the horizon line. Noting the ASI, maintain cruise airspeed. Check the altimeter for confirmation. Don't look outside—that can disorient you.

At this point, you may not be flying the heading you want, but the important thing here is to stabilize the airplane in straight-and-level flight. That done, you now should approach your next tasks methodically, beginning with attempting a turn back into the clear. While a *controlled* 180 immediately on entering cloud is the best course, it could be suicidal to initiate a turn that you can't control. A minute or so of steadied flying and getting settled for the maneuver is less dangerous than a desperate, uncoordinated, immediate effort at escape. That way a spiral dive can lie. Notify ATC or anyone on 121.5 after you make the turn or if you decide not to attempt it. When you tune the radio, move your eyes but not your head. If you are already tuned to Center or another ATC facility, fine. If you do not have someone immediately available, go to 121.5. Don't worry about future repercussions over your being illegally in cloud: You need help now, so seek it; furthermore, you owe it to other pilots for ATC to be able to keep you separated from them while you are in the blind.

Averting a Stall

If your instruments tell you that you are in an unwanted climb or climbing turn, take immediate action to avoid a stall/spin. A high nose dot and perhaps a low wing on the AI, along with low airspeed, are the critical signs. (The altimeter and VSI will confirm this. Also, things will become quieter, and at length, the controls may become mushy, and there may be prestall buffeting, but don't count on it.) To recover, immediately lower the nose to the horizon to regain airspeed and quickly but not violently level the wings. Your critical sources will be the AI and ASI. If you need to increase the power, do it gradually enough to prevent the nose from lifting toward an accelerated stall. If that begins to happen, lower the nose deliberately but not abruptly, for the possible negative *g* of "going over the top" of the vertical curve can cause disorientation or vertigo.

If there is a possibility that you will enter cloud in the cold,
turn on the pitot heat to prevent ice blockage of the pitot tube.
If your airspeed indicator should stop functioning, keep flying
power and attitude. If you are climbing and the ASI continues
to register high speed, don't hold backyoke to slow down. The
reading may be false. Recheck the AI, power setting, altimeter,
and VSI and, as soon as practicable, recheck and turn on the
pitot heat. If you must look for the switch, stabilize the airplane
first.

In cloud, turn off the strobes and other outside lights; turn
up the panel lights; concentrate on the panel; keep your body
and head movements to a minimum; keep your hands off the
controls as much as you can (after trimming), and pressure the
rudder pedals just enough to keep the wings level. Easy does it.
If you spot a hole in the clouds, be sure that it is large enough
to descend through safely, so you won't be suckered into a steep
turn or reentry into cloud.

You must retain the patience to do each job smoothly and
intelligently. If you are caught ill-prepared in IFR, the unfamiliar sensations, information, and stresses will intensify. Fear may
lead you to do the first wrong thing that comes to mind. The
first right thing is, once more, to stabilize the airplane, and you
must know just how you are going to do it.

Knowing demands far more than just reading about it. Hooded
practice and, even more important, actual cloud flying with an
instructor are vital to getting used to how it feels to fly on instruments. Certainly, no IFR trainee should feel well-served by
an instructor who refuses to teach in the soup. A simulator is
also highly useful, especially under an instructor. When you fly
VFR, regularly monitor the panel to note what the needles show
and what the best power settings are for climbout, cruise, cruise
climb, cruise descent, and the approach to landing.

Almost as serious as a failure to read the instruments is a
fixation on one or two gauges. Staring at an instrument, to the
exclusion of others that are important, is bad, in part because
staring does not necessarily mean that you are *registering* what

you see. The longer you fixate, the more likely it will be that the airplane will get ahead of you. This is a major problem for IFR beginners, but it also happens to experienced pilots when they make multiple control and power changes. What stops the scan for the longest time is some sort of secondary task loading. For example, when pilots in simulator tests of scanning habits were made to perform calculations or talk on the radio, they began to stare, usually at the attitude indicator. Some stared for half a minute, but did they really *see* it?

If such problems can beset instrument-rated pilots, they more probably will affect novices caught in cloud or darkness. Reason enough for avoidance.

"IFR . . . at Last!"

Getting your VFR-only self into an IFR scrape is bound to endanger you. You cannot afford to consider a little knowledge of instrument flying as an insurance policy against the worst. Solo IFR can be difficult even for seasoned general aviation pilots. It can wring out a relatively new instrument jock. Pilot Tom Jones tells of a flight when ''getting his ticket wet,'' the time-honored term for real-IFR initiation, was not just a metaphor:

I refused to ruin our trip with a thought about the weather. After all, that's what IFR is all about: No more days of sky watching, hourly calls to Flight Service, and arguments with my wife, Frances, over ''going commercial.'' With my ten-day-old instrument rating, slightly skeptical wife, and full-panel Cherokee 140, the trip from Tennessee to Vero Beach, Florida, had been picture perfect. On Friday, when I called Flight Service for a briefing about the weather on the way back, conditions were so bad I decided to stay a few more days and let them pass. They wouldn't. By Sunday morning, it was time to get tough. What is an instrument rating for, anyway? Making arrangements for Frances to fly back commercially from Melbourne, I would take N55336 home alone—without distractions.

The hop to Melbourne was IFR but fun. Low clouds streamed upward in the noonday heat, and we poked in and out of them with blue sky and sunshine between. An easy ILS into Melbourne was where the fun ended. After scrounging through all the data at the FSS on airports that could be in range and have an ILS, I came up with but one legitimate destination and one alternate. I filed for Albany, Georgia, took an apprehensive kiss from Frances, climbed into 336, set up the radios, and was off. Miami Center sent me up to 8,000, and with the wind out of the south, I thought things were great. My initial fears soon faded.

Scud had formed a solid deck way below me, and I didn't notice how gradually it was creeping upward. Miami was busy. I asked for a frequency change to check weather but was advised to stay on the frequency due to heavy traffic. Maybe in a little while. For some reason, I didn't think it important enough to ask again.

About the time that Miami handed me off to Jacksonville, I observed that it was only about 1,000 feet to the deck below me. I couldn't tell about the deck above me. Also, the last thirty minutes, I couldn't help noticing a "vertical thing" looming at one o'clock. Why didn't I become concerned about it? Center told me I was 20 miles out and gave me a lower altitude. Just before I plunged into the 8,000 feet of scud, I finally noticed the lightning. I asked Center about possible heavy weather in that area and was advised that there was a cell there—12 miles southwest of the Albany airport and moving slowly west. Just before I entered the fungating, purple mass, I asked about my alternate. A solid squall line lay between me and it. The dark curtain had been closed. Rain pounded on the airplane . . . blurred instruments . . . wild, swinging airspeeds . . . stall warnings . . . flying charts.

"This is Albany Approach. You're cleared the ILS Runway 4 approach, circle to 22. Wind is 250 degrees, 15 gusting to 30. Ceiling is 500 obscured, and 1-mile visibility with a thundershower."

They didn't have radar. I was on my own. The urge to run almost got me, but to where? Got to remember . . . attitude, not altitude. ILS without altitude? Albany tried to help, but what could they do? They told me to take my time and relax.

I remember saying "severe turbulence," as I jerked forward against my shoulder harness. And for a split second, I was in the clear. Straight below me I could see the runway. But in an instant, I was back in the storm. I thought I would never get to the beacon. Turbulence bad . . .

outbound finally . . . a little smoother . . . procedure turn outbound . . . rough.

And with me suddenly was the terrified voice of somebody VFR in the same mess with me. He sounded far away. "Severe turbulence"; then, "I've got Albany . . . I've got the beacon." That was his last transmission.

As I wrestled down the glideslope, the turbulence decreased. When I broke out at 500 feet, it was smooth as glass. I told the tower that I had the runway, the best sight I had ever seen. No comment.

At a hangar, I stumbled out of 336. The rain still pounded, as I dropped approach plates in the large puddles. I didn't care. Inside, there was an awesome quiet—not for me but for the silent airplane. Everyone sat huddled around the radio. Then the FSS said that he had landed safely. Later, as my taxi dodged the flooded intersections of Albany, I thought I would never fly again. I do, but not like that.

We will discuss the particularities of thunderstorms later in this book, but the point to note here is that a green IFR pilot allowed his confidence in his skill and the supposed omniscience of ATC to conduct him into violence. Experience can prevent such a thing, but not always. Even airline captains have suffered similar lapses. The instrument ticket is a license to begin to learn through experience about the gritty realities of flying alone in real weather and in a system that holds you responsible for maintaining the safety of your flight. Seldom will ATC just up and ask how you are doing. If you are in trouble or in doubt, it's up to you, the pilot-in-command, to blow the whistle and seek information and, if necessary, some help.

Alone in a Sea of Troubles

Instrument flying requires that the pilot-in-command function simultaneously and expertly as a strategic and tactical planner, manager, communicator, and stick-and-rudder virtuoso. In air-carrier operations, these roles are parceled among two or three crew members who are trained to work in close coordination.

The solo pilot does not have the luxury of concentrating on flying the aircraft while a co-pilot and flight engineer call out checklists, handle communications, navigate, and monitor systems. In an emergency, the solo pilot can delegate lesser but necessary jobs only to himself.

Pilots who fly solo IFR regularly face certain difficulties. A recent study, *Operational Problems Experienced by Single Pilots in Instrument Meteorological Conditions,* prepared by Stacy Weislogel, chairman of Ohio State University's aviation department, is particularly helpful in learning what they are. Weislogel studied reports compiled from the Aviation Safety Reporting System (ASRS) to identify the major nonweather IFR crises. In descending order of frequency, they are: perceptions of inadequate ATC service, altitude deviation, improperly flown approaches, heading deviation, position deviation, and below-minimums operations.

The researchers concluded that three out of four complaints that the pilots' expectations were not met by the System were reasonable. For example, ATC did not always inform pilots when radar contact was lost. Controllers "forgot" about pilots they were working. ATC cleared one pilot to a navaid that was out of service and vectored another toward an area of known, severe thunderstorms. However, pilots do harbor unjustifiable expectations, such as that ATC radar will necessarily cover an entire flight, that ATC will always use radar information to help a flight avoid severe weather or will infallibly vector pilots away from terrain. Furthermore, many pilots unrealistically expect Flight Service specialists to provide current information on thunderstorm activity along proposed routes of flight.

A form of partnership links you to the System. You should not hesitate to request clarification or verification of a clearance when doubt exists, but it makes sense to understand with good will that controllers can make mistakes, especially when their workload becomes intense, and that they must cope with occasional equipment failures. It is eye-opening to visit an ATC facility and observe the controlled frustration and anxiety that greet computer failure or unreliable scope information. The same effects can accompany a controller's having to deal with straying pilots, especially in crowded airspace.

Deviation from altitude can generate such feelings. In many cases, rather than flying his assigned altitude, the pilot settles at the one he has filed in his flight plan, has requested en route, or expects due to previous experience, although that flight level has been given to another aircraft. It can be hard for a controller to change such a "mind set," especially if the pilot chooses self-righteously to debate the issue. The best way to avoid confusion is to read any clearance back on receiving it. Every new clearance and instruction should be jotted down. It is wise always to report reaching an assigned altitude.

Where Accidents Happen Most

The majority of crashes occur during approach and landing. The ASRS reports disclosed that pilots generate crises by executing nonrequired procedure turns, improperly tracking navigational signals, improperly flying missed approaches, tuning navaids erroneously, losing track of their position, and busting minimums. Experiencing vertigo is a major problem. ATC sometimes has to intervene to save pilots from themselves, but controllers are not supposed to be doctors on call. For example, in today's System, you generally can expect radar vectors to the final approach course. Nevertheless, you are assumed able to, say, hand-fly an entire back-course localizer approach and missed approach at an unfamiliar airport, even with inoperative gyros.

Heading deviation is caused by pilots and controllers alike. Again, agreement as to what a clearance requires is crucial. Write down and read back even the simplest instruction, identifying yourself by the number the controller uses to call you. It is sobering to watch a controller rapidly issuing vectors to airplanes with similar numbers, getting non- or misidentifying responses, and seeing aircraft wrongly heading in dangerous directions.

Deviations become even more frightening if the pilot seems to have no clue that he is heading down harm's way—a silent and stupid partner. You must know where you are, where you are being headed, and how you are supposed to get there. Position awareness is key to the safety of single-pilot IFR. If you can maintain an accurate mental picture of your position and track, you will be less likely to deviate from your assigned altitude or heading or to become disoriented during an approach. Especially during lengthy radar vectoring or while watching the DME methodically tick away, one always has a potential for lapsing into complacency. Oblivious pilots have disrupted crowded traffic flows into near paralysis and have allowed themselves to be vectored to the wrong airport and even into terrain. One way of enforcing position awareness is continually to assume that the electrical system, vacuum pump, or both are about to fail. Planning for such a contingency demands knowing where you are.

Another study, this one by the National Aeronautics and Space Administration, reveals other problem areas indigenous to solo IFR. It was based on NTSB accident data for a recent twelve-year period, in which 1,000 general aviation, fixed-wing, instrument-pilot-flown crashes in IFR conditions took place. The researchers concentrated on landing accidents—again, the majority—attributed to pilot error. In half of these accidents, improper IFR operations were cited as probable causes, with low ceilings and fog often present. The pilots either flew too low or off course, failed to execute a called-for missed approach, or entered hazardous icing conditions. In a number of cases, pilot fatigue was cited.

When "Guidance" Stops in a Guided Approach

A number of the landing accidents occurred at night, which is particularly impressive since there are fewer general aviation

IFR approaches at night than during the day. Most of the accidents in which the visibility was 1 mile or less and where fog and precipitation existed occurred at night. There were three times as many ILS accidents at night as during the day. Most of the fatal and serious injuries occurred at night, as did most of the controlled collisions with obstructions and crashes due to spatial disorientation. A lack of approach surveillance radar (ASR) increased the number of ILS initial approach accidents. Heavy pilot workload (e.g., flying a procedure turn to intercept a localizer), a lack of precise position information, and an accustomed reliance upon receiving ASR service were felt by the researchers to be the reasons for the increase. Since lower landing minimums are allowed on ILS approaches, visibility was generally poorer than for VOR or NDB approaches. The median visibility in the ILS accidents was between ¾ and ½ mile.

The grim fact is that, although instrument students spend a great deal of time learning how to track the ILS glideslope and localizer down to decision height and then execute a missed approach, it is after the breakout from the clouds that the majority of ILS landing accidents take place. There are several reasons for this.

First, most IFR training occurs in relatively decent weather, so that when the student raises his hood at the DH, he will probably see before him a clearly defined path to a sharply outlined runway. In real life, an approach near to or at minimums may well include legally visible but partly obscured approach lights and runway. Second, as we saw in chapter 1, visual clues at night can be sparse or confusing, due to the physiology of the eye and interpretive quirks of the mind. Thus, it may be difficult to assess correctly your height above the ground, your distance from the aiming point, your rate of descent, and even how level your wings are. Some pilots have reported breaking out on an ILS and momentarily believing the bright approach lights to be *overhead*. To suffer such an illusion when only 200 feet up and traveling at high speed is, at the least, tricky. Sequence flashers can confuse a crabbing pilot as they race angularly across the windscreen. Furthermore, splattering or streaming rain on the windscreen and patches or wisps of fog can distort the approach lights. Most critically, such disturbances warp depth perception. Depending on their size, drops and droplets can magnify or reduce lights and other objects seen through Plexiglas, causing a false sense of altitude and/or distance as you near the runway.

Flying the ILS is consequently not merely a matter of flying the needles and knowing what to do on reaching the DH; you must be aware of the visibility that you are likely to find near the ground (*likely* because the reported visibility is as seen from the tower, not from an airplane, and even runway visual range values are at surface level)—whether there is rain or snow, if there is a wind shear or gusty or crosswind condition, what kind of approach light display there will be, if there are likely to be fog patches that might call for a last-minute missed approach. What the tower reports is very important but not necessarily the whole story.

The DH can be a major psychological trap. Since you may proceed to a landing if you have the approach lights or approach end of the runway in sight at the DH, your desire to see them may create them out of nonrelated lights. The wish for the sight must not be father to the thought that it is there.

The Nondirectional Conundrum

To shoot a down-the-middle ILS is every instrument pilot's ecstasy. To have to shoot a safe NDB approach is many a pilot's agony.

Nonprecision approaches lack electronic guidance for the prescribed descent. The NDB, the least precise of these approaches, demands the utmost precision from the pilot. It is counted among cockpit crises because a great many pilots regard it as such and try to avoid the confrontation. However, approximately one out of every four published approaches is an

NDB, and at hundreds of airports, the humble nondirectional beacon is the only way in.

While NDB approaches can be mastered, some things about them cause headaches. One is that NDBs are not always reliable navaids. Approach NDBs are often in the LOM (locator outer marker) class; their 25-watt output gives their signals a usable range of only about 15 nautical miles. Another factor is the phenomenon of precipitation static. Precipitation absorbs some of the energy, and therefore reduces the reliability, of the transmitted signal at long range. In addition, the ADF needle is attracted to atmospheric electric discharges. If you hear hissing and crashing noises over the ADF, don't look to the needle for navigational aid. In fact, an old device for detecting nearby thunderstorms is to tune the ADF to 200 kHz and see where the needle points.

Around sunrise and sunset, NDB low-frequency radio waves can bounce off the ionsphere and scatter as they strike the earth's surface. The greater the distance from the station, the more pronounced is this effect. Flying at a higher altitude helps to eliminate this, but that's not much comfort on an approach. Stations with frequencies lower than 350 kHz are less likely to be influenced by twilight effects. Mountainous terrain and magnetic deposits also can deflect weak NDB signals. The best remedy is in stations with high-wattage output: Stations in the H class put out between 50 and 2,000 watts and have a range of about 50 nm; the highest-powered NDBs, the HH class, put out 2,000 or more watts and are good for 75 or more nm. (Unfortunately, NDB classifications are not given on charts or approach plates, though they are found in the *Airport/Facility Directory* of the *AIM*.) Low-frequency radio waves bend as they pass from land to water, so when you are crossing a shoreline in either direction, use bearings that are at least 30 degrees to the shoreline. Fly as directly to or from the station as you can, on a course perpendicular to the shoreline, if the approach allows.

There is also the relatively infrequent occasion when you may be tracking a facility that goes out of service. Always audibly

identify the NDB; the absence of the identifier often indicates
that maintenance is being performed and the signal can't be used.
After you get the identifier, adjust the ADF volume so that you
can monitor the ident throughout the approach. If the ident stops,
the NDB has ceased transmitting. When the signal goes cold,
the needle freezes at 45 or 90 degrees on the card. Similarly, if
you hear a loud hum, muffled voices, or music, the NDB signal
is being interfered with by another radio station.

Setting Up Nonprecision Approaches

Any nonprecision approach calls for certain pretracking
measures to ensure a good margin of safety. Some of them will
depend upon the particular airplane and prevailing circumstances involved, but here are some basics:

• Be aware of the *minimum sector altitudes,* which are included in a circular diagram on the approach chart. The beacon
is at the center of the circle, the radius of which is 25 nm, unless specified otherwise. Sectors are defined by arrows pointing
toward the navaid and by magnetic courses to it. The published
altitudes provide at least 1,000 feet of clearance above the highest obstacles within their sectors. MSAs are meant for emergencies and to preclude confusion between pilots and controllers about
initial approach altitudes. Should you lose the navaid signal or
an engine or become confused, you will want to know these
numbers.

• Study the approach plan view and profile for approach altitudes, the outbound course, headings for the procedure turn, the
inbound course, and any step-down fixes and their facilities.
Again, check the locations and heights of obstacles along the
approach course.

• *Memorize the minimum descent altitude* for your cateogry of
aircraft. One way of keeping it in mind during the approach is
to call out altitudes along your descent, if only to yourself—''At

1200, MDA, six-forty; at 1,000, MDA, six-forty,'' and so on. Be sure you are clear on which MDA, straight-in or circling, applies to the approach you are shooting.

• Calculate the time from an off-airport, final-approach-fix beacon to the MAP and mark it clearly on the approach plate. To estimate the wind at the approach altitude, use the wind direction ATC gives you for your destination or nearest reporting station and add between 45 and 90 degrees; double the surface wind velocity. Your computer can then give you your estimated groundspeed and a good idea of your crosswind correction angle. If working with the computer is awkward at this point, a ballpark estimate should suffice. You can interpolate the navaid-to-MAP time with the aid of the groundspeed–time table on the approach plate.

• Remember that the wind changes just above the surface and that NDB approaches are frequently where there is no on-site reporting of conditions. It makes sense to set for yourself a higher MDA if the field is forecast near minimums or your ADF precision is in doubt. If you are not familiar with the field, study the airport diagram—runways, taxiways, location of obstructions and, if possible, buildings—so that you will know your position when you break out of the clouds. Make sure that what you see really matches what you ought to be seeing, particularly the runway layout, as you approach.

• Review the missed approach procedure, memorizing at least the initial heading, the direction of the turn, and the target altitude.

Tracking on the NDB Approach

While mere homing (keeping the ADF needle on the nose) can be suicidal for NDB approaches, pilots seem to be daunted more by the prospects of tracking, because the procedure seems to be unnaturally complicated. Actually, NDB tracking is not unlike tracking VFR along a long, straight road.

Controlling heading is the most important factor, and that can be helped by your creating a "poor man's RMI," that is, mentally superimposing the ADF upon the DG. If you don't have a rotating ADF card, assume that the zero at the top is the heading at the top of the DG. For instance, if the DG heading is 270 degrees and the ADF needle points 30 degrees right, the course to the station would be 300, where the needle would point on the DG. That line—the road to the station—also represents a radial of 120 degrees (the reciprocal of 300) from the beacon.

To place yourself on the course to or from the station, turn to the course heading, that is, parallel the road. If the needle then points off the upper lubber line (inbound) or the bottom lubber line (heading outbound), you then turn the aircraft toward the needle and double the number of degrees of that deflection angle—to intercept the road. *Inbound*, the needle will cross to the other side of the lubber line. You are *on* the course line when the deflection of the needle equals the number of degrees by which your *aircraft* is pointed off the *course* heading to intercept the course. The nose is pointed away from the road, but your butt is right over it. (For example, you have turned right 30 degrees, say to an intercept *heading* of 120, and the needle points left to 330 on the ADF card.) *Outbound*, the needle will move away from the bottom lubber line *but will stay on the same side of it as your turn*. When the needle is deflected from the lubber line by the same number of degrees as your intercept angle, you are on the course. (For example, if you have turned 20 degrees right to intercept and the ADF needle is at 160—20 degrees right.)

That done, turn to the course heading and observe for wind drift. If there is a crosswind, staying on the course now becomes a matter of crabbing, as if you were tracking above the road. As you hold the course heading, if the needle drifts off center, note how fast it moves to determine the wind strength.

When the deflection passes 3 to 5 degrees, crab into the wind (toward the needle) by 10 degrees. *Inbound,* the needle will cross the upper line (like a road crossing the nose). When that deflection and your crab angle are equal, turn back to the course heading. If the needle is on the nose, turn back to your crab heading. If the ADF needle deflection remains the same as the crab angle, you have bracketed the course and are correcting well.

However, if the needle moves toward or away from the lubber line, you will have to readjust your crab angle. No problem: Only in textbooks and aviation journalists' cockpits is *the* angle hit the first time. You must repeat the procedure, but now you have more to go on. Turn again to the course heading, see where the needle points, double the angle to get back on course. As you drift, crab anew and repeat as necessary.

Accommodating to the Approach

Of course, when you are tracking on an approach, there isn't much time to perfect your correction, especially if you are past the FAF. The point is *to keep your deviations from the course as small as possible.* As you begin to drift, turning back toward the course can protect you, but don't grossly overshoot it. Keep narrowing the adjustments and *hold the heading that works* so as to avoid swooping back and forth across the glidepath.

As you track inbound, the needle at length will begin to twitch erratically. If the ident is strong, meaning no signal interference, station passage is imminent. *Hold your heading* and wait for the needle to swing around to the tail. The swifter the swing, the closer you are to the beacon. On station passage, the needle usually will behave sluggishly and unpredictably. Let it be. If you must start timing at station passage, begin when the needle swings past three or nine o'clock on the ADF. The swing speed may also depend on your altitude, something to remember if you must pass the station both outbound and inbound.

When you are tracking *outbound,* the procedure is the same, except that the crab and needle deflection will both be to the same side of the tail lubber line. Again, mentally superimpose the ADF on the DG (checked against the compass) to keep your headings straight and true. Turn to the course heading. If the needle is at six o'clock, you are on the course. If not, turn to intercept the course, and then follow the above procedure.

The best time for working out the wind correction angle and heading is when you are flying the initial portion of the approach. That is one of the helpful things about procedure turns. An NDB approach imposes a heavier navigational task than do other types. There is more need for preplanning the final descent to the MDA so that the airport can be sighted in time for a normal 3-degree descent to the threshold. Not only solid tracking but a constant-airspeed descent is a must, to make good your timing.

A radio magnetic indicator (RMI) combines the ADF with a DG and VOR and is very helpful. Another aid is RNAV, which can pinpoint the MAP if you have the MAP waypoint coordinates. One way *not* to simplify NDB work is to try what has wrecked several pilots—concocting unapproved, makeshift approaches using nearby VOR radials. The best protection is a firm policy of not doing what you strongly suspect you cannot do. For instance, many smart pilots of high-performance aircraft refuse an NDB approach with less than 1,000-and-3, because they will either have to approach too fast and steeply or drag in at a speed so slow it reduces elevator control.

Going to the MDA

On any nonprecision approach, it can pay to go to the MDA as soon as the procedure allows, as long as you maintain a reasonable rate of descent. This may enable you to break out early on and to see if patches of cloud or fog might obscure your de-

scent from the MAP. Hold that altitude up to the MAP, however, even if the airport is in sight the whole way, to assure
obstruction protection and a safe altitude from which to begin a
missed approach, if needed. If you are flying by radio altimeter,
beware of depressed terrain on the glidepath that may induce you
to descend below the MDA, *which is based on MSL, not AGL
values.* This is particularly important when poor visibility leaves
you uncertain of how the terrain ahead of you may lie.

As you approach the field, beware of VFR traffic in the pattern, especially if the field is noncontrolled and is at or just above
VFR minimums. Don't assume that such traffic will be announcing its position or even be legal. Fly defensively. Announce over Unicom that you are approaching IFR and indicate
your position and intention to make a straight-in or circling
landing.

Circling to Land

Many experienced pilots, including airline captains with their
wide-winged craft, have an aversion to low circling landings.
The circling approach at minimums is, in effect, an IFR maneuver in visual conditions. On paper, with MDAs usually 500 or
600 feet AGL, they look easier than landings from a DH breakout only 200 AGL, but that can be a fooler. Usually, even in
IFR, pilots circle to land in a normal VFR pattern. Consequently, they are not always up for certain surprises:

There is the sudden impression of going too fast. Accustomed to the perceptions of downwind legs at 800 to 1,000 feet,
we find that at 500 or 600, the visual cues increase our *apparent*
groundspeed 50 to 100 percent. It takes concentration to defeat
the urge to slow inadvertently close to or into a stall.

Another surprise is that beneath looming weather, we circle
much closer to the field than we intend or are used to. On downwind, for example, we are used to judging our distance from the

runway by reference to some fixed angle with respect to the air-plane. At about half the normal pattern altitude, this angle-sighting process places the aircraft much closer in than is usual. Furthermore, in reduced visibility, we work hard to keep the runway securely in sight, so we shorten the legs, especially base, and tighten the turns, sometimes actually circling onto final—as when we fly downwind over the runway and reverse course just beyond the approach end, or cross over the runway and then do a tight 270 to final. Especially in a crosswind, such turns induce overshooting the centerline, which can lead to excessive banking at slow speed and a possible stall/spin.

Starting down too soon can bring a jolt. Many pilots normally descend on downwind abeam the threshold. At the circling minimum, that is too early, since there is less altitude to lose. It is illegal to go below the circling MDA until one is "in a position from which a normal approach to the runway of intended landing can be made." It is best to delay departing the MDA until you are on base or turning to final.

One can be caught in all three binds—too low, too slow, too steep.

To avoid that, ask yourself first if you really need to circle. If the conditions are marginal and the wind is not too strong, it may be safer to land crosswind on an ILS runway (which is usually the longest and has the best approach lighting) than to circle to an upwind landing. Towers will accommodate requests for a straight-in if possible. If there is no tower and the airport is unfamiliar, the crosswind or even a slight downwind landing option may be safer, if conditions don't encourage circling.

The key objective is to keep the target runway always in sight and have room for reasonable leg lengths, turn rates, and airspeeds. It may be wise to pass over a nontower field to choose your runway and set up your pattern. Usually, this means left turns, even if you must circle the whole field. Be patient, for if you are finishing a difficult approach after a long flight, it is easy to be misguided by an overeagerness to land.

Complete the landing checklist before beginning the approach, configuring and trimmng the airplane for its circling speed. Memorize the missed approach: Circling at 500 feet in gone visibility is no time to be reading a piece of paper. Save your eyes for the airport or, if needed, the gauges. Be sure you have the local altimeter setting, or the closest thing to it.

Night circling aggravates the problems we have discussed. In addition, the tower may be closed, and the loyal Unicom operator may be home communing with TV. Strange airports seem stranger when the visual guides are unfamiliar lights, which may be swimming in other lights. You may even have to turn on the runway lights by radio. Night circling is not for one new to his aircraft or to instrument flying.

If you lose the airport or can glimpse only vague portions of it, execute the missed approach. On this, Part I of the *AIM* is specific:

• If your visual reference is lost in a circling approach, you must fly the missed approach, unless ATC assigns an alternate procedure.

• To reach the prescribed missed approach course, make an initial climbing turn toward the landing runway and keep turning until reaching the course.

• Since circling maneuvers vary, so do patterns for reaching the missed approach course, depending on where visual reference is lost. You must always be aware of your position with respect to the target runway.

The Missed Approach

This may well be the most critical part of any approach, because if it must be flown, the affecting conditions will leave small margin for error. The transition from final to the missed approach occurs when the cockpit workload is very high. The pilot has shifted his attention from the instruments to the outside for visual references, which can be elusive and illusional. The aircraft is slow, perhaps with landing gear and flaps extended; the weather is, by definition, lousy at the least, and the pilot has not been looking forward to things turning out this way.

Ironically, during training, the majority of our approaches include a miss. We get to the DH or MAP, flip up the hood, see the runway miraculously before us, and then, by prior arrangement with the instructor, climb into the missed approach. That should reinforce the habit of expecting that *every* approach will include a miss—unless it doesn't—so we can be triggered for it. However, in real IFR, most approaches end in a legal landing the first time, and we lose the expectant edge. Reluctance replaces rapid response.

The decision to land or to miss must be quick, yet for some pilots, it is hard to forego a landing that has seemed close at hand. Their temptation is to try to slither in, hoping that the runway will appear before they splatter onto or near it. As in the following case:

• The pilot, a company president, had more than 1,800 hours of flying time, including over 250 in his Cessna 414. Before departing Boca Raton, Florida, IFR, with seven passengers, he received this forecast for Richmond, Virginia, which is about 14 miles southeast of his destination, Hanover County Airport, in Ashland: 800-foot overcast, 1-mile visibility, with the overcast occasionally dropping to 400 feet. Although required by regulation to file an alternate, the pilot did not. He was cleared to intercept the 342-degree radial of the Richmond Vortac, which is the IAF for the VOR approach to Runway 16 at Hanover. The published missed-approach procedure included a climbing left turn to 2,000 feet via the Richmond 324 radial and holding at Annas Intersection. However, the pilot was issued a different procedure by ATC: a climb to 2,000, and direct to the Flat Rock Vortac, 22 nm to the south.

After clearing the pilot for the approach and instructing him to change to Hanover's Unicom, the Approach controller, monitoring the 414's progress, noted that it did not discontinue its descent at 800 feet, the published MDA. The last altitude the 414's radar target displayed was 400 feet—less than 200 above the airport elevation. During its descent, the aircraft drifted east of the final approach course. Witnesses said that it passed over the runway east to west and was flying in and out of clouds, just above the tops of trees near the airport. The 414's right wing then struck a tree; the Cessna rolled sharply to the right and impacted in a steep nosedown attitude. The eight occupants were killed.

Hanover had no weather-reporting facility, but the NTSB believes that the field was below its approach minimums. Richmond was then reporting an overcast ceiling, variable from 200 to 400 feet, and 1-mile visibility in light drizzle and fog.

Apparently, the urge to duck under proved irresistible to the pilot. Or perhaps the assignment of an unfamiliar missed approach unnerved him. Still, under the circumstances, the decision to execute the miss should have been automatic. However, Hanover was his home base, and, according to the NTSB, "the pilot was familiar with the terrain and landmarks on and adjacent to the airport. Therefore, once he could see the lights on the ground, he probably attempted to maneuver for landing by reference to these visual cues alone." The board also determined that on departure, the 414 was carrying more than 870 pounds of load in excess of its certified maximum takeoff weight. While this was not called a major factor in the accident, the NTSB regarded it as an illustration of "the pilot's disregard for safe operating practices and compliance with" regulations.

The Regs and Good Sense

Ironically yet understandably, while the FARs do not prohibit private pilots from initiating approaches in all weathers, air-carrier pilots are enjoined from approaches when conditions are reported below minimums. The general aviation pilot is still prohibited from descending below the DH or MDA, unless "the aircraft is continuously in a position from which a descent to a landing on the intended runway can be made at a normal rate of descent using normal maneuvers." Furthermore, the rule states that the flight visibility—as determined by the pilot—must be at or above the prescribed approach minimum.

Also, at least one of these visual references must be, as the rule states, "distinctly visible and identifiable":

- Approach lights
- Threshold markings
- Runway end identifier lights
- Runway threshold
- Threshold lights
- Visual approach slope indicator (VASI)
- Touchdown zone, zone markings, or zone lights

There are caveats to these options. While flight visibility is a subjective determination and the pilot seems to be the authority on what he can see, controllers must report landings when the reported visibility is ½ mile or less. Those pilots may be called on to explain. Yet, contrary to what you may have read, control towers are not populated by prosecutors looking for work. The regs are based on good sense.

The Bust Not Wanted

It is possible that you may lose visual contact after legally descending below the DH or MDA; if so, not to fly a miss would be a violation. Perhaps more frightening than a willful duck is one that occurs because the pilot is too unaware or unskilled to stop it. The majority of minimums accidents happen that way, for various reasons: The pilot becomes so engrossed in the ILS, he forgets the altimeter and/or how high the DH is, especially if he is diving to recapture the glideslope; the pilot becomes so intent on finding the airport, he lets the descent continue, dives to reach the MDA just before reaching the MAP, or levels below the MDA; the pilot neglects to get a valid altimeter setting; the pilot misreads the approach plate or uses the wrong plate . . . the possibilities are many.

Failure to stay abreast of altimeter changes while approaching a nontower airport is high on the list. In bad weather, barometric pressure can change rapidly, and a setting thirty minutes old can become obsolete. Numbers become misplaced in transmission or receipt; for every 0.01 of barometer discrepancy, there is a difference of 10 feet, so a "small" mistake set in the Kollsman can lead to a large altitude error close to the ground. Another lethal flaw is the pilot's inability simply to hold altitude. Be it due to nervousness, a misunderstanding of trim technique, an inability to handle pitch changes with gear or flap operation, whatever, a pilot under stress can stray below a minimum altitude, although he need only fly level.

Missed approach points for many nonprecision approaches do not leave much room for a normal descent and landing. To ease matters, *visual descent points* have been published for many straight-in nonprecision approaches. A VDP, identified with a *V* on the approach profile view, provides room for a normal descent from the MDA to the runway. If the usual sighting requirements are not satisfied upon reaching the VDP, the pilot continues to the MAP and then initiates a missed approach.

Making a Hit on the Missed Approach

Successfully completing a missed approach requires preparation, discipline, and sound technique. At the DH or MAP, do not hesitate or let temptation mar your concentration; apply climb power, pitch the nose to a climb attitude, clean up the aircraft, and tell ATC what you are about, including your intentions after completing the missed approach. Completing the miss success-fully demands alertness and quickness.

Your intentions upon completing the miss must include hav-ing a workable alternate, one that is forecast for your ETA there to be above 600-and-2 for a precision approach (ILS or PAR) or 800-and-2 for a nonprecision. Far from being a formality to "satisfy the Feds," selecting the alternate is potentially a life-and-death commitment. If the bad weather that prevents your making it in to your primary destination covers a large area, your alternate also could go below minimums, even as you fly your first approach. If your fuel supply leaves you no other choice, you could have to face the hazards of a below-minimums ap-proach to an alternate that goes sour as you fly to it. Update your weather information and ask ATC or Flight Service about possible open alternates even as you fly to your primary desti-nation. If the weather is grandly going to pot, your departure airport could prove to be your best or only reliable alternate.

In retrospect, it may seem peculiar that certain basic IFR op-erations such as we have been discussing should be described as cockpit crises—they weren't designed to be that way. But they *have* become matters of crisis for many pilots and even harbin-gers of disaster. Instrument flying is a difficult, challenging, and taxing occupation. It demands the fullest powers of intelligence and skill from a pilot, and it calls for an attitude of steadiness, professionalism, and that blessing, "grace under pressure." For the airman who carelessly stumbles into cloud or confidently and legally makes a highway there, such an attitude is truly a saving grace. That is the good word.

The bad word is that IFR pilot errors have accounted for hundreds of lives in recent years and that neither the System nor the pilots who inhabit it are failure-proof. All the more reason to adhere tenaciously to the elements of righteous practice. As we shall see in the next section, these elements lie even more at the heart of survival when the pilot encounters violent elements of another kind.

Part Two
WIND HAZARDS

3
Thunderstorms

From the first, aviators have perceived that he who knows not the wind may reap the whirlwind. Headwinds, tailwinds, crosswinds; gusts, shears, and storms; the constant and frivolous currents of the ocean of air have always had to be reckoned with and handled.

Reckoning with the wind does not banish the whirlwind, but knowledge can render it manageable, if we learn how not to challenge it beyond our powers. The ways of the atmosphere are today far less a mystery than in the past, but these forces still tax a pilot's skills, however much power and strength he carries in his aircraft. Airliners and bombers commanding thousands of pounds of thrust are still vulnerable, and unique would be the pilot of lighter craft who has not at some time faced a grave crisis in a cockpit buffeted or wrenched about by rampaging masses of air.

In this section, we will confront not only winds that nature stirs to bedevil us but man-made blasts. We will begin with the most consistently awesome and complex of wind phenomena, the thunderstorm. To understand how to "manage" flight when thunderstorms are a factor, we must understand how they are created. In the space of this book, our examination cannot be exhaustive—this subject occupies shelves of volumes devoted exclusively to it—but it is intended as a means toward recognizing basic signals, on the weather charts and in the sky, and toward using sound techniques and tools in making weather flying decisions.

Battles without Bullets

Many reports of encounters with thunderstorms have quali-
ties of accounts of outnumbered fighter pilots diving into huge
enemy formations. For combat pilots, initiating battle is necessary. From the first, their survival is problematic, even impossible, but more important objectives dictate that they do it. Not
so for us civilians, who are trained to avoid any violent confrontation in the sky. For us and those who fly with us, survival
is the thing, and timidity is an honorable means to that end.

All the more tragic, then, is a report such as this:

• The noninstrument pilot, 34, received a telephone weather
briefing and was advised to expect instrument flight conditions
along his projected route, including rainshowers, thunderstorms,
and moderate turbulence. The aviator had 186 total hours and
had logged 10 hours, including 3.3 of simulated instrument flight,
in his Cessna 210L. He departed an Indiana airport for his Georgia destination between 2:00 and 3:00 P.M. EST on a VFR flight
plan. No radio contact with him was recorded after his departure. Meanwhile, a Sigmet calling for flight precautions over
Tennessee and warning of embedded thunderstorms with tops to
35,000 feet was issued. It was valid from 2:55 to 5:00 P.M.

At approximately 5:30 P.M., several witnesses observed the
aircraft spinning out of a 3,000-foot overcast ceiling with a large
section of the wing falling beside the main structure. The airplane struck some trees before burrowing into the earth. The flier
and five passengers, all relatives, were killed.

The National Transportation Safety Board found that the
probable cause of the accident was the pilot-in-command's "improper inflight decisions or planning, operation beyond experi-
ence/ability level, continued VFR flight into adverse weather
conditions, spatial disorientation, and exceeding design stress
limits of the aircraft." The board also noted that the weather
forecast was substantially correct.

We can only wonder at what happened. Were the destructive stresses pilot induced, or did the forces within the storm doom the airplane, no matter what the pilot might have done? Would the pilot have had the wit to find his way out had nature granted him a little more time? At what point did the pilot pass from being able to evade the storm or extricate himself from it to being involved in something stronger than his or his aircraft's ability to survive? Know your adversary, the wise combat pilots say, so he won't take you unawares. Did this pilot recognize the adversary when he first saw it? Considering that he had been warned and had so little experience, was the worst adversary he faced *himself?* As we shall see, this accident and our questions about it reflect on basic principles of thunderstorm management.

A Little Knowledge . . .

Statistically, thunderstorms are not a major cause of general aviation accidents. In 1982, for instance, there were 34 fatal general aviation accidents involving thunderstorm activity. Pilots lost control of their aircraft while attempting to penetrate thunderstorms; loss of control in other accidents caused the aircraft to break up before hitting the ground; other pilots struck trees or flew into mountains while trying to fly underneath or near thunderstorms.

The smallness of these numbers indicates the respect that thunderstorms command among most pilots. Yet there is a nagging possibility that embedded in any year's weather-flying experiences is an unhealthy number of unreported close calls. In some pilots, unfortunately, experience does not engender wise respect but arrogance. Some "experts," well-meaning as they are, have a way of diluting their admonitions about thunderstorm dangers by encouraging too much of a taking-a-look-won't-hurt mentality. Even the new knowledge and technology we have developed for dealing with thunderstorms in recent years—information that tends to be more scary than soothing—has encouraged some pilots to press the flesh of a beast they may feel has lost most of its surprises.

It doesn't take a cavalier attitude to get caught. Even if, like Jeff Richmond, you are a pilot armed with a professional's discipline and a strong airplane equipped with weather-piercing eyes, you may find it hard to "watch your six" in a gaggle of turbulent bogies:

My first flight as captain on a Convair 240 was also my co-pilot's first flight as a qualified crew member. We were flying a routine training route from Sacramento, California, and had spent nearly six hours flying over southern California, while other members of the crew, under the direction of a navigational instructor, tried to locate the Pacific Ocean. It was their first flight, too—their instructor was the senior crew member that day.

Our first hint of trouble came after a check was made with the Sacramento Flight Service Station. We were warned of heavy thunderstorms stretching between us and our destination, and, up ahead, we could see menacing cumulus clouds forming a forbidding horizon.

According to the FSS briefer, the line extended from the Sierra Mountains to the San Francisco Bay area. From our position south of Lodi, California, a detour to the east meant confronting mountain peaks 10,000 feet high in the doubtful, surely turbulent, weather conditions. Diverting to the west would add two hours of flight time to the (still lost) Pacific Coast to get behind the storm line.

We had several minutes to consider our options, and in the process, we asked Air Traffic Control if it had any reports of severe weather and if the line of thunderstorms appeared to be solid. The controller replied that no one had flown through since the storm had appeared, but he thought he could see a gap between two heavy cells. If we wished, he would vector us through the area.

The controller sounded positive, at least to a crew that wanted to avoid the two-hour detour. Our navigator began adjusting the ground mapping radar, which, in a pinch, could provide some weather detection. Over the intercom, the navigator informed me that he could not see any gap between the cells. I attributed this to the limitations of the navigation radar. I asked the co-pilot to call ATC and accept the controller's offer for vectors between the storm cells. We were nearing the storm line rapidly—the dark clouds grew up out of the Sacramento Valley like a newborn mountain range.

As soon as the controller gave us our first heading, we entered the clouds. Immediately, we were engulfed in darkness; there was only a hint of turbulence, but my stomach tightened. I soon realized that we were in a maze, depending on someone else to find an open path to the exit. Within seconds, the controller called again. His voice sounded tense: "Another cell is beginning to appear on the radar directly in front of you. Maintain heading. Expect a turn in two minutes."

My cool, professional "roger" was the product of a false sense of confidence in the controller's ability to detect fully the intensity of the storm. But our navigator knew, and the intercom cracked, "Sir, I can see that cell on the nav radar. It is directly ahead, less than 5 miles. We'll be in it in less than three minutes."

"Roger." The cool was wearing off fast.

I poked the co-pilot. "Call Approach and say we want a 180, and then we'll take the detour to the west."

ATC did not respond. Lightning began to appear in the gloom. Still no response from ATC. "Tell it we are going to make that 180 now." I had made my decision, but I wanted some advice. "Hey, Nav, which way should I turn?" I shouted into the intercom. His response was not encouraging. "It looks like those two that we flew between have come together behind us."

I picked a left turn, but the storm had other ideas. Immediately, the aircraft went into a 60- to 70-degree uncommanded right bank. Using both hands, I twisted the control wheel to the left. Lightning ricocheted through the blackness. The spinning propellers appeared frozen in the quick flashes of energy. Thunder crashed over the drone of our 2,400-horsepower radial engines. Huge raindrops—they sounded like stones—pelted the cabin. Gradually, the artificial horizon began to return to a familiar attitude.

Then the vertical speed indicator began to show a climb of 2,000 fpm. The old Convair was a good airplane, but for those 44,000 pounds of nuts and bolts to climb at that rate would have required takeoff power and a zoom maneuver. We were caught in a vicious updraft. My first reaction was to try to hold my assigned altitude of 5,000 feet. With the nose pointed down, the airspeed was approaching red line, and we still were climbing like a runaway elevator.

Quickly, a long-forgotten textbook diagram of a thunderstorm flashed through my mind. Where there are updrafts, there probably are downdrafts. Suddenly I saw the diagram superimposed on an exaggerated image of the Sierra foothills below, reaching up toward us. I decided to let the aircraft climb and allowed the airspeed to slow to maneuvering speed. I concluded that altitude—high altitude—would be better than being caught in a downdraft, with my nose pointed down, near the sharply rising mountains.

The co-pilot finally raised ATC, but it was unable to find us on radar because the storm was too dense. Radio communications were intermittent. Then the navigator, sounding irritated, called, "Hey, pilot, I can't find the ground!"

The Pacific I could understand, but the ground? In the few seconds that we had been fiddling with the radios, the aircraft had rolled into a 90-degree bank. No wonder he couldn't find the ground. "There, how's that?" I asked, as the co-pilot and I twisted the earth back beneath the airplane, where it belonged. The navigator's answering grunt was less than enthusiastic.

As I tried to maintain control of the aircraft, the co-pilot was busy just trying to find somebody to talk to. In less than two minutes, we had gained 4,000 feet of altitude and were still climbing. I sought to hold a heading that would be the most direct path through the storms, but the turbulence was severe, and the heading indicators looked more like spinning tops than compasses.

All this time, lightning was shooting through clouds like angry arrows hunting some unseen prey, while rain continued to hammer the cabin. I did not want to admit it, but I was scared. I concentrated on holding the aircraft relatively level. Again the navigator called: "Sir, it looks like it is not quite as thick to our right. I think if you turn right we may fly out of this [stuff]."

At his first mention of "right," I had already begun the turn. My mind ran through a series of broken thoughts: "Standard rate turn for thirty seconds—hope this works—roll wings level. How much longer? Hold the wings level—wish I knew just where we are." Then, in the next instant, we flew out of the wall of clouds into bright, clear sunshine. Directly ahead, about 5 miles away, we could see our base.

When we had shut down the engines, I stayed in the cockpit for a few minutes, not wanting the rest of the crew to see my shaking legs. As the students were leaving the aircraft, one would-be navigator stuck his head into the cockpit. "Wow! Is it always like this? That was really fun." I just gave him a lame smile and nodded.

Enemy Forces

In this account, we can see most of the effects that constitute a thunderstorm's order of battle. First, there is the rapidity with which an airplane and a storm can make contact, especially if the storm is growing as well as tracking toward the aircraft. A flight path in an area of developing cells can be a series of collision courses, and when the cells are embedded in cloud, the "maze," as Richmond calls it, becomes far more sinister.

Next, there are the violent forces—up, down, and around—that can literally flip even a heavy, multi-engined machine into hazardous attitudes. Such turbulence can jolt a tightly strapped-in pilot to the point where the yoke is hard to hold, where his hand reaching for a knob only flails ineffectively, and where the vibrating instruments become "spinning tops" before his eyes.

Researchers have found that turbulence can affect a pilot's judgment, decision-making ability, reflexes, motor actions, and perception. The air force discovered that a sudden onset of moderate or severe turbulence can startle a pilot and cause him to make involuntary control movements. (During its investigation of one fatal clear air turbulence-related accident, the NTSB found that the pilot had moved the fuel/air mixture control to Idle/Cutoff during the initial climb.) Turbulence can also affect sensory illusions. During tests conducted by the air force, subjects consistently reported their instruments to be unreadable, when photographs showed them to be indicating clearly.

Such punishment, especially compounded by fear, is quickly fatiguing. In such conditions, vertigo and a general disorientation can betray even an accomplished instrument pilot. Finally, hoped-for outside help may be lost as radio contact fails, radar vectors prove useless, and onboard radar, assuming one has it, spells no relief. What light may be thrown upon the scene may be only from sudden, blinding electrical flashes that compound these other effects upon the pilot and may do physical damage to the aircraft—which is, of course, also structurally endangered by the storm's winds and hail.

During his battle, Richmond remembered diagrams he had seen of thunderstorms, with their neatly curving arrows and shadings representing the forces, masses, and materials of a storm. By visualizing the updrafts and downdrafts, he could see the potential benefit of being elevated well above his assigned altitude, since a powerful downdraft could just as easily drive him into the ground.

Diagrams neatly illustrate the "machinery" of a thunderstorm and suggest the extent of its violence, but they can also invest storms with more predictability than may be warranted for a particular disturbance. Thunderstorms form, rage, and die according to physical laws, but so varied and complex are their elements, that any thunderstorm and its accompanying environment should be considered an erratic individual whose properties will include a dirty, mean streak.

Modest Seeds

The makings of a thunderstorm crisis can at first be absurdly humble. On a summer's day, a pilot sweats through his preflight walkaround, cursing the heat and humidity and impatiently looking forward to lifting off to where the air is sure to be cool and refreshing. The sky is blue, except for increasingly numerous cumulus puffs that seem to form and then slowly fizzle. Aloft at last, he notices a light-to-moderate chop as he heads for his destination. If he is a glider pilot, he may be thinking of the lift he could be getting in his sailplane from those bumps: They are thermals, columns of heated, lighter air naturally rising to top surrounding, cooler, denser, "heavier" air. Almost a hundred miles ahead of him he sees a solid cirrus overcast and large cauliflower heads of cumulus rising thousands of feet above his altitude. At first, the heads seem well separated, but even as those buildups begin to dissipate, other large, increasingly menacing cumulonimbus clouds loom upward around them, and the gaps narrow. The pilot remembers that in the area of his destination, the surface temperatures have been reported at about 85 degrees F, with dewpoints in the 40s and low 50s. The reports spoke of "chance of thunderstorms," and now there is clearly trouble ahead. A weather update is in order, as is some consultation with the appropriate Center or Approach facility for radar reports and, possibly, vectors around the boiling mass. It is also time for making some hard decisions about the general outlook for the flight.

Thunderstorms are compounded of unstable air—warm air *underlying* or surrounded by cooler air—the presence of significant water vapor, and the operation of something that can lift the warm air smartly upward, so that it cools faster than at the normal lapse rate. Heat radiating from land baking in the sun will do it, as will winds converging or blowing over hills, or as will frontal action forcing a mass of warm, moist air into overlying cooler air. The body of warm air continues to rise, like a bubble through water, until it cools to nearly the temperature of the surrounding air aloft. Very warm air can contain large amounts of moisture. That moisture condenses, forming cloud and also creating heat. In an air mass thunderstorm, the simplest kind, the ingredients of unstable air, a lifting agent, and sufficient moisture can thus combine into a temporarily self-perpetuating machine. As the warm air rises, the space beneath it is filled by other warm, moist air, which is also drawn upward, et cetera, et cetera. That air may be cool air that has sunk to the surface, to become warm and ripe for rising. (It is important to know that thunderstorms can occur in any season, including winter, under the right conditions.)

Thunderstorms can gain tremendous momentum during their growth stage. One factor that helps is the creation of heat as moisture condenses. The formation of cloud tends to retard the cooling of the warm air, so that it keeps lifting and remaining warmer than the air around it. It is not uncommon for a thunderstorm to begin to grow at a few hundred feet per minute and quickly accelerate to 3,000 to 8,000 fpm, reaching up to 30,000 feet and quite possibly higher. If there is instability or low pressure aloft, the vertical flow and condensation can be sustained as high as 60,000 feet.

As the water vapor continues to rise, it cools to its saturation point (dewpoint), which results in clouds of water droplets that collide and form larger, heavier droplets. A thunderstorm with extremely strong vertical development can hold very large droplets suspended above the freezing level, so that they become supercooled and freeze on contact with ice nuclei, such as dust particles, producing hail. If the rush of upward flowing air is strong enough, a hailstone can be kept suspended and grow to larger than a baseball. At some point, however, the water droplets and the hailstones become too heavy to be supported by the rising air, and they begin to fall.

The precipitation, in turn, generates downdrafts—and heat— that blow through the bases of the clouds and spread swiftly along the ground, creating a violent gust front and wind shearing— layers of wind flowing in abruptly differing directions and speeds. Downdrafts betoken that the storm has reached maturity. Unless something happens to break the pattern for such an air mass thunderstorm—and things do happen—the machine will lose energy. Falling rain produces drag that slows the vertical drafts; cascading cooler air also tamps down the fury. Anywhere from twenty to ninety minutes after such a storm begins it will probably die, unless something rechurns the explosive mixture.

Does Simple Mean Safe?

Such a storm is relatively simple in structure and is short-lived. It billows energetically in its youth, stabilizes in its maturity and then wears out, consumed by the precipitation and cooling it has spawned, until its winds are reduced and its crown of cloud is lopped away by high-altitude currents. It is, nevertheless, a dangerous animal. For a pilot who flies too close to them, those winds, those pellets of hail, and the lightning that is integral to a thunderstorm can be lethal.

An airplane penetrating such a storm can ride it out—*if* the gust-produced and shear-induced stresses upon the airplane are not stronger than the designed *g* load; *if* the pilot is skillful enough not to overstress the plane himself; *if* hail or lightning or ice or water ingestion don't fatally tip the balance. Furthermore, there is no guarantee that a given storm will be as simply constructed or isolated as the "typical" air mass disturbance, which is not categorized as severe or extreme. There are other, more dangerous kinds, as we shall see, and conditions can change rapidly. Even with radar or other storm-detection gear, a pilot may face many unknowns.

There are tactics that a pilot can bring to bear in such a situation, and we will discuss them in the next chapter, but in using them he may be like an outgunned fighter pilot who blunders too far into a melee to be able to run: He must do what he can, but the odds won't be in his favor. His best policy would be to see and avoid.

What do we mean by *avoid?* The advice of experts and experienced pilots counsels anywhere from a 5-mile to a 20-mile berth. Don't try to fly over a growing thunderstorm unless you are already sufficiently high to clear it by at least a couple of thousand feet or unless you know for sure that your airplane has a climb rate capable of clearing the fast-rising drafts and the turbulent, often ice-laden cloud tops. Down below, attempting to sneak beneath the cloud bases could be inviting encounters with a devastating gust front, wind shear, downdrafts, heavy precipitation, and terrible visibility near terrain.

That a wide berth is advisable in the extreme is attested to by pilot T. L. Barber:

On a flight to Columbus, Ohio, in his Cessna Skyhawk, Barber had been plagued by the suspicion that a threatening cold front and its attendant heavy weather had not actually passed through the Columbus area. As he neared Columbus, he writes, assurances by Flight Service and EFAS notwithstanding, "we could see the entire storm. I estimated it to be 150 miles long and the tops to be 40,000 to 50,000 feet. It appeared to be some miles to the west of us, but the northern end was almost straight north of Columbus." In gathering dusk and the darkness of the visible storm, Barber continued on his way. Radio traffic, including the Columbus ATIS and the tower at his destination, Ohio State University Airport, indicated that all was normal. Suddenly, when the Skyhawk was approximately 10 miles north of Circleville, Ohio, the OSU tower issued a Sigmet: "Severe thunderstorm southwest of the city, moving northwest . . . possible hail and winds up to 50 miles per hour. Suggest small general aviation aircraft in the area make Port Columbus, as it is still open."

Barber chose to return to Circleville to land and wait out the storm. But the enemy was already at his six o'clock:

. . . Executing a faster-than-standard-rate right turn, I came face-to-face with the trailing edge of the storm coming up behind me, and it was too close to make Circleville. Again I executed a faster-than-standard-rate turn, this time to the left, and headed for Port Columbus. A few minutes later, we were just east of Rickenbacker AFB and about 8 miles in front of the storm.

Suddenly hail, approximately ¾ inch to 1 inch, was striking the airplane, sounding like a line of .30-'06 rifles. A split-second thought ran through my mind that, if the size or intensity of the hail increased, the windscreen would not stand, to say nothing of the prop and the aircraft skin.

Like a shotgun being fired inside the cabin, an explosion sounded, and the windscreen disintegrated. The first piece, approximately 12 inches by 12 inches, caught my mother-in-law on the left cheek at the edge of her eyeglasses and then fell into her lap. The next piece, about the same size, went by the right door under the Skyhawk's wing. The remaining shattered pieces fell inside. A piece about 8 inches wide hung precariously in place directly in front of me.

The rush of the wind into the cabin instantly pushed the 172 into about a 60-degree dive. The wind's force and my reaction time cost me an 800-foot altitude loss before the airplane was back in a flying attitude. The hail had ceased to fall, or by then we were out of range of it. Our total time in the hail had been approximately thirty seconds.

Even with full power and practically full elevator, the Skyhawk did not want to fly, because of the drag produced by the open cabin. I picked up the mike to call Port Columbus—and discovered that the radios were out. A glance showed that most of the breakers on the panel had been tripped. The demands of the airplane convinced me that I did not have the time or the available hand to reset them.

I attempted to coax the Skyhawk to gain a little altitude but instantly felt the impending stall. As I eased the nose over, the wind flowing through the open cabin took away another 100 feet. Feeling now that I would be unable to keep the airplane in the air long enough to reach Port Columbus, and having inadequate control to turn for Rickenbacker, I looked for a place to put down. With nothing but houses in sight, I started easing north to the interstate bypass loop.

By then, we were riding a roller coaster. Each time I raised the nose enough to hold altitude, I could feel the shudders of a coming stall; and as I eased back pressure, the wind slammed the nose down. The indicated airspeed reached 80 knots on the down side of the roller coaster and dropped off to 75 and lower as I attempted to level out. At this rate, I was sure that we would run out of altitude well before reaching Port Columbus.

We came up on the loop, but traffic did not allow a clear spot to put the 172 down. My mind raced: "At least the median or the right-of-way edges will keep me out of the houses, and there will be nothing but the airplane involved if we come down, so I'll stay with the interstate loop." Following the loop also was taking us in the direction of Port Columbus, which I could now see we were approaching.

No runway has ever looked so good to me as Runway 31 at Port Columbus did that day. However, there was a Boeing 727 on final for 28L. I would have to stop short of the intersection some way, since I could not know if the tower was aware of my approach. No time to worry about that.

The IAS was still roller-coastering between 74 and 80 knots. Stop the yaw somehow, no flaps—fly it onto the runway—the rudder is mush—wind approximately 220 degrees and gusty. Left wheel down first, but not enough control to hold it smooth, so the right wheel is down immediately and the nosewheel instants later. On the ground. Hold short of the intersection—and a glance overhead as the 727 passes at 500 feet.

Soon after, we were just rolling the hangar doors closed when the storm struck Port Columbus. We have all been taught the hazards of thunderstorms, including that hail can be thrown several miles from the top of a storm. Many pilots continue to believe, nevertheless, that we are immune. I was 8 miles out in front of the storm—and it did happen to me.

What kind of power can fling volleys of hail 10 miles and more? Forces of the same order that can keep a storm alive and at full destructive fury for many hours, that can lay waste to miles of communities over which they pass. Such storms operate by *essentially* the same principles as do air mass storms, but there are other features to their making and careers that increase their severity by many degrees.

A critical point about Barber's experience is that the clear air surrounding a thunderstorm can be as dangerous as the atmosphere inside its clouds. Given enough updraft force, hail can be flung out of the top of a storm, and horizontal winds within the machine can hurl it out the sides. Another cause of caution is the fact that as air is drawn into a storm's flanks, areas of strong turbulence and high rates of sink develop at altitude around and well outside the standing cloud.

Similarly deceptive may be the conditions within the immediate sphere of activity. In fact, one may enter the cloudy area and find the situation to be less threatening than expected. But then . . .

Pilot David G. Wood describes what can happen then:

Wood had been wary about making this flight, for the forecasts and reported weather had warned about thunderstorms and wind shear. Nevertheless, his passenger, a campaigning political candidate, was anxious to go, so Wood decided on a "look-see" attempt. His Cherokee Six entered cloud containing moderate turbulence and flashes of lightning, but with help from ATC, Wood was able to circumnavigate what was showing to be the worst weather. Soon Jacksonville Center was reporting no problems between the Cherokee's position and its destination, Moultrie, Georgia:

. . . Without warning, a brilliant white flash and a shotgun-like roar exploded through the cabin. Everything went black. Our nostrils were suddenly burned by the heavy smoke of an electrical fire.

I told Jim, my right-seat passenger, to run his hand across the circuit breaker panel to see if he could get anything to work and to get the flashlight out of the glove compartment. Just the post light and a frequency selector dial light came on. I adjusted the post light to cast a faint glow across the artificial horizon. With my nose 2 inches away, I could barely see the instrument. I feared the onset of vertigo. Then Jim lit the panel with the flashlight while he worked at the circuit breakers.

I needed now to clear out the smoke, which I did by slowing the airplane to 80 mph and opening the side vent window. When the air was clear, I closed the window; no more smoke appeared, so the damage apparently had already been done. I then asked my passengers if they were all right. From one came a mumbled yes.

I thought, "The airplane seems to be flying well; there's no visible external fire, but I can't see the tail section." I had to assume that it indeed was burning to a crisp. I had to take the appropriate action to blow it out. Besides, I could see no advantage to remaining in a cruise configuration at 5,000 feet under the circumstances.

I decided that, since I had been flying off-route, the danger of a midair collision with another aircraft at lower altitudes was remote, so I went into a high-speed dive to blow out any possible fire and to lose altitude. I decided to level off at 2,000 feet and hoped that I would break out of the bases by then. Meanwhile, I had selected code 7700 on my transponder and was switching back and forth on both radios, trying 121.5 and the JAX frequency, as I broadcast a Mayday in the blind. Just as I leveled at 2,000, I reestablished two-way communication with JAX. They had lost radar contact with me ten minutes previously. When I requested the nearest airport with emergency services, they suggested Albany as being closest to my last known position. With a DF steer from Albany Flight Service, I soon found the airport and gingerly made the best landing of my flying career.

Capriciousness is a characteristic of severe weather, which the behavior of lightning well illustrates. Lightning is caused by differences in temperature and electrical charges. Only recently have we come to know enough about it to determine just how it is generated and how lightning strikes do their damage.

Lightning strikes have often caused small perforations in aircraft skin, and they have also taken out many an antenna. Radios and magnetic compasses have been destroyed. Strikes have been known to damage wings and other airframe structures, freezing control hinges and even causing fuel to explode. Their ability to damage aircraft skin and structural members, to start fires at vulnerable points, and, perhaps more dangerous because more frequent, to cause panic and momentarily blind and disorient pilots is sufficient to make lightning a prime enemy.

Icing is another peril associated with thunderstorms. The upper portion is the coldest portion of a thundercloud, and it is the area where water droplets lifted by updrafts condense most rapidly. This does not mean, however, that icing can be avoided by staying below the upper regions. The critical boundary is the freezing level. In a thunderstorm, any area that is below freezing—even when colder than -10 degrees C—is quite capable of seriously icing an airplane. Considering what a rapidly building load of ice may do to the controllability of an airplane, icing up could be a catastrophic development for a pilot to face as he works to keep the airplane upright at a relatively slow airspeed in strong turbulence.

The Larger Environment and the Jet Stream

Out of Wood's report, another crucial fact emerges: Within a thunderstorm environment, even when you are flying between cloud layers, abatement of the turbulence does not necessarily mean that the crisis is over. Seeking out "clear" areas is a wise approach, but it cannot be assumed that this will bring peace and quiet. A thunderstorm exists in a larger environment, in which storm-breeding forces are present, active, and long-lasting. There are storms that just won't quit, and they are especially nasty.

Thunderstorms are influenced by the jet stream, which plays a forceful, often a dominant, role in the upper reaches of the atmosphere and at lower altitudes. It is important to know what the jet stream is and how it makes its presence felt, wherever you fly, not just because of the high winds it contains but also because of its profound effects on the formation of low-pressure centers, the ground track of large-scale bad weather, and the creation of clear air turbulence.

The height of the troposphere—the lower layer of air, in which weather occurs—can reach 50,000 to 60,000 feet over the equatorial regions and 25,000 to 30,000 feet at the poles. The variation is due to the differences between the relative lightness of warmer and the greater density of colder air. At around 30 degrees north latitude, depending on the season, these two very different tropospheres meet, causing a zone of temperature and pressure discontinuity and an abrupt break in the height of the *tropopause,* the boundary layer between the troposphere and the stratosphere. The jet stream lives in this break, at the northernmost edge of the warmer tropospheric air mass (FIGURE 1).

The jet stream is a narrow, undulating, high-speed river of wind that flows from west to east in the northern hemisphere. Its speed is greatest at the center of the stream and diminishes outward, as if in concentric rings. Like a snake, the jet stream core can whip up and down, latitudinally and altitudinally, in its travel around the globe. It typically curves northward, then southward as cold and warm air masses exert themselves as pressure centers. In addition, the strongest wind zones do not maintain an even speed whenever a jet stream appears. Rather, the centers of highest speed are fragmented, with the highest core speeds occuring to the west and east of a lower pressure center

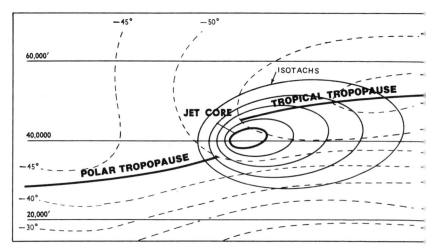

FIGURE 1   A cross-section of the upper troposphere and lower stratosphere showing the tropopause and associated features. Note the "break"
between the high tropical and the lower polar tropopause. Maximum
winds occur in the vicinity of this break.

or trough after the jet stream's air is bent in its travel from west
to east around it.

A very well-developed jet stream can be of continental proportions, with a length of 1,000 to 3,000 miles, a width of between 100 and 400 miles, and a thickness of 3,000 to 7,000 feet.
Seasonal changes affect the height, location, and speeds of the
stream, and those speeds are formidable. The maximum velocities in the core can reach 300 knots in winter, although a more
common value would be about 150 to 200 knots.

In the summer, the tropopausal break moves upward after
the retreating polar dome of air, so the jet stream trends northward while warmer air pushes it aloft. The typical summer jet
stream will be around 60 degrees north latitude at an altitude of
35,000 to 40,000 feet. In the summer, a secondary, southern jet
stream can flow as far south as 20 degrees north latitude—roughly
the location of Florida.

Come winter, the situation reverses. As the polar air mass

encroaches on the temperate regions, the tropopausal break lumbers southward, bringing the jet stream with it. Then the stream tends to settle at about 40 degrees north latitude, right over the United States. At the same time, as the air temperatures cool, the jet stream descends, so that its core may be only 20,000 feet above the surface.

Jet streams derive their strength from several sources. First, there is the steepness of the temperature gradient. In the rarified strata above 18,000 feet, it doesn't take a large temperature change to effect strong winds. A 2-degree or 3-degree change across a 300-mile-wide stretch can help to produce winds of more than 100 knots. The jet stream coincides with a ''packing'' or narrowing of isothermal separation. The farther south the tropopausal break goes, in winter, the steeper the temperature gradient becomes and the stronger grow the jet stream speeds. If two jet streams are present, the southernmost will contain the higher winds.

Orographic features also can help to form jet streams. There is, for instance, a semipermanent, very strong jet stream situated off the east coast of the huge Asian land mass. A strong pressure gradient will generate a strong wind in the upper levels, just as it will in the lower altitudes. Add the ''pushing'' effects of a polar low or trough with the resultant concentration of energy as the warm and cold air masses collide and rub against each other, and the stage will be set for a truly well-developed jet stream.

The jet stream easily plays a critical role in the formation and movement of low-pressure centers, and is an influence in the development and positioning of major thunderstorms.

Storms of a Different Order

Air mass storms are fueled essentially by vertically flowing air. Precipitation weakens them. In such storms, new air is pumped upward mainly from the ground. But what if low pressure associated with a weather system causes the storm to ingest substantial amounts of air at higher altitudes? Those winds will be strong enough to be able to blow rainfall out of the cloud, leaving the circulating winds to move free of weakening drag. Such a *steady-state* storm may last for days and travel from the Midwest to the Atlantic coast.

The winds may be encouraged by sloping action in mountainous terrain or by the jet stream (FIGURE 2). With far less water drag to contend with, the updrafts remain very strong, and the storm builds even higher, usually to create substantial hail which the high winds can fling to the rear of the storm or downwind, from the characteristic, overspreading anvil. Tornadoes may develop. The area surrounding the visible thunderstorm is likely to be treacherous with shearing, vertical currents.

Cool, dry air rushing into the storm from the flanks wreaks

FIGURE 2   A classic jet stream situation. The areas of highest speed are at *A* and *C*. Maximum vorticity is at *B,* where the upper winds bend around the leading edge of a trough. Surface lows and storms tend to form and deepen at *D,* an area of vorticity and diverging air flow.

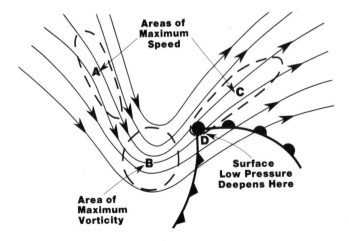

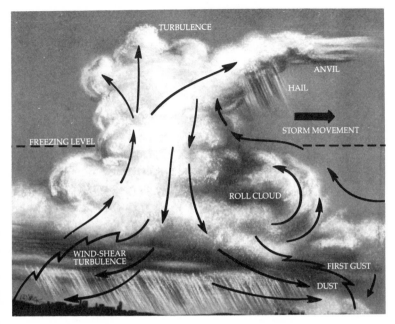

FIGURE 3 The circulatory machine that is a thunderstorm at its fierce maturity. Note the roll cloud and the forces that can toss hail great distances from the mass of the storm. Air ingested from the surface or the sides may be twisted or spun by the storm's movement or internal forces to produce tornadoes that descend through the base or remain spinning, sometimes horizontally, within the mass. Clashing updrafts and downdrafts create severe turbulence and wind shear.

other, worse, changes. It evaporates the rain falling out of the thundercloud. Equally important, because it is cool, the air sinks rapidly and, on striking the ground, drives a tremendous gust ahead of the storm that displaces moist, warmer air upward and into the cloud, creating the effects of a miniature cold front. This mechanism is visible as a great, looming roll cloud (FIGURE 3). The effects are violent, as more and more air is driven vigorously upward. The wind speeds at the surface can be more than 70 knots, and the gust front can precede the main body of the storm by more than 20 miles. Such storms tend to develop in lines, with a broad gust front preceding them. The 70-knot winds of the advancing line are but harbingers of updrafts with velocities of up to 5,000 to 6,000 or more fpm, and downdrafts of as high as 12,000 fpm within the storms. Because of this, to traverse a line from the back side—usually west to east—is to fly into increasingly rough conditions, with the savage gust front at the far boundary.

Such storms are not the worst that a line can contain. The agents that create severe storms are still unstable air, a lifting mechanism, and moisture. Add to that more instability, greater wind velocities at the lifting stage, and more moisture, and the resulting storm clusters can become the stuff of legend.

Spinning Out Tornadoes

Consider the winds accompanying an advancing low-pressure system over relatively nonencumbering terrain, such as flatlands. This low-level jet stream can reach velocities of around 50 knots. Then add substantial moisture from a large source, such as the Gulf of Mexico, and you are already confronting a major disturbance. If that air is lifted over a warm front, the thunderstorms that will result will be severe. Then, if that system is hit by the winds of the high-level jet stream, a new and more vigorous triggering takes place. The high-level winds, at, say, 30,000 feet, will be flowing at an angle to the lifting air and will tend to spin and roil it considerably. The spinning action can spawn tornadoes, which will not necessarily announce themselves by popping out of cloud bases. In fact, *horizontal* tornadoes do occur in severe thunderstorms. They may also exist in clear air on the right flank of the storm or line of storms, away from the visible mass of clouds and precipitation.

The severe storm, like its "milder" brethren, exists in a larger environment than its visual presence suggests. The three-dimensional repercussions of colliding, rising, and spinning air, not to mention currents rushing in to fill low-pressure voids, churn and twist far and wide, even spawning clean air tornadoes as far as 20 miles from the visible storm line. The unwary pilot, thinking he is steering clear by avoiding the "ugly" clouds, may actually fly into a tornado or wind shear. Differences in rainfall also affect wind-flow boundaries and the speed of the gust front.

Since conventional radar only picks up strong precipitation, tornadoes are not likely to be visible to it; they spin out what water they originally contain. A visible tornado is essentially spinning dirt and debris. Even though the winds of a tornado within a thundercloud, or outside it, may top 200 knots, such a tube of raw energy will not be discernible to radar pulses. Radar can detect areas of possible tornado activity—the classic "hook" shape on a radar return. (As we shall see in the next chapter, Doppler radar with computer assistance can see strong winds, certainly including tornadoes.) However, even with radar, entering a thundercloud can well end in an encounter with the whirlwind.

The problems of avoidance are compounded at night, although lightning gives clearer warning of storms by night than by day. At night, you may not know where the thundercloud is until you are actually in it; gauging distances is very tricky. Watch the lightning for its direction of movement, its extensiveness and for the cloud it illuminates. Keep in mind, again, that a thunderstorm can consist of several cells in various stages of growth, maturity, and development, and that a single cell can last several hours.

Wind Shear Awareness

With the crash of an Eastern Airlines Boeing 727 at John F. Kennedy International Airport on June 24, 1975, the wind shear effects of a thunderstorm's gust front and downdrafts became the objects of intensive research. These are not new phenomena, of course, but recent studies have enabled us to understand their specific characteristics and to develop ways of avoiding and coping with them.

The Eastern jet encountered a decreasing headwind after flying through a severe downdraft. It crashed short of the runway, and 113 people were killed (FIGURE 4). A University of Chicago meteorologist, Dr. T. Theodore Fujita, began to study the behavior of downdrafts and came up with some new observations. He coined a term—downburst—to describe a phenomenon he had found, an intense and localized downdraft with forces, as he defined them, "comparable to or greater than the approximate rate of descent or climb of a jet aircraft on final approach or takeoff

FIGURE 4   At JFK at 4:00 P.M., June 24, 1975, a thunderstorm generated several intense downbursts—2 to 3 miles in diameter and spaced at 3-mile intervals—which produced a characteristic spearhead echo on radar. Several airplanes heading toward JFK experienced wind shear and wild airspeed fluctuations. Eastern Flight 66 crashed just short of the runway.

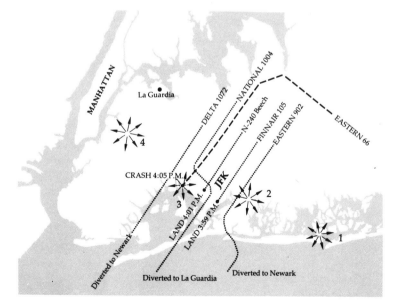

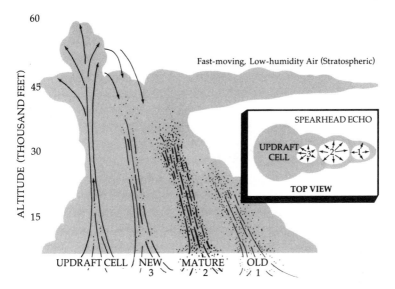

FIGURE 5   Dr. T. Theodore Fujita first described how overshooting storm tops contribute to the intensity of a downburst when they collapse into the body of the storm's circulation. A spearhead echo often turns up on radar when the most severe downbursts occur.

at 300 feet above the surface." For Dr. Fujita, this amounts to a downward force of 720 fpm or greater. Anything less than that is a downdraft. Downbursts, he claims, are about 3 to 4 miles in diameter aloft and affect an area approximately 15 miles in diameter, once the downburst strikes the ground and splatters outward.

Fujita studied several takeoff- or landing-phase crashes that took place near thunderstorms and noted that a characteristic "spearhead" radar signature of downburst conditions was usually found to the north of each accident site. The most severe downbursts are associated with thunderstorm tops collapsing in the mature phase of the storm. The high horizontal speed of the spearhead formation helps to intensify the downward transport of precipitation and air associated with the collapsing tops (FIGURE 5).

In 1980, Dr. Fujita discovered another phenomenon, a small-scale downburst called a *microburst,* which can be as powerful as a downburst but affects a surface area of only 1 mile in diameter. Some indications of microburst activity are found in blowing dust devils, virga, falling tree limbs, and extremely heavy rain. Studies have found that downbursts and microbursts also can exist at high altitudes within thunderstorms.

When the Bottom Falls

On November 12, 1975, the weather at Raleigh-Durham Airport, in North Carolina, was reported as 1,000 scattered, 2,000 overcast, 4 to 7 miles visibility in light to moderate rain, and winds variable from the south at 4 to 7 knots. An Eastern Airlines 727 was on an ILS approach to Runway 23. As the aircraft descended through 300 feet, the captain saw the lower rows of lights for the visual approach slope indicator change suddenly from white to red. Along with this signal from the VASI, the 727's ground proximity warning system activated just as the captain increased the thrust and pulled back on the control wheel. By doing this, he was able to check the aircraft's sink rate, regain the glideslope, and land on the runway.

The captain had encountered a low-level wind shear, and he had done everything right, recognizing the situation and reacting immediately to penetrate the shear.

At the time, another Eastern 727 was approaching Raleigh-Durham from the southwest. While approaching the airport, the flight crew had to deviate from course several times to circumnavigate thunderstorms. However, no thunderstorms were evident in the immediate vicinity of the airport, and the aircraft's radar was displaying no areas of heavy precipitation.

The crew was cleared for an ILS to Runway 23 and was informed that the pilot of a Beech Queen Air had reported a strong left crosswind between 900 and 1,200 feet. The 727's first officer replied, "Okay, thank you, sir. Looks like you have quite a storm coming your way."

As the 727 descended on the ILS, the crew was advised that the surface winds were shifting to the southwest and becoming stronger. Also, the visibility was deteriorating rapidly. At the time, the aircraft's descent rate was stabilized at about 700 fpm. About 500 feet above the surface, the first officer told the captain that he had visual contact with the ground. At 200 feet (decision height), he reported the runway in sight.

During the next five seconds, several things happened: The 727's rate of descent increased suddenly to 1,250 fpm, then to 1,400 fpm. As the captain applied thrust to arrest the sink, all forward visibility was lost when the aircraft entered heavy precipitation, which the captain described as a "wall of water." The 727's main landing gear struck the localizer antenna screen and contacted the ground 282 feet short of the runway. The main gear and the right engine separated from the aircraft as the 727 bounced onto the runway and slid 4,150 feet, coming to rest off the right side of the runway. Of the 139 people aboard the aircraft, 7 sustained minor injuries and 1 suffered a broken ankle. There were no fatalities.

After a six-month investigation, the NTSB determined that the captain's failure to execute a missed approach when he lost sight of the runway below decision height was the probable cause of the accident.

At that time, as we have seen, our knowledge about the effects of wind shear on aircraft performance was relatively small. In 1978, the Air Line Pilots Association petitioned the safety board to reopen the investigation, because the severity of the weather conditions and the circumstances encountered by the crew had not been adequately considered. Further investigation led the NTSB to revise its findings to a recognition that the crew had had to cope with heavy precipitation *and wind shear* and that the captain had not had enough time to arrest the aircraft's sink rate.

Considering the high fatalities suffered in other wind shear accidents, this crew and its passengers were fortunate. As many studies have indicated, some wind shears, like some thunderstorms, are so powerful they cannot be penetrated, but, unlike thunderstorms, wind shear is almost impossible to detect with equipment now *generally* available.

In the period from 1980 through 1982, fifty-four accidents were attributed by the NTSB to the effects of wind shear. Six were fatal, seven others involved serious injuries. Eleven of the accidents occured on takeoff. In one, a Beech 35 Bonanza was 500 feet above the ground and was configured for cruise climb when its airspeed dropped suddenly from 96 to 77 knots. According to the NTSB, the pilot applied full power but then became disoriented. The Bonanza was destroyed when it crashed into trees, and the pilot was seriously injured. Wind shear was involved in forty-one landing accidents, five of which were fatal.

Hammer and Scissors

How a downdraft or downburst is capable of driving an airplane—especially a low-powered airplane—into the ground is not hard to visualize. In a downdraft, an airplane's ability to climb may deteriorate by 100 fpm for every knot of downward wind. Even immediate application of full power may not be able to counter such a hammer blow. A reciprocal-engine airplane may be able to respond instantly when full power is called for, but its full power may not be enough. Jet engines may have the power, but they must spool up over a period of several seconds, so that, as we have seen, the pilot may not have sufficient time— in effect, altitude—to arrest the descent and climb out past the draft or burst.

Wind shear presents a different set of problems, for it does not hammer an airplane but rather catches it between the scissorslike motion of abruptly changing flows of air. If an airplane *suddenly* passes from air going in one direction into air headed in another, the airflow over the wing will change dramatically; a headwind can suddenly become a tailwind, and vice versa. Thus, an indicated airspeed of, say, 120 knots can instantly decrease to less than the airplane's stall speed, as the airplane flicks out of a headwind layer into a tailwind.

When this happens, the airplane swiftly seeks a flyable airspeed, its trim airspeed, and dives. In one recorded incident, a cruising airliner that encountered wind shear dove 12,000 feet before the pilot could halt its descent.

If the pilot has enough altitude and/or power in reserve, he may escape. If he is too near the ground and lacks the thrust to help him out of the stall, he is in the same bind as a pilot caught in a downdraft. If he is dragging his plane to a runway behind the power curve and suddenly enters a tailwind, he may lack the reserve power to overcome the sudden stall. If he is climbing out under full power—as most lightplanes do—and a shear drops his airspeed to below stall, there will be nothing for it until the descending aircraft can pick up flying speed.

Conversely, flying rapidly from a tailwind into a headwind will increase the airspeed and induce an unwanted climb. On an approach, and especially on short final to a short field, that could be very inconvenient. Furthermore, a sudden pitch-up due to increased lift would have to be compensated for lest the airspeed dangerously bleed off due to the high angle of attack.

The Forging of Shears

Dangerous wind shears can occur anywhere that the wind is blowing strongly and the direction and strength of the wind is subject to sudden alterations in direction and speed.

We have seen the power that can precede a thunderstorm in the form of air blasting down from within the cloud—winds of 40 knots and much more. Furthermore, as the storm operates, it sucks in air so that above the level of the gust front—especially at 2,000 to 3,000 feet—there may be a contrary wind of some 30 knots or more. That differential, at or above 70 knots, is obviously enough to overwhelm an airplane in the rolling turbulence of the gust front, through the loss of airspeed in flying suddenly from a headwind into a tailwind, or by the bludgeoning and destabilizing effect of a 70-knot change from tailwind to headwind. An airplane trying to land or take off in such conditions obviously faces severe hazards. Several accidents have involved pilots who tried to beat gust fronts into or out of airports.

If you are contemplating a departure near an advancing thunderstorm, wait out the storm's passage. Remember that a thunderstorm is not only its visible self but its environment. Even if you take off after the gust front has passed, the conflicting winds will still be present, and a takeoff into a good, steady headwind could suddenly become a climbout to, and a stallout in, a tailwind. The gust front may precede the storm clouds by 15 or 20 miles, and it will not necessarily be visible. The wind whips across the landscape like a speeding wall.

It is just as dangerous to race a gust front to an airport. If a safer alternate is available, use it. Even if you are able to get through the shear line and/or the front on the approach, if you have to go around, you may have to attempt your second approach in heavy turbulence and precipitation.

Other phenomena to beware are downdrafts and potential shears underlying virga, the ragged-looking shafts of rain that fall from clouds but evaporate above the ground. The rain dissipates in dry air as it falls from clouds whose bases may be 6,000 feet or higher, but the accompanying downdrafts continue to the ground and then spread out. An airplane can lose altitude rapidly in the downdraft, and the crisis would be compounded by a sudden loss of airspeed in wind shear.

It is easy to find oneself beneath a relatively high ceiling, in dry air and light to moderate winds, and suspecting no trouble aloft. One way to kindle a healthy wariness is to look for a combination of warm, dry air and middle-altitude clouds in ragged bases. The chances are that the warm air is rising by convection to form those clouds, in which updrafts and destructive down-drafts may be churning.

Severe wind shears can be created by fronts moving at 30 knots or more or causing a 10-degree-F change in temperature. That speed means that the system will be carrying substantial power. The high temperature differential of 10 degrees F or more indicates that the line between the cold and warm air masses is thin and that the pilot can expect a rapid shift in the wind while crossing from one to the other.

As in the case of virga, the threat may be hidden, for frontal action does not always spawn heavy cloud. Furthermore, as we have seen, cold fronts are not always the villain when frontal action creates adverse winds. Experts generally recommend taking care when you are nearing an airport from behind a cold front and before an approaching warm front. Occluded fronts are particularly dangerous, but any frontal activity that swiftly lifts warm, moist air in an unstable atmosphere can create thunderstorms. Even stationary fronts have proved to be storm contributors when the moisture and airflow were ripe for it.

Supersharp Shears

Mountain waves and low-level jet streams, which are frequent in the West and Great Plains and usually whistle along below 7,000 feet, are also sources of severe wind shear. This can be expected where there are strong low-level winds of 40 knots or more. Mountains, hills, treelines, and obstructions such as large buildings can cause surface winds to shear. A microburst, the most severe form of vertical shear, is hard to detect, but it offers clues in blowing dust clouds, virga, trees with limbs flailing wildly, and extremely heavy rain.

Most violent atmospheric phenomena either offer direct evidence of their presence or can be deduced from what we have learned about severe weather formation. Thunderstorms usually have the socially redeeming feature of announcing themselves spectacularly, though what you see doesn't necessarily tell the whole story of what is going on. What you see should be enough to persuade you to avoid the system by a wide margin. A pilot going against a storm in a general aviation airplane, especially a little airplane, is a lone fighter mixing it with a squadron of troubles. In the next chapter, we will look at the pilot's available arsenal for survival, from an early-warning system to stick and rudder tactics that he may have to call upon if he hasn't heeded what the warnings foretold.

4
Thunderstorm Management

The best way to "manage" severe weather is either to keep your mind on the sky while keeping a safe distance between you and the trouble or to keep your body planted safely on the ground. There are airmanship techniques that a pilot must know in order to survive in rough weather, but they are fall-back measures, not the first line of defense.

The first line is a good and thorough weather briefing obtained shortly before the flight, a probing question-and-answer session with Flight Service or the National Weather Service, augmented by constant updating during the flight. Airborne weather radar, Stormscope, and ATC radar information provide some protection, but you may not have the airborne devices, and ground radar consultations are not always reliable, as ATC readily admits. A venerable aid for thunderstorm detection in a pinch is ADF tuned to the lowest band. The value of all these information sources will depend upon the soundness of your judgment, the strength of your decisiveness, and the steadiness of your internal discipline. Finally, if you couldn't bear to wait it out and now find yourself too intimately checking it out, you may just have to ride it out, falling back on your best airmanship and perhaps a prayer.

How critical *all* the information-gathering measures at a pilot's disposal can be is pointed up in the background to this fatal event, which good management—meaning the use of established procedures, available technology, and common sense—could have prevented. This story has relevance for all pilots, including those in general aviation.

The Air Wisconsin Disaster

On June 12, 1980, a Swearingen Metro of Air Wisconsin crashed, causing the deaths of the crew and eleven passengers; there were two survivors. The pilot was an 8,400-hour ATP, with 6,000 hours in type; his co-pilot had a total of 4,000 hours.

The Metro was on a scheduled commuter flight from Appleton, Wisconsin, to Lincoln, Nebraska, with an en route stop in Minneapolis. Before leaving Appleton, the crew obtained a thorough weather briefing that included a forecast for thunderstorms in Lincoln. By the time the aircraft reached Minneapolis, a Sigmet had been issued pertaining to an area of thunderstorms, with tops to 40,000 feet, moving eastward through central Nebraska at 20 knots. It is doubtful that the Metro received this Sigmet, for the National Transportation Safety Board, in its postcrash investigation, found no evidence that the pilots had sought to update their weather information. However, while on final approach to Minneapolis, the crew talked with another Air Wisconsin pilot, who had just returned from Lincoln. That pilot reported that he had had no weather problems along the route and that the weather to the west of the route appeared to be dissipating.

The Metro departed Minneapolis at 2:30 P.M. and climbed to 12,000 feet. About thirty minutes after departure, the flight crew was advised by the Minneapolis Center controller of a "large area of weather" 35 miles ahead of the aircraft. The controller did not know how severe the weather was, but he reported that another pilot had "found his way through it" inbound to Lincoln.

The Metro crew responded, "Wilco. According to our radar, it looks okay for us now. We'll continue direct for the time being."

Based on the information they had at this time, the weather ahead did not appear to be particularly bad. Pilots had flown into and out of the Lincoln area with no problem. Nothing significant was showing on the weather radar display. But the weather ahead was very bad. Pea-size hail was striking the ground, and 3 inches of rain had fallen within thirty minutes. Winds of up to 100 mph were blowing down trees and powerlines. These reports were transmitted by the National Weather Service to ATC supervisors, but the supervisors decided not to relay the information to the working controllers. They believed that sufficient warning of severe thunderstorms had already been included in Sigmets.

The Metro crew had not asked for or received the Sigmets. They had learned from ATC that there was weather out there, but pilot reports (made before the thunderstorms arrived) and their X-band weather radar (which was attenuating) indicated that the weather was not severe.

The Metro was descending to land at Lincoln when it entered a Level 5 (intense) thunderstorm. The flight crew reported moderate to severe turbulence and lightning. One passenger later described the encounters as running into a "wall of wind and rain," and he recalled holding onto the seat in front of him to steady himself against the turbulence. Another passenger described the flight conditions as a roller coaster, "except that you did not know when you were coming down or going up."

The crew requested and received clearance to descend to 3,000 feet, ATC's minimum vectoring altitude for the area. Shortly after advising ATC that they were descending to 3,000 feet, the crew reported that they had lost both engines.

(The Garrett TPE-331 engines had flamed out from water ingestion. During certification tests, the TPE-331 was required to keep running after encountering a simulated rainfall equivalent to about 4 percent of engine airflow weight. The NTSB said that the Metro's engines actually ingested more than twice that much water when the aircraft flew into the Level 5 thunderstorm. The safety board said, "It is not realistic to expect an engine or an airframe to be designed to sustain the extreme forces and conditions which were encountered in this severe thunder-storm.'')

The NTSB determined that the Metro's engine flamed out at the same time the aircraft encountered a severe downdraft. Its rate of descent increased suddenly from 1,600 fpm to nearly 5,000 fpm. With a combination of a flameout and a downburst at such a low altitude, an accident was inevitable, said the board. The pilots were able to restart both engines, but there was not enough time for them to spool up to full power before the Metro hit a level, muddy field in a slightly nose-down and right-wing-low attitude.

The NTSB's report states that "the probable cause of the accident was the flight crew's continued flight into an area of severe thunderstorms and the resultant precipitation-induced flameout of both engines at an altitude from which recovery could not be made." The board also indicated that the flight crew did not have enough information to complete their flight safely, that the pilots did not use all the available sources of weather information. The board also faulted ATC for not disseminating critical weather information to the crew. The limited ability of X-band radar to reveal the extent and intensity of severe weather was also ascribed as a contributing factor.

In effect, the decision of the ATC supervisors to put bureaucratic line drawing ahead of assuring an extra margin of safety, and the flameout once the Swearingen was in the storm, were concomitant causes of the pilot-in-command's failure to double-check a tricky weather environment. In this, as in so many other accident cases, the weather briefing and updating process was, at least in part, taken for granted and slighted.

Basics of the Briefing

Such slighting also takes the form of shortcuts made during briefings. A proper briefing methodically touches all the bases, of which there are several when it comes to establishing a defense against a thunderstorm encounter.

First, determine whether any thunderstorms have been detected along or near your route of flight, where they were last reported to be by weather stations, radar, and pilot reports, and where they are moving and how fast. On the basis of these reports, you may decide to wait things out or should at least devise a route well clear of the weather. A negative report, however, should not be an automatic all-clear signal. Storms may not have been reported, but if the conditions are ripe, assume a high probability of their showing up.

Check for any *current convective Sigmets,* which will provide warnings of tornadoes, lines of thunderstorms, embedded thunderstorms, scattered severe thunderstorms, or hail 3/4 inch or more in diameter.

The NWS correlates thunderstorm activity with the amount of rainfall being produced. Less than 1/2 inch of rain per hour is produced by Level 1 and Level 2 thunderstorms. A Level 1 thunderstorm is considered to be weak; a Level 2 is moderate; in either, a pilot can expect to encounter lightning and light-to-moderate turbulence. A Level 3 (strong) and a Level 4 (very strong) thunderstorm produce 1/2 to 2 inches of rain per hour, as well as lightning and severe turbulence. Two inches to more than 8 inches of rain per hour are produced by Level 5 (intense) and Level 6 (extreme) thunderstorms. Severe turbulence, lightning, and organized wind gusts can be expected in a Level 5 storm, and hail is likely. Large hail, severe turbulence, lightning, and extensive wind gusts are characteristics of a Level 6 thunderstorm.

Degrees of Turbulence

Terms describing the relative severity of turbulence have specific meanings for the NWS, pilots, and flight crews:

• *Light* turbulence momentarily causes slight, erratic changes in altitude and/or pitch, yaw, or roll. The occupants may feel a slight strain against their seat belts or shoulder straps. Unsecured objects may be displaced slightly. Aboard a transport-size airplane, food service may be conducted, and walking is not difficult. Reports of *light chop* refer to light turbulence or turbulence that causes slight, rapid, and somewhat rhythmic bumpiness without appreciable changes in altitude or attitude.

• *Moderate* turbulence is a term that can be deceiving to the inexperienced pilot. Moderate turbulence is not a comfortable condition. It is of greater intensity than light turbulence, though similar to it. Changes in altitude and/or attitude occur, but the aircraft remains in positive control at all times. There are usually variations in the indicated airspeed. However, there may be rapid bumps or jolts without appreciable changes in the aircraft's altitude or attitude. The occupants feel definite strains against their seat belts or shoulder straps. Unsecured objects are dislodged. Food service and walking are difficult. Reports of *moderate chop* refer to moderate turbulence.

• *Severe* turbulence causes large, abrupt changes in altitude and/or attitude. It usually causes large variations in the indicated airspeed. The aircraft may go momentarily out of control. The occupants are forced violently against their seat belts or shoulder straps. Unsecured objects are tossed about. Food service and walking are impossible. Such turbulence is reported as *severe*.

• *Extreme* turbulence tosses the aircraft about so violently that it is practically impossible to control and may suffer structural damage. It is reported as *extreme*.

Pilot reports of turbulence should indicate what type of airplane was involved, for what may be moderate turbulence to a large, powerful aircraft can be severe to a smaller, lighter one. Also, while these definitions may suggest that all but extreme turbulence can be handled by virtually any pilot, the fact is that even moderate turbulence can occur in conditions that can render it beyond a pilot's capacity to handle.

Good News and Bad from Flight Service

In the late 1980s, we have at our disposal sophisticated techniques and technologies for understanding and predicting thunderstorms. This is due in large part to the National Severe Storms Laboratory of the National Oceanic and Atmospheric Administration, which has done exceptional work since its creation in 1960. In wind shear research alone, such an effort as JAWS (Joint Airport Weather Studies) has used new weather radars and other tools to multiply our knowledge and avoidance capabilities. In general, the ability of meteorologists to predict and characterize thunderstorm development and behavior has made life easier for pilots—if pilots are willing *and able* to use the information.

Working with these data sources is central to any good weather briefing. The convective Sigmets we have mentioned are but one element of the whole battery.

The best way to get a reliable briefing is to see for yourself what is on the charts the meteorologists compile to form a mosaic of long-range and on-the-spot intelligence—something like a running compendium and analysis of an enemy's order of battle and probable movements. Nothing beats studying them with the help of a NWS meteorologist or a patient, knowledgeable FSS specialist. Patience and determination are often required to get the same kind of job done by phone. Many pilots are sufficiently intimidated by the process to request and accept less information than they need. Automated phone briefings, as one would expect, are the least detailed and helpful of the lot, especially if conditions are unsettled, with the dangers and options still not set clearly in perspective.

Next Generation

A superior system for detecting incipient severe weather conditions is being developed by the Air Force Weather Service and the FAA. Based on widespread use of Doppler radar and computerization, the system, called Nexrad, for Next Generation Weather System, has been in development since 1976, with an eventual goal of 160 such radar installations dotting the country.

In 1962, the NSSL, in Norman, Oklahoma, began working with Doppler radar, which measures the frequency phase shift of returned radar energy. Conventional radars measure how much signal energy is reflected back to their receivers. Doppler radars can do this, too, but they also can detect where and how fast precipitation is moving, not just where heavy precipitation *is*. With the help of computers, Doppler radar has also been able to identify the locations of gust fronts, turbulence, and downdrafts, and for this, significant amounts of moisture are unnecessary.

With this kind of power and resolution, this system can detect very small amounts of moisture. Since there is some moisture in any air mass, Doppler can show gust fronts, wind shear, and turbulence even on clear days. It can detect areas of convergence before clouds form. It can identify the cyclonic circulation in a storm's middle levels thirty to forty-five minutes before a tornado forms. The scientists at NSSL have been able to predict routinely and with a high degree of accuracy where and when tornadoes will form.

Until Then . . .

The Nexrad system is not yet operational for all concerned, so until then, the information we are likely to receive in a briefing will emanate in large part from Oldrad, the system of ground-based, conventional weather radar that has been used since 1957. Three elements of this system have special meaning during the thunderstorm season, yet are often ignored.

Summertime briefings often warn of a "chance of thunderstorms" as part of terminal forecasts and area forecasts. Transcribed weather broadcasts carry the same message. "Chance of" is a vague term, and a FSS specialist, if goaded to define it, may add a slight, pessimistic elaboration. He or she isn't a meteorologist, after all, and wants to be covered in the event of an accident investigation. There are, however, ways of delving into the background of the forecast the briefer reads to you.

Twice daily (usually at 0800 and 1500 Zulu) the National Severe Storms Forecast Center (NSSFC), in Kansas City, Missouri, issues a *convective outlook*—or severe weather outlook—which is called an AC by those briefers who know that this forecasting tool exists. If the briefer has not volunteered information from the latest issued convective outlook and specifically identified it as such, ask him to call it up on the teletype. The code for him to use is RQ MKC AC. The convective outlook delineates those areas of the country where thunderstorms are most likely to occur. It consists of two parts, a map and a written section, and is simple to interpret (FIGURE 6).

FIGURE 6   The Convective Outlook or Severe Weather Outlook chart delineates areas of the country where thunderstorms are most likely to occur. It is issued usually at 0800 Zulu and 1500Z by the National Severe Storms Forecast Center in Kansas City.

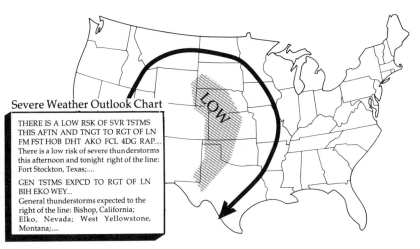

Severe Weather Outlook Chart

THERE IS A LOW RSK OF SVR TSTMS
THIS AFTN AND TNGT TO RGT OF LN
FM FST HOB DHT AKO FCL 4DG RAP....
There is a low risk of severe thunderstorms
this afternoon and tonight right of the line:
Fort Stockton, Texas;....

GEN TSTMS EXPCD TO RGT OF LN
BIH EKO WEY....
General thunderstorms expected to the
right of the line: Bishop, California;
Elko, Nevada; West Yellowstone,
Montana;....

On the convective map, a line with an arrowhead delineates an area of probable activity. Facing in the direction of the arrow, you may expect thunderstorms to exist to the right of the line. Areas of probable severe thunderstorms (those with 50-knot or greater surface gusts, 3/4-inch or larger hail, and/or tornadoes) are indicated by *hatched lines;* tornadoes will appear as *crosshatched areas.*

Along with the graphic presentation will be a notation: *low* means that there is a low risk of thunderstorms, 2 to 5 percent of the area indicated is expected to have severe thunderstorms; *moderate* means that there is a risk of severe thunderstorms covering 6 to 10 percent of the shaded area; *high* means that there is a high risk of thunderstorms covering more than 10 percent of the indicated area.

When you obtain your briefing by phone, have the written part of the convective outlook read to you. In the written form, the boundaries of an area that is likely to experience severe thunderstorms are indicated through airport identifiers. The arrowhead line is defined in the same way.

More familiar to most pilots is the *radar summary chart* (FIGURE 7), which is issued several times a day and provides a means of checking on the development of storms. Areas of radar echoes are plotted, along with their direction of movement and *precipitation* tops. Cloud tops may be 2,000 feet higher than the numbers given on the chart, because conventional radar sees only larger moisture particles. Boxes enclosed by a dashed line indicate areas where a severe weather watch is in effect. Bear in mind that the information on the radar summary chart can be two to four hours old by the time it comes off the facsimile machine. The chart is valid only at the time of issuance. When briefing by phone, ask where the boundaries of the boxes are and what the behavior of the lighter echoes has been, for they could indicate building thunderstorm conditions.

Space-age technology may also be available to the inquiring pilot. Geostationary Operational Environmental Satellites (GOES) provide imagery of most of the western hemisphere. GOES

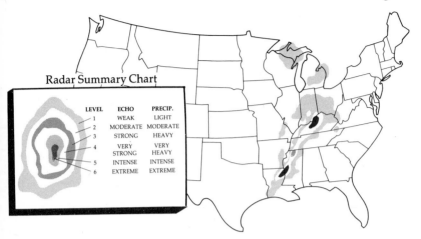

Radar Summary Chart

LEVEL	ECHO	PRECIP.
1	WEAK	LIGHT
2	MODERATE	MODERATE
3	STRONG	HEAVY
4	VERY STRONG	VERY HEAVY
5	INTENSE	INTENSE
6	EXTREME	EXTREME

FIGURE 7   The radar-summary chart, which is issued frequently during the day, is useful for checking on the development of storms. Keep in mind that the information may be two to four hours old by the time it is reproduced for Flight Service Stations.

transmit visible-spectrum and infrared-spectrum imagery to the FSS network. GOES imagery allows a pilot to locate precisely areas of extensive cloud development, day or night. Also, selected FSS are equipped with weather radar units that are capable of reproducing the radar imagery received by the National Weather Service's nationwide system of weather radars. Using this remote radar weather display system (RRWDS), a pilot in one part of the country can look at the radar information being received by any one of NWS's ground-based radars. These provide the pilot with real-time radar imagery, anywhere.

The Vital Stability Chart

The *stability chart* (FIGURE 8) is particularly helpful, for it shows areas of stable and unstable air and is a means of visu-

Stability Chart

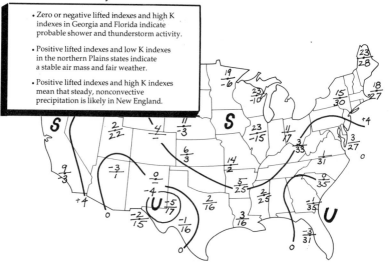

• Zero or negative lifted indexes and high K indexes in Georgia and Florida indicate probable shower and thunderstorm activity.

• Positive lifted indexes and low K indexes in the northern Plains states indicate a stable air mass and fair weather.

• Positive lifted indexes and high K indexes mean that steady, nonconvective precipitation is likely in New England.

FIGURE 8   The stability chart shows areas of stable and unstable air. A large negative number over a high positive number in the fraction means a high probability of thunderstorms. Unstable areas are often marked with a *U* and stable areas with an *S*. Contour lines connecting lifted index values of +4, 0, and −4 also are plotted for easy interpretation.

alizing rapidly which regions of the country are most likely to have cloudiness, precipitation, and convective activity. Unlike the convective outlook, the stability chart describes conditions throughout the country.

On the chart, stations are plotted in the form of a fraction. The top number is the *lifted index,* which is a measure of the stability of the air. The index is computed by "lifting" a parcel of air to about 18,000 feet. A *positive* lifted index indicates that a parcel of air at the surface, if lifted to 18,000 feet, would be cooler than the air already existing at that altitude. This means that the air is stable. The higher the positive number, the more stable the air.

A *zero* lifted index indicates that the lifted air would be the same temperature as the air existing at 18,000 feet. The air is thus "neutrally" stable—neither stable nor unstable.

A *negative* number is a warning. That lifted air would be warmer than the air already at 18,000, signifying unstable conditions. We need only recall that the mechanism by which a thunderstorm builds involves warmer air being propelled upward through cooler air. Large negative values mean that the air is very unstable and that thunderstorms could occur.

The bottom number in the fraction is the *K index*. The formula for determining the *K* index is rather complicated, but the point is that a high *K* index indicates not only an unstable lapse rate but a high degree of atmospheric moisture, which, too, is an ingredient of thunderstorm formation. Therefore, on the stability chart, *a large negative number topping a high positive number indicates a high probability of thunderstorms*. For quick reference, meteorologists mark unstable areas with a *U* and stable areas with an *S*. Contour lines connecting lifted index values of +4, 0, and −4 are plotted for easier interpretation.

In constructing a picture of the weather area, we essentially try to create a three-part conception of what the air is like and is going to be like when we will be flying through it. We are concerned with (1) relative temperatures, (2) amounts of moisture, and (3) wind action.

Relative temperatures tell us much about the presence or probability of lifting due to the heated surface warming its blanket of air. The temperature is also important in that it affects the likelihood of tornado formation. These temperatures are actually dewpoints. Lifting can be expected when the dewpoint is at least 40 degrees F. At a 53-degree dewpoint, tornado activity becomes a serious prospect. Another surface condition to watch for, strangely enough, is hot, *clear* air, for without cloud cover, the surface heats more, and it is the heat radiating from the surface that determines the warmth of the air.

Temperatures, dewpoints, and low-level wind conditions are described on the *surface map*, which also depicts frontal and squall line activity. By tracing the movements and extensiveness of front and squall lines (the latter are indicated by alternating dots and dashes, unless the line coincides with a front) and by determining the dewpoints (at the lower left of each station data block) and their trends, you can gain a good idea of what is happening to the air over a large area. For more details about the actual weather, check the *hourly sequence reports* for airports along your route, reasonably distant from it, and at locations where changing developments may affect you. This will suggest alternative routings and indicate trends, since the sequences describe the weather that *has happened* at those stations, not necessarily what is happening by the time you read the reports. It is particularly important, again, to check the sequences not only for reports of thunderstorms and towering cumulus but for temperature and dewpoint readings, wind velocities and directions, and cloud layer information. Pilot reports are golden, if you keep in mind that they are generally not up to the minute. Check them for thunderstorm sightings, cloud tops, turbulence, and temperature data.

It Pays to Be Trendy

Where the air is unstable enough to spawn thunderstorms, things can happen very fast, so watch for trends. Winds aloft information can help you to chart the nature of the changeability. If the charts and numbers indicate a strong flow from large sources of moisture—say, the Gulf of Mexico or large lakes—be wary. Note also gusty conditions where no thunderstorm activity has been reported *yet*. Like an intelligence officer sizing up the possible battle, check out any potentially menacing indicator, if only to have the security of knowing for sure that it can be safely disregarded. In that respect, consult the relevant prognostic charts and terminal forecasts—recent and current—to determine what was being predicted and how righteous the prophets were. If they erred, why? If they spoke truth, why? Ultimately, your decisions have to be based initially on the picture you build *now*.

With so much information to be gathered at your preflight briefing(s), it is obvious why being at the FSS is superior to using the phone. If you must call, keep asking questions as you see the need. It's your right, and it's your fate you're asking about. If the specialist hasn't consulted a chart that you would have looked at were you there, request that he do so. The importance of this is heightened, of course, if you are going IFR, possibly into clouds where thunderstorms could be embedded.

No competent commander rests secure with old reports if the battle is still raging. As we have seen from the Air Wisconsin crash—other, similar cases could be cited—updating while en route and at each pit stop is a necessity. The En Route Flight Advisory Service (122.0) was created to make updating easier. Especially if you are IFR, use ATC to obtain the currrent radar observations—but remember that their radar does not see thunderstorms perfectly. If you are VFR, check with ATC and when you are in range, monitor the Approach Control frequency at your destination, or Unicom, if you are heading for a nontower field. If there is trouble out there, pilots may well be talking about it. You can also monitor certain VORs and NDBs for TWEBs. ADF tuned to the low-frequency band may detect and point to the electrostatic activity associated with thunderstorms. In the Florida area, the Hazardous Inflight Weather Advisory Service provides valuable updates.

Above all, if what you hear from these updates suggests changing your flight plan (filed or mental), get ready with a new plan to request or initiate before you reach a state of crisis.

Radar Vision and Radar Blindness

Some pilots who carry airborne radar believe that their scopes provide just about all the updating that is necessary. They hold to this in spite of a painful history of airborne radar's failure to protect airplanes— including airliners—from destruction or savaging by storms. The sad fact is that weather radar is far from being invulnerable to error. Radar can actually be fooled into depicting the worst parts of a storm as relatively clear areas. These "shadows" become traps for the unwary, cell-dodging pilot.

This flaw is caused by *attentuation* of the radar signal. The antenna's signal can be deflected or absorbed by a heavy precipitation or hail, so that the beam does not penetrate the storm or line. As a result, intense areas of the storm can appear as shadowed areas that falsely suggest "avenues." In other words, the affected return signal hides the fact that there is more storm out there than meets the eye glued to the scope. Such eyes have belonged to several trained airline pilots who have been lured into the very violence they were trying hardest to dodge.

Obviously the foremost lesson to be learned from this is that such shadows should be avoided. Never head for one.

Also, however sophisticated your equipment, you must recognize that this generally supremely helpful device cannot be used by itself, in an informational vacuum. You must be aware of the atmospheric environment; you must know what conditions have been reported and are being forecast, and you must use these data to interpret what your radar is telling you. Only then can you confidently make decisions on where to go to avoid trouble.

Keep in mind certain storm characteristics, such as the velocity, moisture content, height, and relation to the tropopause, echo-level intensity reported by the NWS, and the description provided in the convective outlook. Needless to say, the higher a storm tops out (it may even rise above the tropopause) the more vicious it is likely to be. Similarly, if the storm is large but does not have a large moisture content, the convective activity needed to create the system would be greater than for a high-moisture storm. The winds involved are likely to be far stronger. It is therefore important to know if the airflow dominating it is off a large body of water like the Atlantic or the Gulf, or has been traveling over land. It is also important for the pilot to be able to factor the groundspeed in with the velocity of the storm's winds, since they combine to make up the force with which his airplane may have to contend.

Knowing how bad and how extensive a storm or line is likely to be should help you to interpret your radar's reports realistically and to be alert for any anomalies that may appear. Always lean on the side of wide avoidance and away from any temptation to use radar to ''thread the needle'' between cells, so that you won't think you are heading for the eye of the needle while you are really aiming for the heart of the storm.

To determine how your equipment may be used to best advantage and with least confusion, take a course in weather radar operation or consult an instructor who is expert at operating *your* equipment. Check with your radar's manufacturer, but remember that they may not be willing to admit that their radar can fail to paint the whole picture with true realism. If necessary, consult an *authoritative* publication. Be sure that your source is appropriate to your equipment and needs and is up to date.

Here are some general guidelines:

• Turn on the radar and adjust the antenna tilt, lowering it until the display screen is filled with ground returns, then raising it until those ground returns appear only in the outer third of the display.

• Look for precipitation echoes. Especially hazardous signatures in thunderstorm depictions include hooks (possible tornadoes), pendant shapes, and steep reflectivity gradient contours.

• Radar screens have range markers. When flying above the freezing level, be sure to avoid all storms by at least 20 nm. When flying below the freezing level, avoid all storms by 10 nm. If you fly between cells, they should be at least 40 nm apart.

• Do not fly into any area of radar ''shadows.'' Some color radar displays portray these shadow areas with a blue return. This indicates the presence of severe weather that cannot be displayed.

The Stormscope Alternative

Although airborne radar has come a long way in sophistication, sensitivity, and availability—radar antennas now grace the wings of many singles—most general aviation pilots are prevented by cost or the nature of their particular aircraft from making use of it. Furthermore, as many owners have discovered, to use radar to its full effectiveness can demand more training and application than is realized at the time of purchase. A more recently invented device, the 3M Stormscope, has been adopted by many pilots. This invention of electrical engineer Paul Ryan has been flight tested on aircraft ranging from the Cessna Skyhawk to the BAC 1-11 to the F-104, and it has been used in several aircraft of various types as a complement to radar.

Neither Stormscope nor airborne weather radar displays turbulence and hail, but a proper interpretation of what they do show can help a pilot to avoid thunderstorm violence.

Stormscope displays intracloud electrical discharges that are associated with convective wind shear. Radar displays the intensity and size of precipitation. The two systems, therefore, can complement each other. Of the two, Stormscope has the advantage of being less expensive.

The discharges are shown as dots on a cathode ray tube. The device retains the dots until its memory is filled, at which point the first dot drops off and is replaced by a dot representing the latest electrical discharge. Periodically, the dots are cleared from the scope so that the storms will be depicted in their proper relation to the nose of the aircraft. By avoiding the areas represented in dots, one has a good chance of staying out of the most severe weather. Stormscope's range of detection extends to beyond 200 nm, and the range can be set closer, to, say, 40 and 100 nm.

The heart of the device is a computer processor, which is programmed to accept vertical intracloud discharges and reject horizontal discharges and many types of lightning ground strokes. In essence, Stormscope is a passive radio receiver, similar to an ADF, that picks up signals in a narrow range around 50 kilohertz. Ryan determined that this is the frequency range within which emissions from vertical intracloud discharges (the type associated with convective wind shear in thunderstorms) can be found. A microprocessor plots each such discharge on a grid. The image on the Stormscope CRT is a representation of that grid. Since the first models were marketed, Stormscope has undergone many refinements, including a mating capability with certain airborne radars and a "synchro-digital converter," to accommodate heading changes.

To make comparisons between Stormscope and radar is not only to evaluate the equipment but also to see in sharp relief the challenges of accurately reading thunderstorm activity from the cockpit (FIGURE 9). For instance, Stormscope cannot show precipitation or map terrain. Radar cannot show electrical activity, present a 360-degree view, or operate safely on the ground. Which system is better largely depends on personal preference. The FAA allows either system to be used on commuter aircraft that are required to have thunderstorm detection equipment, although transport-category aircraft must have radar.

Many pilots who have both claim that the combination provides more information on which to base decisions. Some say that Stormscope portrays weather that lies behind the attenuated portion of a radar image—that shadow, which, as we have seen, can be created by very heavy precipitation and which can look deceptively like relatively nonviolent air. They also report penetrating areas of heavy precipitation but no electrical activity, without encountering more than moderate turbulence. Their general feeling, nevertheless, is that radar provides a more precise definition of the area of a thunderstorm and a better indication of its distance from the airplane.

Just as with radar, Stormscope does not provide the pilot with instantaneous wisdom. For instance, it is sometimes hard to distinguish where a storm ends and "radial spread" begins—when

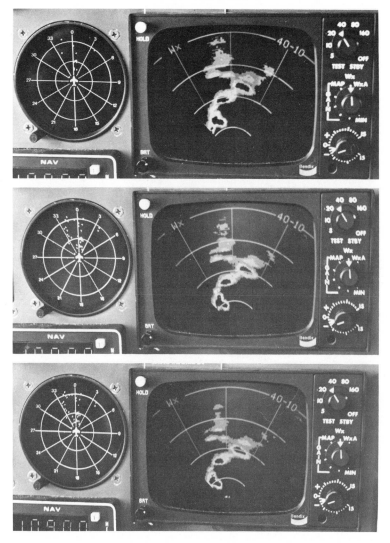

FIGURE 9   An actual comparison of Stormscope and radar storm detection displays. This series of photographs was taken over a period of
about 30 seconds inside a Cessna 414 that was at 17,000 feet and approaching a storm. Tops were reported above 30,000 feet. The Stormscope and radar were operating on 40-mile ranges, and the radar tilt

energy emitted by strong storms causes the Stormscope to depict a trail of dots from the storm center to the center of the screen. To sort out the real storms from this false "radial spread" indication, the "clear" function of the instrument must be frequently used. There are Stormscope models that reduce this effect.

Wind Shear Detectors

The new technology of thunderstorm management is also attacking the problems of wind shear, the foremost of these being early warning. One detection system available at several airports is the FAA's low-level wind shear alert system (LLWAS), which comprises up to five anemometers placed around the airport periphery (usually near ILS middle markers). A microcomputer compares wind velocity readings obtained from the peripheral anemometers with a centerfield sensor. If the difference exceeds a certain value, usually 15 knots, a visual signal (a flashing light) alerts tower controllers, who pass the information to pilots.

LLWAS can alert a pilot to the presence of wind shear, but it cannot pinpoint its location or quantify its severity. For instance, on July 9, 1982, the flight crew of a Pan American 727 was advised of wind shear alerts from all quadrants of the airport before they took off from New Orleans. The captain used

was adjusted for the best presentation. In the upper photo of Figure 9, the Stormscope displayed several dots immediately after the displays had been cleared; additional dots continued to accumulate in the following pictures. Discernible clusters of dots near the 20-mile range marker closely correlate with Level 3 contours on the radar display. Stormscope also indicates electrical activity farther to the left of course than the radar's rainfall presentation. A pilot using Stormscope to avoid areas of turbulence would make a course correction to the right or left and then clear the display, allowing new information to appear for more accurate course selection.

his weather radar to check the departure path for any areas of heavy precipitation. He decided to take off but instructed his first officer, who was flying the aircraft, to ''let the airspeed build up on takeoff'' and to leave the air-conditioning packs off to increase available engine power.

The 727 crashed, killing 153 people, 1/2 mile off the departure end of the runway. The aircraft had flown into a microburst. Dr. Fujita, in examining the crash, determined that in encountering this combination of horizontal and vertical wind shears, the 727 crew flew from a 17-knot headwind into a 31-knot tailwind and was struck, at the same time, by a 420-fpm downdraft. The NTSB attributed the probable cause of the disaster to wind shear. Significantly, the board cited as a contributing factor the limited capability of LLWAS to provide definitive guidance on wind shear avoidance.

The crash of Delta L-1011 at Dallas–Fort Worth International in August 1985 has cast additional strong doubt on the ability of the LLWAS and tower-to-pilot warning system to prevent wind shear accidents. In that crash, 137 people died.

While inbound, the pilot had received a routine ATIS report, which had given no cause for concern. Still, ten minutes prior to the crash the controllers at the airport received a thunderstorm warning—but they did not pass it on to the pilot. As the crew initiated an approach to Runway 17R, they were told about variable winds from the east at 5 knots gusting to 15 in connection with a ''shower on short out there north end of DFW.''

Witnesses later reported that the electrical storm had moved in from the northeast, growing very rapidly and, after moving to the right of the runway, spreading onto the approach path. An American Airlines pilot waiting to take off reported that the wind sock rapidly shifted around from south to north. Lightning bolts were also seen.

The approaching Delta pilot was requested by the tower to slow to 150 knots to maintain separation behind a preceding Learjet. The pilot complied, eventually slowing to 150. In his last transmission he reported heavy rain but no problem.

The tower first saw the L-1011 approaching as low as 50 feet and still outside the field perimeter. The controller instructed a go-around, but the plane had already bounced short of the field and was on its way to a breakup crash.

To the NTSB, the evidence indicated that the airliner had encountered a microburst and a sudden tailwind, which, combined with the pilot's slowing of the aircraft, forced the aircraft to fall to the ground.

Not until 12 to 14 minutes after the crash did the LLWAS system sound a wind shear alarm. It was speculated that the system's sensors had not detected the wind shear earlier because the cell had passed between them.

LLWAS is a temporary measure. The FAA is working with the NOAA and the Department of Defense in using Nexrad, the Doppler-based system we have discussed, as a means of detecting and *measuring* wind shear. Meanwhile, an airborne wind shear warning system has been developed by Safe Flight. The system measures horizontal and vertical wind shear and provides aural and visual warnings of performance-threatening shears. The system can also provide the pilot with pitch guidance to minimize altitude loss. It is available for air-carrier craft, general aviation turbojets, and some turboprops.

Airmanship, the Ultimate Defense

We have been looking at technologies designed to warn us away from trouble. They don't always succeed, and many pilots lack the requisite airborne equipment for storm avoidance. Furthermore, weather briefings and inflight updating, including vectors from ATC, may also fail to protect entirely from high- and low-altitude hazardous turbulence. What then? If your early warning system fails, you will have to fall back on eyes-peeled, hands-on airmanship for survival.

Take gust fronts and wind shears: The departing pilot's first line of defense is in knowing that a storm is approaching, which should dictate delaying the takeoff unless he *knows* there is no danger of advance-gust or wind-shear action. He should observe his departing predecessors to see how badly they are buffeted on climbout. What may be moderate chop when they go could quickly strengthen into serious problems for pilots who follow. A pilot preparing to land at an airport where storm activity is imminent should also think twice about trying to beat the disturbance to the runway, since his airplane will be flying at a low altitude and airspeed and in a high-drag configuration.

On landing, if you find that the windsock or the reported wind values indicate a windflow direction and speed that are belied by the crab angle you must assume to make a good downwind track or glide path on final, you may well find yourself flying through a shear line close to the ground. When you are still miles from your destination, you may notice there a clearly demarcated layer of haze or smog, like an ugly floating pancake, topping in a sharp line about 1,000 to 2,000 feet above the surface. If there is thunderstorm activity close by, that could be the boundary between contrary airflows.

At any time, a whipping or full but inconsistently pointing windsock is an omen. When wind shear is possible, plan to climb out about 10 knots faster than normal.

Wind shear can particularly bedevil the IFR pilot. Let us say that you are given an approach to Runway 36 and the winds are reported as 350 to 15. As you make your northward approach, with your IAS where it should be, you find that you must power back and keep a high sink rate to hold the glideslope, or that, when you break out, you are farther along the glide path than your timing led you to believe. As you descend, your tailwind is about to become an instant headwind. More dramatically, if you are flying an ILS into a stiff headwind, as indicated by a need for a lower-than-normal sink rate and a higher power setting to maintain the glideslope, keep a close tab on the wind report from the tower. Whether you are flying a circling approach or an unavoidable straight-in to the active, a report signifying a tailwind at low altitude could mean that you will hit a shear line, with a sudden drop in airspeed, at the worst possible time.

If you are in real doubt about the situation, think hard about missing the approach and heading for your alternate. If you continue the approach, leave the flaps retracted or at an intermediate setting and be ready to apply full power and bring the nose up. The less drag, the better your acceleration capability. Make your decisions about gear and flaps early so as not to be fiddling with those controls or abruptly altering the configuration of the airplane if it stalls or the pitch suddenly changes.

Any suspicion that you may be flying into a sudden tailwind should prompt you to add insurance power. When you hit the shear, the nose will drop, and the airplane will sink. Immediately go to maximum power and lift the nose. You will be trading some airspeed for altitude, which, at a low height, is a dicey but necessary situation. If ground contact still appears imminent, increase the pitch to 20 or 25 degrees while maintaining maximum power, and keep flying the airplane.

A sudden increase in headwind (or decrease in tailwind) will increase your airspeed. The nose will pitch up and the airplane will balloon. In short-field conditions, a go-around may be your automatic best bet. But be careful, for you may soon be climbing back into a tailwind: Go to full power and keep the nose low enough for insurance airspeed as you ascend.

Regard any IFR circling approach where there is a threat of wind shear as simply dangerous, especially if the field is near circling minimums and/or there is threatening terrain. A low circling approach near minimums can be difficult enough, especially at an unfamiliar field, without treacherous winds compounding the hazards. Whatever your airplane's attitude, if the approach becomes unstabilized below 500 feet AGL in a difficult wind, do not hesitate to miss the approach or go around.

Turbulence Flying

As we shall see in the next chapter, turbulence can stem from many sources, natural and man-made. The methods for coping with thunderstorm turbulence, then, are generally applicable to other rough-air conditions.

First, tighten all seat belts and harnesses so snugly that they are uncomfortable. A belt or harness with "play" can leave you rattling about in your seat, at the mercy of the plane's oscillations. Your body may be repeatedly lifted off the seat, your feet off the rudder pedals, and your head into the roof, while you strain for a firm foundation from which to control the airplane. A co-pilot undergoing such torture will be of little use to you, and rear-seat passengers so flung about can easily reach hysteria and worse. Similarly, all loose items must be secured, lest they become projectiles within your closed environment. Small things, such as pencils, Jepp books, charts, and so forth, should be in pockets, in you flight bag, or lodged where they can't get out. Have a flashlight secured but in quick reach, in case you lose your instrument and cabin lights.

If you enter cloud, turn the internal lights on full bright, turn on the pitot heat (before entering the cloud, if possible), and turn off the navigation lights—strobes and rotating beacon—for they become distractions that can encourage vertigo. Landing and taxi lights are left off. Flaps are kept up.

There are two schools of thought about the best airspeed to maintain in turbulence: at the airplane's published maneuvering speed (V_a) or slightly below it. The maneuvering speed is the maximum airspeed for an aircraft flying at gross weight at which full and abrupt deflections of the flight controls can be made without overstressing the airframe. Pilots are taught that at V_a the airplane should stall before the airframe will suffer a pilot-induced failure. V_a or slightly below is thus somewhere between 60 and 40 percent above the flaps-up, power-off stall speed and is established to ensure that the airplane will stop flying before it can be brought to endure a load factor of 3.8 g's, for which most general aviation aircraft are certificated.

Flying at the published V_a can impose trouble. The gross-weight, power-off stall speed probably will not reflect the actual conditions under which an airplane will be flown in turbulence. The power will most likely be on, and the airplane will most likely be somewhere below gross weight. Furthermore, heavy, gusty conditions can mean wind shear at any altitude, and, as we have seen, a sudden headwind increase abruptly raises the airspeed; that raises the load factor. A shear-induced speed increase from the published V_a will be more than 60 percent above the *power-on* stall speed and is far more likely to overstress the airframe.

How Slow Is Safe?

Although penetrating turbulence at the published maneuvering speed can bring on the overstressing it was meant to prevent, flying too near the power-on, clean stall speed of an airplane can also induce stalling and overstressing. Flying slowly does tend to lessen gust shocks and some of the dangers of overcontrolling, but very slow flight can mean mushy controls and the constant imminence of a stall. That is bad enough in light chop; in significant turbulence, especially with shearing action, when you have to work at keeping the wings level and the pitch stable below the critical angle of attack, you can't allow the margin above the stall to be reduced too much.

The usual general aviation aircraft is susceptible to overstressing from a sudden, violent drop of virtually the same g magnitude as from an instantaneous, savage lift. Certainly, a drop of that kind may well induce a rapid overcorrection by a startled pilot. Overstressing is, in fact, usually pilot induced.

Just which turbulence-flying speed is best depends on the airplane and its overall weight at the time. Beyond question, if the chop is building toward karate intensity, the airspeed needle is to be kept well away from the yellow, the beginning of which is V_{no} or the maximum structural cruising speed. To determine where in relation to the published maneuvering speed you should be flying, determine what the wing loading of your airplane is. The heavier the wing loading, the more the gust suppression. That will give you some idea of the relative effects of varying degrees of turbulence on your airplane. As a help to pilots, aircraft manufacturers increasingly are developing recommended turbulence penetration speeds for more aircraft as well as publishing the V_a for various weights.

A suggested rule of thumb is to fly at about 1.7 times the power-on, clean stall speed. That is a good compromise between stall and the usually listed maneuvering speed. But, of course, the real trick will be to establish that speed and hold to it in the bucking and jerking that turbulence can bring. The secret lies in competent attitude flying.

A Good Attitude in Bad Conditions

We have already discussed attitude instrument flying in connection with simple penetration of cloud and fog (see chapter 2). Steady attitude flying is easily as critical in turbulence. When in the toils of gusts, shears, and drafts, the object is to keep the airplane flying as near to the selected speed as you can get, in as close to a constant level attitude as conditions will allow. One of the worst things a pilot can do in turbulence is to chase the airspeed needle by hauling back on the yoke and shoving it forward. In turbulence, an airplane will gain altitude in updrafts and lose it in downdrafts, but as long as the pitch attitude remains constant, airspeed excursions can be relatively minimized, even to some extent in shear conditions. Power changes can help. For example, if the sink rate is increasing and the airspeed is decreasing, add power to avoid a stall. If the airspeed is increasing dramatically, lessen the power until the target airspeed is reached. *Such measures are for dramatic changes and trends.* In strong turbulence, the airspeed is bound to fluctuate some—in fact, the airplane may periodically stall and recover so quickly that no recovery input is needed from the pilot. Generally speaking, if the airspeed is holding near the target, maintain a constant pitch and power setting. Proper trimming helps enormously. Lowering the gear (be sure it's at below the gear-extension speed) also dampens shear-induced fluctuations. Keep in mind that loss of control in turbulence more often than not means loss of *pitch* control.

Lateral control inputs should also be kept as light and smooth as conditions permit, although the airplane may be rolled this way and that. The experienced pilot learns when he can afford to surrender a bit of roll momentarily, knowing that a countergust may well roll him back the opposite way. No problem, if the roll rates are small. Concurrently, he won't have to be hit too hard by turbulence to know when to exert muscle to maintain lateral control. He learns, also, that while there are times when the rudder pedals can help to keep the airplane straight and level, too much rudder can lead to stressful yawing.

Drafts and Altitude: Give and Let Live

An autopilot can be an aid as a *wing leveler* in turbulence, but it should not be used to hold altitude. In fact, holding altitude is not a goal when there are powerful updrafts and downdrafts. As we have seen in one pilot's thunderstorm battle, trying to maintain altitude in heavy turbulence leaves you no choice but to fly a series of dives and climbs, with the airspeed fluctuating into forbidden areas and overstressing becoming a distinct possibility. Put an autopilot in charge of maintaining altitude in strong turbulence, and it will act like a ham-fisted, unthinking human: It will constantly retrim the elevator and readjust the pitch, and, therefore, the airspeed, until the airplane breaks.

The reality is that in such turbulence, you may well have to accept altitude fluctuations to preserve your aircraft. In a light-plane, it's no contest anyway. How many general aviation aircraft can overcome downdrafts in excess of 2,000 fpm? The chances are that the updrafts and downdrafts will average out. Furthermore, keep in mind that any aircraft above or below you are probably rising or descending when you are.

If you cannot safely maintain your assigned altitude, tell the controller and request a different altitude along with storm-escaping vectors, if you have good reason to believe that a higher or lower assignment could make for a smoother ride. Be cautious. Going lower could put you to close to terrain in the event of strong downdrafts, and climbing could put you into worse turbulence, hail, and icing conditions such as reside in the upper reaches of a thundercloud.

Flying Blind in the Whirlwind

If you blunder into a thundercloud, your chances of flying through it successfully will depend greatly on your ability to avoid panic and to concentrate on basic attitude instrument flying. This is easier said than done, especially if you are inexperienced. If you are instrument rated, you will have a far better chance of success than if you are not, but instrument training that hasn't included extensive practice in actual cloud is not good preparation for blind flying in heavy turbulence. The less training and actual instrument experience, the more likely you will be to revert to older habits of relying more on physical sensations than on the instruments to know how the airplane is flying. Or you may find yourself incapable of interpreting the gauges, as spatial disorientation and fear take over. "Unusual attitude" exercises do not convey the relentlessness of vertigo and the general confusion that can occur when you are coping alone in a cockpit that has lost its recognizable up and down.

In spite of such gloomy prospects, the fact is that in cloud, salvation for the pilot lies in the panel. Try to relax as much as possible, keep up your scan, and concentrate on flying the plane. Follow the method described in chapter 2. Scrunch down in your seat so as to concentrate on the gauges, try not to keep a death grip on the yoke, and fly *as if* you were as cool as Chuck Yeager. Fiddle with no more controls than you must. Once the power is set, change it only if things start to get out of hand. Carburetor heat should be on. Stay with one radio frequency, if you can. Needless to say, a headset and boom mike are godsends in such a situation. As long as keeping the airplane upright and under control is a full-time task, give little or no time to dialing, tuning, adjusting, chart scanning, or talking—anything that can disturb your concentration on flying. If you have a knowledgeable co-pilot, let him or her handle the secondary things you haven't the time to deal with.

Retractables tend to lend themselves to swift speed buildups during descents—intentional or not. As briefly suggested above, many experts hold that if the V_a is less than the maximum landing gear extended speed (V_{le}), it could be better to ride through the turbulence with the gear out, to add lateral stability in rough air and, more important, to create drag in case of an upset. This practice also allows a higher power setting without adding airspeed, which in turn provides a better control capability.

If you should lose control, you will not have run out of options—just almost. If the nose is down and the airplane is gaining speed, retard the throttle to lessen the airspeed buildup, and begin a *gradual* pull-up. *Don't abruptly haul back.* This is a critical maneuver, for in turbulent air, any abruptness during a recovery attempt will increase the risk of structural failure. Once you have leveled the aircraft, go to full power and establish a definite rate of climb to clear the terrain. If you are diving in a spiral or spin, retard the throttle and determine which way the airplane is turning. If you are in a spiral, level the wings. If you are in a spin, kick opposite rudder and neutralize the controls.

Remember that in a spin, the airplane is in a stalled condition, so let it build flying speed before you pull up. Trying to pull out of a dive while banked could induce a spin.

Once in cloud or in severely restricted visibility, go to your instruments and stick with them. Trust them, whatever the seat of your pants or your instincts may tell you to the contrary. If you *feel* that you are entering an unusual attitude, check and trust the instruments to tell you what is really happening. Usually in such cases, nothing is happening but stable flight, though your scared body and disturbed inner ear are clamoring otherwise. If your attitude indicator, airspeed indicator, altimeter, and VSI tell you that you are climbing, banking, and losing airspeed, level the wings, lower the nose, and put on power until you are again in stable flight.

Is Turning Around Wise?

A turn out of a storm cloud is not generally recommended, once you have made penetration. An exception might be a case in which you know you are going into much worse conditions—say, if you have entered the back side of a squall line, where the leading edge of the line is the most violent area. Besides placing additional stress on the airplane and making it more susceptible to an upset, a turn may invite vertigo or other disorientation. For an inexperienced instrument pilot—certainly, for a nonrated one—it is much more difficult to maintain a constant, shallow angle of bank in cloud and turbulence, referring solely to instruments, than in level flight.

A 180 could betray you. In thunderstorm-forming conditions, cells develop and clouds build very fast. What minutes earlier was clearer air could close up in the time it will take to get back to it. It makes more sense to spare yourself and your plane the dangers of a turn into you know not what—that is, unless your radar and/or Stormscope or radar-inspired instructions from the ground suggest a more reliable way to go. Continuing on through a storm is surely not an enjoyable option, but it may well be the least of several evils.

Also, the turn itself poses dangers. However shallow the bank, and it can't be too shallow if you want to make any progress, gusting can aggravate the bank into one that is far more extreme, which, added to wind effects on the pitch attitude, could cause a wing to stall. In a bank, the lift component is decreased as the angle of bank steepens.

If you can do so without incurring these dangers, select and hold a heading that will lead to the quickest exit from the storm. Your weather briefing and updates should offer some idea of which way to go. For example, if you have been told that the storm activity was expected along a line oriented north-south, a penetration heading of east or west should mean the shortest way through—avoiding the widest part of the storm.

If you are in and out of cloud or between layers and you detect a clearer area for which you might head, judge carefully. You may be seeing an area marking a differential between precipitation intensities. The clear area may be drier, but the drafts may be stronger. There have been cases of airliners turning and heading into destructive turbulence that occupied tempting "light" areas. In like manner, underflying thunderclouds toward lighter-looking areas can be a mistake. There may be little rain, but those bases may be harboring severe downdrafts or updrafts or creating violent wind shears. This is no time for creative scud running.

Avoidance is paramount. If you are VFR, keep well clear by eyeballing the conditions. If you are IFR (or VFR), request vectors from ATC to help you deviate from thunderstorms in your path, but know that vectors are not always reliable; lacking such help, deviate as best you can and land at the most practicable airport (possibly your departure airport), notifying ATC of your intentions. Use what onboard devices you may have, with the understanding that they are meant for avoidance, not penetration, and that no warning system is perfect.

Wind hazards do not always come in huge doses served up by thunderstorms. In smaller portions, they can bedevil the pilot mightily, be they blows created by nature or by other pilots.

5
Hazards Natural and Man-Made

As the Wright brothers proved on the swept dunes of Kitty Hawk, preparation for adverse winds is the prime preliminary to freeing oneself from the ground. Great storms are awesome and by their visible enormity recommend evasion. Other wind hazards are more insidious, and they, too, should be avoided when they promise to be too much for pilot or plane. Mountain winds, severe crosswinds, and vortices generated by other aircraft are some. More treacherous because it is invisible and nearly unpredictable is clear air turbulence.

A Killer High and Low

Commonly, clear air turbulence is considered a hazard mainly to high-flying airliners. By definition, however, CAT includes all turbulence outside and away from *visible* convective activity, such as thunderstorms. The NTSB has shown that the majority of CAT accidents involves general aviation aircraft flying at relatively low altitudes. Of the ninety-two CAT-related accidents that occurred from 1977 through 1982, only fourteen involved air-carrier craft. CAT was a direct cause in twelve of the general aviation accidents and was a contributing factor in the remaining sixty-six. In a large number of the crashes, the aircraft stalled when they encountered turbulence on initial climb, during approach, or while maneuvering at low altitude.

Undetectable to the eye, airborne radar, and Stormscope, clear air turbulence can cause sudden, wrenching excursions of airspeed and attitude, leaving the pilot of a stricken aircraft little time to react and recover. One aircraft was rolled inverted while cruising at 17,500 feet. Its wing structure was substantially damaged, but the pilot managed to regain control and land safely. Another airplane was so jolted that it descended out of control after the pilot was blinded when his head struck the cabin roof. At lower altitudes, especially where the terrain is high, CAT can be amazingly vicious:

• One private pilot (2,382 hours) departed for a flight along the Cascade Mountains in his Piper Arrow. He obtained no weather briefing and filed no flight plan. He reported cloud tops over the mountains at 7,000 to 8,000 feet. The weather was CAVU with gusting winds. An Airmet valid for 1:15 to 8:00 P.M. called for occasional moderate turbulence within 5,000 feet of the terrain and occasional strong updrafts and downdrafts along the slopes of mountains.

The pilot had leveled at 8,500 feet but, after encountering rough air, began a climb to 10,500 feet. The Arrow didn't make it. The airman later reported that the airplane "fell out of the sky at 9,400 feet" after encountering a strong downdraft. Even with full power and one notch of flaps, the Arrow could not climb. The pilot attempted to maintain an airspeed of 120 mph, but the vertical speed indicator was pegged at a 2,500-fpm descent. In an attempt to turn out of the downdraft, 1½ miles from a peak, the Arrow struck the side of a mountain at 7,400 feet in a slightly nose-up, left-turn attitude and was destroyed. The pilot and one passenger survived but were seriously injured. One passenger was killed.

Certification standards require that most general aviation airplanes be able to withstand a vertical gust as intense as 3,000 fpm while flying at the maximum structural cruising speed (V_{no}). Yet severe turbulence can quickly exceed the stress limits of any aircraft. Two examples: In the period 1977–82, one airplane lost its right wing, and another, a turboprop twin, lost its elevator assembly during CAT encounters.

According to the FAA, meteorologists know very little about the causes of CAT, so forecasts are unreliable: Where CAT is forecast, "the pilot experiences control problems only about 0.2 percent of the time; odds of this genuinely hazardous turbulence are about 1 in 500." It is important to note, however, that many CAT-related accidents occur in areas where turbulence had been forecast. Still, warnings of CAT in Sigmets (severe) and Airmets (moderate) usually are based on pilot reports.

Since clear air turbulence is associated with high-altitude disturbances, pilots should expect it when they operate near the tropopause, the boundary between the troposphere and stratosphere. The height of the tropopause varies from about 55,000 feet over the equator to about 28,000 feet over the poles. The severe turbulence generated where the jet stream shifts its direction is also part of the CAT phenomenon.

Again, the Convection Factor

Convective (or thermal) turbulence is caused by ascending and descending columns of air and typically is encountered in flights over deserts and arid land. Solar heating causes the air to rise, and as it rises, the air expands, cools, and starts to descend, usually moving less quickly than the rising air. A result is strong vertical shearing. Of course, we recognize this as part of the mechanism for the building of thunderstorms. What is missing is sufficient moisture, but the energy is there. In checking the weather, therefore, don't be too quick to relax if the dewpoints are not high or if other signs of moisture aren't present. If the air is unstable and convective activity seems likely, beware, as you launch yourself into the cloudless sky.

Wind shear turbulence not associated with thunderstorms can

also be expected when 20-knot isotachs (lines connecting points of equal wind speeds, regardless of wind directions) are spaced closer together than 60 nautical miles and when the wind velocity changes more than 5 knots per 1,000 feet of altitude. Frontal movements also cause wind shear, which again calls to mind the caveat, be especially cautious when you are flying near cold fronts and warm fronts that are moving over the ground at 30 knots or more or are causing a temperature change of 10 degrees F or more.

CAT in the Upper Reaches

At high altitudes, clear air turbulence is caused by shearing between layers of different wind speeds as the jet stream converges and diverges around upper air systems. Severe CAT is especially probable north and east of a developing low as the low intensifies on its way north under the path of the jet stream. The turbulence frequently shows up where the isotachs are most concentrated, on the stream's northern edge and directly above and below a well-defined jet stream core. The steeper the temperature gradient between the air masses involved, the stronger the CAT.

Experts say that clear air turbulence can appear at any altitude between 15,000 and 45,000 feet, but it most often surrounds the jet stream core, near 28,000 to 30,000. These are fairly broad ranges; the science of predicting the location of the turbulence is still relatively new, and meteorologists find it easier to predict jet stream positions than to prognosticate clear air turbulence locations.

Yet more and more of us are flying general aviation airplanes at airliner altitudes, and we need all the forecasterial help we can get. The airlines have their own full-time meteorological services, of course, and their information is processed by computers geared to an airline's route structure. The result is a suggested flight plan and climb/descent profile that maximizes the airplane's performance and takes into account the avoidance of adverse conditions. General aviation pilots must live with what the NWS, its Flight Service clients, and our analytical powers can provide. As with working out defenses against thunderstorms, the pilot is best served by a briefing at the FSS than by phone when planning a high-altitude flight.

Too often, when pilots transition to high-altitude flying, they bring their low-altitude habits with them, which means concentrating on surface-condition information. High-altitude flying calls for studying high-altitude analysis and upper-winds charts. Low- and high-level significant weather prog charts will help you to visualize expected conditions at cruise altitudes. The radar summary chart is also a must if there is a chance of low-pressure or thunderstorm activity.

Constant-pressure analysis charts, which are issued twice daily, tell at a glance the strength and direction of the winds aloft and the locations of any natural "fast lanes." Just as important, they also show pressure patterns by means of isobars (lines connecting points of equal barometric pressure). The millibar designations correspond roughly to various altitudes. For example, the 700 mb chart represents about 10,000 feet MSL, 500 mb is 18,000, and 300 mb is close to 30,000. Isobars identify the height (in meters) at which, for example, a pressure of 500 mb of mercury is exerted in the atmosphere. By observing the differing heights of a pressure level, you can visualize the declining slopes, which signify a low, and the rising contours, which indicate a dome of high pressure.

One thing to look for is the distinctive *U*-shape of a low-pressure trough. In the straighter portions of the *U*, you will find the areas of highest wind speed. Areas where isobars converge or diverge are apt to produce CAT. The straight portion of the *U* on the east side of the low is especially important, because this is the area that is prone to produce adverse surface weather, maximum vertical cloud development, *and* clear air turbulence.

Breeds of CAT

Meteorologists have three criteria for determining the probability of CAT. If the vertical difference in wind speed is from 4 to 5 knots per 1,000 feet, they predict moderate CAT. A difference of 6 knots or more per 1,000 feet will bring a forecast of severe CAT. That is the vertical profile for a likely CAT situation. If the wind speed varies by more than 40 knots in a 150-mile horizontal distance, meteorologists suspect that CAT is imminent. Since forecasters expect CAT in 6,000- to 8,000-foot layers beginning at the tropopause and extending downward, it is easy to see that the probability of clear air turbulence should not be overlooked when you are flying a turbocharged airplane at its optimum altitude near lows or troughs.

You can foresee CAT by using the constant-pressure analysis chart and another source of information, the upper-winds prognosis charts. These charts cover eight altitudes, from 9,000 feet to 39,000 feet, and offer a less cluttered view of the forecast winds aloft. From the analysis charts, find the isobar orientation that indicates possible clear air turbulence; then go to the upper-winds charts and figure the vertical differences in wind speeds at various altitudes as reported by a station in the suspected CAT region.

Forecasts of clear air turbulence are available in several forms. Area forecasts will indicate the expected nature and extent of any clear air turbulence. Significant weather prognosis charts are perhaps the best way of locating any possible forecast turbulence or other adverse conditions aloft. The low-level prog chart is fairly well known to pilots. The high-level prog chart is a useful tool that most pilots do not even know exists.

This chart depicts turbulence and clouds from 24,000 to 63,000 feet. Because the high-level prog chart covers such high altitudes, the clouds shown are either cirrus (depicted in widely scalloped outlines) or cumulonimbus (densely scalloped outlines), and the turbulence shown will be CAT. Unfortunately, most FSS choose not to receive the high-level prog chart; a pilot must contact a NWS office, which is usually helpful in *any* case. Depending on your location, this information may be impossible to get without dialing long distance and having the chart interpreted for you, secondhand. That is why a basic knowledge of CAT forecasting from the analysis and upper-winds charts is valuable.

Mountain Waves

Since air behaves like a fluid, it naturally forms waves when a strong current piles up and spills over a large obstruction, such as a tall ridge. Like a breaker, it smoothly flows up the upwind side of the ridge and then lofts and curls over to rush turbulently, in great drafts, down the downwind side. Wind blowing perpendicularly to a mountain ridge at 50 knots or more can create a mountain wave extending to the tropopause or higher and 100 miles beyond the downwind side of the ridge.

Every year, many pilots get caught in bouts with such turbulence or variants of it in hilly regions.

One pilot, Rogers H. Wright, describes a battle he waged with mountain winds in a Cessna 150. Wright is an instrument-rated, commercial pilot. He had departed Los Angeles on a flight to the Monterey area. The coastal forecast at noon, when he first departed, called for clouds with tops pushing 8,000 feet. "The briefer," Wright reports, "gave me no reason for concern other than the usual precaution about 'turbulence and updrafts and downdrafts within 5,000 feet of rough terrain.' Pilot reports indicated smooth air."

Wright's 12:30 P.M. IFR departure was into heavy cloud, but at 7,500 feet, he broke out into a beautifully clear day. Suspecting a mechanical problem, he made a precautionary stop at

Santa Paula prior to flying over 100 miles of sparsely populated mountains, the Santa Susannas. There he was reassured by the resident mechanic, topped his tanks, and, as the afternoon wore on, took off for Paso Robles across the mountains:

Santa Paula lies deep in an old river valley between two parallel ranges of mountains that block radio communication until the airplane gains considerable altitude. After several efforts to contact Los Angeles Center or Santa Barbara Approach Control, I busied myself with flying and made no further attempt to establish contact to procure a weather update. The air was smooth, with no significant wind, as my passenger and I laboriously climbed out from Santa Paula Airport, making large circles trying to stay near the center of the valley.

As we approached cruise altitude, the air began to be mildly turbulent. But given a lightly loaded 150 and typical late-afternoon onshore winds, I was not particularly concerned —my attention was still on the fuel flow [the suspected mechanical problem] and achieving sufficient altitude to clear a defined ridge line ahead.

I recalled from an AOPA mountain-flying course I had taken that the best way to approach ridge lines lying perpendicular to the wind is at a 45-degree angle. What I conveniently forgot was that frequently there are tremendous rotors and downdrafts downwind of those ridge lines. [Rotors are horizontally rotating masses of air under a mountain wave.] With 8,500 feet of altitude and a 45-degree intercept angle, I began my run. At last, I began to relax; the fuel problem was resolved, and I would reach Monterey by late afternoon.

Suddenly I felt as though I had hit a wall head-on. The aircraft shook as I made a quick instrument scan. To my dismay, I was descending at an accelerating rate already approaching 2,000 fpm. The ridge line, so comfortably stationary at the bottom of my windscreen only a moment before, was now rapidly reaching the top of the Plexiglas. There was obviously no way I was going to cross that ridge safely.

Frantically recalling that the advantage of flying a 45-degree angle to a ridge line is that it permits a quick and safe turn toward lower ground, I immediately changed course away from the ridge.

The VSI swung past 2,000 fpm and continued its counterclockwise rotation until it began to stabilize at the 1,000-fpm *ascending* calibration. Extrapolating that, I must have been going down about 3,500 fpm. I began to search desperately for a solution and came up with another recollection from the mountain-flying course: Hills or mountains facing into either the sun or the prevailing wind occasion substantial updrafts. Inasmuch as I had just crossed a smaller mountain before making my run at the ridge line, I continued my escape turn in the hope that, before I lost all my altitude, I would somehow make it safely over to the sunny, 4,000-foot mountain.

Incredibly, in almost no time, I had already lost nearly 4,500 feet. It was an all-out race against time. Continuing my turn, I quickly glanced at the VSI and saw that for the first time in many, many long seconds, my descent had slowed to slightly less than 2,000 fpm and that the rate was again readable on the correct portion of the instrument. Though lagging behind the VSI, the altimeter also seemed to be slowing in its indication of lost altitude.

I then remembered how I once had turned off the engine of a Cessna 172, changing a heavy metal airplane into a glider, and wondered if such alchemy could be repeated. Cautiously and gingerly, I began to test the control movements. With gentle banks, I discovered that I was moving deeper into the updraft of the sunny slope.

Now I had nearly 500 feet per minute of indicated climb. With full power and a tenderly executed bank, I kept myself in a fairly small, climbing circle, continually attempting to feel my way around the outer edge of the updraft. From what appeared to be a safe altitude, I cautiously began to extend the downwind part of my climb, ready to dive back into the safety of the updraft at the first indication of descent.

As my strategic withdrawal and the howling northwesterly put increasing distance between me and the ridge line, I grew bolder in my ascent. Finally, at 10,500 feet, I rolled out and pointed north again.

Even though I was a good 4,000 feet above the ridge, I again began to experience the tremendous downdraft as I approached the ridge line. Putting the aircraft into a slightly nose-low attitude, while maintaining the crosswind, 45-degree intercept angle, I calculated that the increased speed from the shallow dive would move me through the downdraft and into the updraft on the windward face of the mountain.

My plan worked, and with the loss of only a little more than 1,000 feet of altitude, I found myself in the 2,000-fpm updraft on the northwest side of the ridge. Upon reaching 10,500 feet, my VFR cruising altitude, I decided that I now could turn my attention from piloting to communicating.

As I called in my pilot report to San Francisco Center, I learned that, in the time from my first takeoff to the time I spent in Santa Paula, the winds out of the northwest had risen to such a velocity that Sigmets for extreme turbulence and extreme updrafts and downdrafts in the passes and at ridge lines had been posted for California from San Francisco to the Mexican border.

You can never entirely trust rules of thumb when it comes to flying. Staying current on techniques and receiving continual weather updates are a must for mountain flying.

As Wright points out, there are some basic principles to observe when you fly in areas of high terrain and mountain winds. First, always file a flight plan, in case you may need rescue. Using the Sectionals, select prominent checkpoints, and be sure you know the altitudes of the peaks and ridges along and near your route. Plan the flight to traverse populated areas and well-known passes. Whatever the visible conditions, check and update the weather before the flight and en route, paying special attention to the winds aloft. In the mountain states, expect the winds above 10,000 feet to be prevailing westerlies.

If the winds at your proposed altitude are above 30 knots, don't fly. Any bad or threatening weather, especially including snowstorms, is good reason not to go. Be sure to check the freezing level to avoid any chance of icing.

Know the wind direction at all times, and visualize the wind as water flowing up, over, and down the slopes. Watch for abrupt changes in wind direction and velocity, and keep in mind that the winds will be much greater in passes than will be reported at stations a few miles away. Approach mountain passes with all the cushioning altitude possible, since downdrafts may be expected on the downwind side. Approaching the pass over a ridge will lessen this effect significantly. Two thousand feet or more of clearance is best on windy days. Plan with the fact in mind that nonturbocharged engines develop less horsepower at high altitudes. Approach passes and ridges at a 45-degree angle so that you will be able to turn approximately 90 degrees into a valley or lower terrain in case you encounter severe downdrafts. If you do run into a downdraft, don't be alarmed. Keep the nose down and maintain normal airspeed. If you have altitude, continue through the downdraft and expect a compensating updraft. If you are in doubt, turn back and try crossing again at a different location, and if possible, attempt crossing at a higher altitude. Strong downdrafts, however, can render crossings impossible. Keep in mind that the actual horizon will be near the base of the mountain. If you use the summit peaks as the horizon, you will end up keeping the aircraft constantly in a climb attitude. When you are flying through a valley or canyon, the best path is on the updraft side. If you must fly low-level, fly through the valley or canyon from the high end to the low. Don't fly up the middle of a canyon, but on the downwind side, in order to take advantage of updrafts and to provide room to execute a turnaround.

Don't be suckered into a blind canyon while climbing out of a valley. Avoid flying closer than is necessary to terrain such as cliffs or rugged areas; dangerous turbulence may be expected there, especially with high winds.

When hazardous factors in mountain flying make a connection with forces usually found higher up, life can become bizarre. Dr. W. B. Bradley describes the strange turn that his flying career took when he was still a relatively new airman but in a position to get some fast seasoning:

This happened one spring when I was essentially a neophyte pilot (200 hours and VFR capability), living in Monte Vista, in the San Luis Valley of Colorado, 135 miles west of Pueblo and on the western side of the massive Sangre de Cristo Mountains. In the spring, the passes in this range are made especially hazardous by low visitations of the jet stream's high-velocity air movements and turbulence.

Shortly before this particular flight, from Pueblo to Monte Vista, the weather had deteriorated somewhat. Small, lens-shaped clouds had begun to cap the northern ridges and passes of the Sangre de Cristos, and the winds were increasing. The routes through La Veta and Mosca passes were, however, uninvolved, so my passenger and I readied to make the trip in my C-model Bonanza.

However, all the passes were now capped with clouds. Their shapes were indiscernible, since they were oriented on an east-west axis. The headwinds and turbulence told me precisely, however, what meteorological conditions were producing the clouds. It only remained for me to accept the facts. I firmly believe that pilots, even early in our careers, are not so prone to make errors in weather evaluation as we are to lie to ourselves about the analysis. I did so that afternoon.

La Veta Pass was completely closed, but a thin ribbon of blue sky was visible between the narrow defile in the mountain range and clouds overlying Mosca Pass. I convinced myself that I had a safe margin under the cloud base. I knew when I did so that I was practicing self-deception. I flew directly under the lee edge of the cloud and was "surprised" to find more room there—a natural consequence of flying under the concave base of a lenticular cloud. So I "took advantage of the opportunity" and climbed.

I had committed another serious error. When I accepted the gain in altitude, I knew instinctively that I would have to face the consequences of this act. I shortly did. Because of the climb, I was flying in an elongated, inverted bowl with sharply restricted lateral visibility. The flanks of the pass were thinly visible by looking downward at about 45 degrees, and the peaks, which I knew to exist on either side, were well above the cloud base.

I was committed—no room to turn back—go directly through—no options. The windward apron of the cloud became a swirling, hellish turmoil shortly before I entered it—like a mobile sculpture gone insane. At the instant of recognition, I tried to reduce power and dive underneath—too late.

But hadn't I had an hour of hood time in obtaining my license? "I'll only be in it a few seconds, and I can fly an attitude indicator that long." Already haunting me were the lies I had conveniently told myself while I pursued this course of action. Any time before the last two minutes of the ordeal I could have avoided it but would not.

I've experienced turbulence since that day, but never like what I found on that day. In seconds, my attitude gyro tumbled. When I was aware of it (not frequently), the airspeed indicator was fluctuating wildly, and the buffeting in the cabin produced real physical pain—blunt head trauma and seatbelt pressure.

I had no awareness of the Bonanza's attitude until I perceived that I was probably spinning out of a power-on stall. As the forward motion slowed, the buffeting subsided and the seatbelt pressure told me with certainty that I was inverted. I was still in the cloud but anticipated an inverted spin when I came out.

When ground contact was reestablished, I was beyond the highest point in the pass (about 10,000 feet), which, with the cheap altitude I had bought a short time before, improved the terrain clearance. My first impulse was to assume the fetal position and ride it to the ground. I distinctly remember uttering a piteous whine, a fleeting, fatalistic impulse I immediately dismissed as I forced myself to think.

Stall with power on leads to inverted spin . . . what do I do . . . keep the nose down . . . but down is up . . . *DO IT, FOOL! OKAY, OKAY, DAMMIT.* Mind racing, groping for reality, I recognized Mount Blanca moving rapidly on an inverted horizon. The nose is coming up . . . don't get flat . . . yoke *all* the way back . . . *DAMMIT, ALL THE WAY!*

Okay, Okay . . . Now I'm gaining . . . Mount Blanca again . . . close the throttle . . . situation improving. The nose is dropping off, Mount Blanca again appears in my peripheral vision. Anticipate the peak by about 30 degrees, then full reverse rudder and full throttle. *Now! Do it now!* (To this day, I do not remember the direction of the spin.)

The engine coughed and produced power. It worked! Well, now—inverted flight with a standard carburetion system flying toward the biggest mountain in southern Colorado. Not exactly a solution. Reduce power again . . . slowly, slowly . . . forward pressure on the yoke . . . God, let the seatbelt hold . . . it's hard to reach the rudder pedals. The airspeed's dropping . . . somewhere in the green arc now. Okay, yoke back . . . What's a split-*S?* I'm about to find out.

I can see the Alamosa sand dunes sliding into view at the upper edge of the windshield. The nose is pointed straight down now . . . the dunes righting themselves as rotation progresses around the lateral axis . . . seatbelt pressure lessening . . . I can feel the *g* forces building . . . body very heavy now . . . slight gray-out. Let up the yoke pressure, then straight and level at 235 mph indicated just above the sand ridges west of San Creek.

"God, we made it." Neither of us spoke during the ten minutes to the airport. Since then, I have looked for another pilot who has flown a Bonanza out of an inverted spin. I know he's around somewhere, but I haven't found him yet.

I also learned some things: When tensions build in a flying situation, talk to someone—even if it's to yourself—and be sure you answer. It's the most certain way I know to initiate an orderly thought process. I also learned that lenticular clouds are where you find them—not at some arbitrary altitude where light aircraft don't fly—and that they are as relentlessly cruel as the weather manuals say. I learned that it is possible to fly a Bonanza out of an inverted spin. Finally, and most important, I learned not to deal in self-deception where flying is concerned.

The Deceptive III Wind

Every year, hundreds of pilots suffer misfortunes ranging from embarrassment to death out of their failure to handle winds that are far less powerful and dramatic than those we have been examining thus far. These accidents occur, in the main, on landing. To many pilots, that they happened at all may seem incomprehensible. Perhaps the key lesson, therefore, is that they did happen:

• A 300-hour pilot occupied the right set of the Cessna 182-A, and a student pilot with 46 flight hours occupied the left seat, as they made an approach to the runway. The student had recently acquired partial ownership of the airplane, but there was no entry in his log to indicate that he had flown the aircraft in the past or that he had been properly checked out for solo flight in it.

The airport manager reported that the plane was high and fast during the approach, with the flaps up. The craft touched down with 1,300 feet of runway remaining and continued the rollout on the runway for 600 feet. The runway was inclined, and the airplane was moving up it with an 8-knot tailwind. Power was applied, and the Cessna lifted off 350 feet from the end of the runway in a nose-high attitude. In a slow left bank, the 182 struck trees about 50 feet above ground level and 250 feet from the end of the runway. According to the NTSB, it was "destroyed by impact forces and a postimpact fire which occurred while moving the aircraft during the rescue operation." Both occupants were killed.

The board found that the private pilot-in-command "misjudged distance and speed, delayed in initiating a go-around, and selected the wrong runway relative to existing wind." It also cited high density altitude as a factor.

• On a planned flight from Fort Lauderdale to Tallahassee, Florida, the 122-hour pilot of a 172 Skyhawk advised Miami Flight Service that he was "going to have to land. . . . I can't get through." There was heavy coverage of the sky by dark clouds and rain approximately 8 miles north of the airstrip the pilot selected for a landing. Witnesses on the ground saw the airplane make three approaches to the 3,900-foot runway with full flaps in a quartering tailwind in gusts up to 20 knots. A windsock was located at midfield.

On the third approach, one witness said, a gust lifted the left wing and caused the right wing to dip. The right wing struck a tree and the aircraft cartwheeled to the ground, coming to rest on its back. The pilot and his wife were killed on impact. A third occupant was seriously injured.

• This pilot's destination airport had a single 5,300-foot runway. The pilot, who had 340 total hours, was cleared to land his Piper PA-28-180 on Runway 32 and was told that the wind was from 240 degrees at 30 knots. By the time the airplane was on final approach, the wind had shifted; the pilot was now encountering a direct crosswind of 23 knots. (The maximum demonstrated crosswind component for that airplane is 15 knots.) The pilot initiated a go-around, and tower controllers observed the Piper drifting east of the runway in a nose-high, wings-level attitude. The airplane stalled and crashed 2,000 feet east of the runway. One passenger was killed; the pilot and two other passengers were seriously injured.

The NTSB determined that at the time of impact, the airplane was 83.6 pounds over maximum certificated takeoff weight.

• In this case, the pilot, who had 50.7 hours, departed on a local, nonsupervised solo training flight in a Cessna 172. He had not obtained a weather briefing. About an hour later, he returned, entered the traffic pattern, and called his downwind entry over Unicom. His flight instructor was in the airport office at the time and heard the radio call. He noted that the office wind indicator showed the wind to be from 180 degrees at 10 knots, gusting to 25.

The instructor watched as the student turned final for Runway 17. According to the CFI, ''he was lined up well but appeared to be oscillating in the pitch axis very slowly, as if he was chasing his airspeed indicator.'' The airplane descended to within 50 feet of the ground when it suddenly bounced over and impacted the ground at a 45-degree angle. The Cessna then bounced forward 20 feet and came to rest inverted on the runway. The pilot was killed instantly.

The flight instructor stated that he believed the student had ''encountered a stall condition coupled with a gust downdraft and failed to recognize it until the aircraft was out of control.''

Withstanding Drift

A wind is violent if it threatens to take control of your airplane away from you. Against its force, the pilot must compensate with decisive action. A common theme in these crashes was the vagueness with which the pilots approached their last landing attempts. Allowing the airplane to drift, selecting the wrong runway, losing it when the landing should have been secure, and trying to do more with an airplane than its design and the laws of aerodynamics would permit—these lapses suggest a lack of recognition that an airplane must be *directed* if it is to hold its own against the wind.

The chief accident-producing wind problems are excessive

crosswinds and gusting conditions in the landing phase, downdrafts and updrafts when operating close to the ground, and wind shear. Pilots also fall victim to such winds on takeoff; accidental downwind takeoffs and landings are surprisingly frequent. It's as if to many pilots, wind consciousness is some sort of arcane and superfluous pastime.

Behind every successful crosswind landing is a winning battle to prevent drift. As we have seen in these examples, a drifting airplane close to the ground is very much a lost and wandering bird, with a pilot who may have been reduced to a mere left-seat passenger. Crosswind approaches and landings require positive antidrift measures to maintain directional control.

The most frequently used tactic is the *forward slip,* which involves banking into the wind and simultaneously holding against a turn by pressing opposite rudder. Stronger crosswinds require stronger inputs, but there is a limit to what pilot and plane can do. If you find that you are still drifting away from the imaginary extended centerline of the runway, call off the approach and either try again—if you have *good* reason to believe that a successful adjustment is feasible (be honest with yourself)—or find an airport with a more favorable runway alignment to wait until the wind conditions improve. You must be willing to concede that the wind can exceed your airplane's ability to compensate. Every airplane has a published maximum crosswind component, arrived at by flight testing, to be respected.

It is especially vital in a slip to keep your airspeed at least 1.3 times the stall speed for your airplane according to the configuration and power setting you are flying. Absentmindedly bleeding off your airspeed to a stall with crossed controls can easily snap your airplane into a spin, which would not be readily recoverable close to the ground. By the same token, if you are wrestling with a crosswind on a turn from base to final, don't let the struggle translate into crossed controls with a lowering airspeed caused by a pilot who is at odds with the approach and his airplane. A common stall/spin accident results from a pilot's banking hard to line up on the runway, inadvertently or purposely pulling up the nose to lessen his rate of descent, and pushing opposite rudder to halt the drift of the nose or to level the wings. Concentrating hard on maintaining or gaining direction and perhaps fighting a gust-produced roll, the pilot fails to notice the impending stall until too late.

Many pilots deal safely with crosswinds by simply crabbing into the wind and straightening the airplane just before touchdown; combining the two techniques is also popular.

A crosswind factor demands that the approach be well planned and executed from pattern entry to turning off the active. Once you have gauged the strength and direction of the wind, plan your downwind and base legs accordingly to allow yourself sufficient airspace and time to obviate vigorous, last-second adjustments. As you approach the downwind leg, lay out a landing pattern for yourself based on the one in use, setting up landmarks that will be aiming points for your turns to base and final, custom chosen for the present wind conditions. Having them to aim for, you will automatically begin to accommodate for the wind, taking up the proper amount of crab, setting your leg lengths, and so on. If the base leg will be with a tailwind, pick the aiming points so as to allow you room for a *stable* base leg *and* a comfortable turn to final. A steep turn to final from a headwind or tailwind, especially a gusting wind, can lead to drifting and overbanking, two principal approach destabilizers.

Just before touchdown, to point the nose down the centerline, you will need to kick out with rudder any crab you may be carrying, at the same time maintaining enough aileron to keep the upwind wing lowered to prevent its being lifted. Touchdown may therefore be on one wheel. To do it smoothly and precisely takes coordination and practice.

Flaps and Speeds

When you anticipate landing in strong winds and gusts, you would be wise to carry a reduced flap setting and a slightly higher than normal airspeed. The added lift produced by a full-flap extension may cause a sudden ballooning or loss of control if a gust occurs at the moment of touchdown. Extra airspeed is advisable because the sudden loss of a headwind component at a normal 1.3 V_{so} approach speed could cause a stall. Directional control is easier with more airspeed, since there is more relative wind flowing over the control surfaces. Most instructors recommend adding a "gust factor" of one half the gust value. If the winds are 20 knots gusting to 35, you would add approximately 7 knots to the normal approach speed.

There can, however, be disadvantages to approaches such as these. To be sure, you will have good control against the crosswind; but without a proper descent angle, you could find yourself overshooting. The higher the airspeed, the more time you may spend floating (and anxiously correcting) as you prepare to put the upwind wheel on the runway. On the ground, any swerving caused by the wind or by lapses in your technique will be magnified by the aircraft's higher speed.

In most cases, full flaps should be used for crosswind landings, assuming the wind is steady and not strong. Pitch and power can be used to keep airspeeds at a safe margin above the stall and provide controllability. The touchdown will come at a slower speed, the tires will be preserved, the landing roll will be shorter, and any swerving moments after touchdown will be lessened.

Romping on the Rollout

What can happen after the touchdown is the stuff of hangar legends. Nothing in flying is so awkward, so ungainly, and so humbling as a thumping ground loop. Weathercocking (or weathervaning) is something airplanes love to do. Airliners have done it in strong winds, and airline pilots are expected to hold a tight rein all the way from the runway touchdown zone to the gate. Light planes need nothing heavy to turn their tails, so proper nosewheel steering is demanded.

Some airplanes have nose gear that is fixed to the rudder pedals. This arrangement does not allow for automatic centering of the nosewheel when in the air. Landing an airplane with an uncentered nosewheel in a crosswind may result in a violent swerve, a ground loop, or even an accident if rudder pressure is held at the moment the nosewheel touches the pavement. Check your operating manual for any recommended nonstandard crosswind procedures.

Sometimes a ground loop will be the fault of the nosewheel. Sometimes it will be by default of the pilot, as John C. Pickels candidly recollects:

It occurred during the pilot's studenthood, as he labored in heavy air on his second solo just to get his 152 onto the ground:

. . . I was apprehensive and certainly concerned, but not panic-stricken. My fourth and final approach finished close to the threshold. I added fairly heavy left rudder, straightened from the crab, dipped the right wing and eased back on the yoke a little more gently than before. The right main touched on the numbers just a little hot, but I knew all was well, because I was on the ground and pointed down the runway.

I thought I had completed my second solo safely. What I had really done was reach my first plateau. I relaxed; I dropped my concentration; I thought I was finished. I had landed maybe fifty times before, and the rollout had always been uneventful.

As the right main touched, I relaxed pressure, the Cessna dropped to the left main and slid sideways to the left (a terrible sound). About that time, the nosewheel touched, and the nose jerked to the left. My foot flew off the left rudder pedal as if it were burned, and I did what any automobile driver would have done—I turned the wheel right to arrest the left turn of the nose. That was not such a bad idea as the leftward scrubbing of both mains was replaced by a right bank back up on the right main. With the arrival of the increased right crosswind from a tree line and the removal of the left rudder pressure, the agile 152 pivoted on the right main and weathervaned into the wind, heading briskly toward the lights to the right.

Whereas my automobile-driver reflexes were not so bad before, they certainly did not help on my next maneuver—turning the wheel to go left. As the gusting right crosswind got under the right wing, the out-of-control aircraft lifted on the left main and turned sharply back to the left. The wide arc of the left wingtip raced toward the pavement. At that moment, I knew the 152 was going to cartwheel. I was amazingly calm—I think—but I had no control over what was happening. I had stopped flying at touchdown; now I was just a passenger.

The wing did not touch. There was plenty of room to run diagonally to the left. I must have returned the wheel to the right. I would like to say that I had regained my senses, but the airplane continued to fly itself, and I merely was reacting to reflexes long ingrained from driving cars, not flying airplanes. The forward speed had bled off, and the airplane became "drivable."

Caution: Wake Turbulence

Thus far, we have been looking at the fierce winds nature blows our way. Other airplanes can do a good job of flinging us about, too. In earlier days, pilots used to talk about the effects of passing behind or beneath another airplane, calling the jolt of such turbulence "propwash," as it usually was. The advent of jets, with their great size and high speeds, created a far more serious problem

By the mid-1960s, several accidents had occurred that seemed to indicate that the power of a jet transport's trailing wingtip vortices was enough to cause uncontrollable rolls and descent rates. Propwash became a dated term. By 1972, we had a new one—wake turbulence—and a new set of rules concerning its behavior and avoidance. There has also been recognition that it doesn't necessarily take a jet airliner's wake to drive a small airplane into the ground. For example, the following case:

• A 266-hour pilot with commercial license and instrument rating came to grief in his Aero Commander A9B, flying behind a Grumman Ag-Cat, while dusting cotton near Nolan, Texas. The lead aircraft completed a spray run and turned back to begin another. The Aero Commander was following close behind, when it suddenly rolled to the right, and the nose pitched down. Flying at less than a hundred feet above the ground, the Aero Commander had too little altitude to recover before it crashed. It burst into flames and was totally destroyed. The pilot was fatally injured.

The NTSB determined that the crash was caused by "vortex turbulence" and that the pilot had "misjudged distance."

At the other end of the spectrum, this happened:

• In 1972, a Delta Air Lines DC-9 crashed during an attempted go-around after an aborted landing during a training flight. As the aircraft passed the runway threshold, it began to oscillate about its roll axis, and a wingtip struck the runway. The aircraft crashed and burned; its only occupants, four crew members, were killed. The NTSB determined that the probable cause of the accident "was an encounter with a trailing vortex generated by a preceding 'heavy jet' [an American Airlines DC-10] which resulted in an involuntary loss of control of the airplane during the final approach. Although cautioned to expect turbulence, the crew did not have sufficient information to evaluate accurately the hazard of the possible location of the vortex."

One more incident illustrates how unexpectedly such "man-made tornadoes," as they have been called, can attack an unwary crew:

• This accident involved a Piper Navajo, piloted by an ATP with 3,670 total hours, 117 in type. On a scheduled commuter trip, the Navajo, designated Flight 501, was 14 miles northwest of its destination, Philadelphia International Airport, when Philadelphia Approach told the crew to fly a right base leg for Runway 27 Right. Soon after, the co-pilot reported the airport in sight, and Approach came back with a request to report over downtown Philadelphia. Then the Approach controller advised Flight 501 that it was number four in line to land, following a United Airlines Boeing 727—Flight 555—which, at the time, was over the Walt Whitman Bridge, 5½ miles from the runway. The 727 was on an ILS to Runway 27R.

When the Navajo reported the 727 in sight, it was told to follow United 555 and contact the control tower. The co-pilot did so, and the tower asked if they had the 727 in sight. The co-pilot replied that he did, and the tower requested another call when the Navajo was 1 mile out on its final approach. The tower cleared the 727 to land and then advised the Navajo where the 727 had turned on to the final approach course.

A minute later, the Navajo was cleared to land. Tower personnel observed it flying a stabilized approach ½ mile out from the runway. The wind was calm. By this time, the 727 had finished its landing roll and was turning off the runway.

At this time, the tower supervisor noticed that the Navajo was making "erratic movements." He drew the attention of everyone in the tower to its behavior. Witnesses in the tower stated later that the airplane first rolled from side to side with as much as 70 degrees of bank. Then the nose pitched up as the Navajo rolled to the left, reaching an inverted position. Then the nose fell through and the airplane descended—inverted—and impacted the ground nose first. All three persons aboard the Navajo were killed.

During the postaccident investigation, the tower controller stated that at no time did he feel that a wake turbulence warning was warranted, and, therefore, no cautionary warnings were issued to the Navajo's crew.

Perhaps the most useful clues to understanding this accident came from the automated radar terminal system III (ARTS III) ground-track data. The NTSB plotted the stored radar data in three dimensions. The board discovered that the United 727 joined the extended runway centerline gradually. Four nautical miles from the runway, it was 1,800 feet north of the centerline. Three quarters of a mile out, it joined the centerline and made a constant descent on the ILS's 3.6-degree glideslope. At 7:11.20 P.M., the 727 was 2 miles from the runway and at an altitude of 800 feet. The ground-track and altitude information for the Navajo showed that it turned onto the final approach course 2 miles from the end of the runway at 7:12.12—fifty-two seconds after the 727 passed the same point—but with one important difference. The Navajo at this point was flying at 500 feet, and it was flying a flatter approach. The NTSB estimated its glideslope descent angle to be approximately 2.3 degrees. At this point, the flight was not yet in danger. The United aircraft's wingtip vortices had, by the time the flight reached the 2-mile point, descended below 500 feet.

Witnesses concurred that the Navajo's flight became erratic between 1 mile and ½ mile from the runway threshold. The last two radar targets from the Navajo showed it to be 1½ to 2 miles from the threshold and 100 to 150 feet below the flight path of the 727. The NTSB believes that, as the Navajo continued its descent, it flew into the 727's wingtip vortices. Since the airplane rolled to the left, an encounter with the right wingtip vortex was suspected. The probable causes of the accident were listed as "loss of aircraft control due to an encounter with wake turbulence from the preceding aircraft at an altitude too low for recovery, and the pilot's failure to follow established separation and flight-path selection procedures. . . ."

High Versus Low at the Tips

Wake turbulence is a direct result of the pressure differential between the air flowing over a wing's curved upper and relatively flat lower surfaces. The curvature of the upper surface accelerates the air passing over it, creating a region of lowered air pressure; the air passing beneath the wing has a higher pressure value, since its velocity remains virtually unchanged. This differential, of course, causes lift. Lift is also augmented at the span of the trailing edge, for the accelerated air coming from the top of the wing causes a downward flow.

But at the wingtips, a different phenomenon occurs. The higher-pressure air flows up over the tip of the wing to fill the partial vacuum created by the top of the wing. Instead of a downward flow of air, there are trailing vortices of swirling air. These vortices' flow fields generate a clockwise rotation of air (when viewed from behind) from the left wing and a counterclockwise rotation from the right. The wingspan also greatly influences the strength of an airplane's wake turbulence. The larger the span, the larger the flow field. Generally, trailing wingtip vortices have dimensions corresponding to two wingspans in width and one wingspan in depth. The angle of attack, gross weight, and configuration are also important. A slow-flying heavy jet in a clean configuration (gear and flaps up) will produce the most severe wake turbulence. Tests have shown that vortex velocities can reach 133 knots.

Since trailing vortices are generated whenever the wings are developing lift, they are present from the time an aircraft rotates on takeoff until it rolls out after landing (FIGURE 10). There are

FIGURE 10   As long as an airfoil generates lift, it generates vortices. It is crucial to note the point where a preceding airplane rotates or touches down, to avoid its turbulence. Heavy, slow-moving transports are especially hazardous to general aviation aircraft.

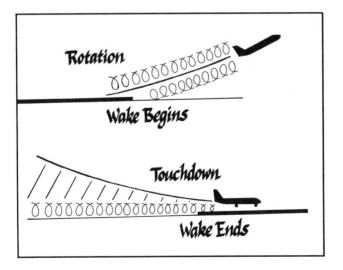

visual clues to the presence of vortex turbulence, but not many. The normally invisible vortices may be identified when engine exhaust gases, moisture, or dust are drawn into the rotating air. However, even though they are not usually seen, the potentially dangerous disturbances have predictable characteristics that can aid a pilot in avoiding them.

Vortices trail behind the generating aircraft and descend at 400 to 500 fpm until they settle 800 to 900 feet below the aircraft's flight path, where they stop their descent, weaken, and begin to break up, especially in strong winds (FIGURE 11). Their lifespan at altitude may be as long as five minutes, and they may linger as much as 20 miles behind the generating aircraft. The descending vertical flow may reach 1,500 fpm. The swirling air rotates inboard, and the diameter of the vortex core may range from 25 to 50 feet, although the field of influence may be equal

FIGURE 11   Vortices sink at a rate of 400 to 500 fpm and level off about 900 feet below the heavy aircraft's flight path. Vortices from a heavy aircraft flying within about 200 feet of the ground spread outward along the surface at a rate of about 5 knots.

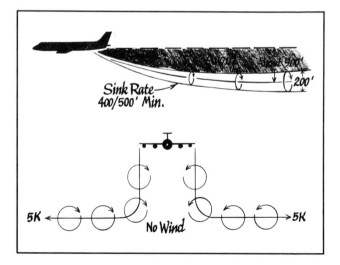

to the wingspan of the aircraft. The vortices tend to parallel each other, remaining about three-quarters of a wingspan apart.

The force of a vortex can easily exceed the aileron control capability or climb rate of some aircraft. A NASA study recorded one instance where the induced roll rate was nearly 100 degrees per second while the pilot was holding more than half the available opposite aileron. And that pilot was flying an F-104 behind a heavy jet.

In calm wind conditions, the vortices drop almost vertically behind the airplane and, if they reach the surface, spread outward at a rate of 5 knots. They gradually diminish in one or two minutes in calm air and more quickly in rough conditions. On takeoff, the vortices begin forming at the rotation point, for where the nose is raised and, therefore, the angle of attack is increased, there lift-generation begins. In fact, the strongest vortex turbulence is generated by heavy aircraft that are on takeoff, when the angle of attack is high, the airspeed is slow, and the wings are in a clean configuration. Flaps and spoilers tend to reduce vortex strength.

In crosswinds, wingtip vortices travel downwind and therefore can affect a nearby parallel runway or airplanes flying tight patterns on the downwind side of a runway. A crosswind will decrease the lateral movement of the upwind vortex and increase the movement of the downwind vortex. A light wind of 3 to 7 knots could result in the upwind vortex remaining in the touchdown zone for a while. Likewise, a tailwind component can move the vortices forward along the approach path and up the runway.

To avoid wake turbulence when you are landing behind an aircraft larger than your own, keep your approach path above the other plane's. Note where it touches down and land beyond that point. When you are landing behind a departing larger aircraft, note the point where it rotates and arrange your approach to land well short of that point. If you are landing at an airport with parallel runways, request a runway upwind of landing or departing larger aircraft.

If you are instructed to use a runway that intersects one being used by a large airplane, put your airplane on the ground short of the intersection, if the departing aircraft rotates past it.

When you are taking off behind a departing large airplane, safety lies in lifting off well short of its rotation point and climbing out at a sufficiently steep angle to avoid its wake. In fact, when you lift off, you may want to ease over upwind of its rotation point and flight path if there is a crosswind.

Controller Protection?

Controllers are supposed to issue wake turbulence advisories whenever they believe such turbulence is an operational factor, but since wake turbulence is invisible, it is the pilot's responsibility to use his judgment whenever the potential for wake hazards exists. This is especially true in VFR weather conditions at airports where large and small aircraft are mixed together. A controller who issues a visual approach is not obligated to provide wake turbulence advisories. By accepting a visual approach, the pilot becomes responsible for providing a safe landing interval.

Controllers are required to apply specific separation intervals for airplanes flying behind heavy jets, for the weight of these airplanes creates the strongest wake effects. Small and large aircraft flying behind a heavy jet at the same altitude or less than 1,000 feet lower are supposed to be given a 5-mile separation. Furthermore, controllers are required to provide a 6-mile separation for small airplanes landing behind large ones. Takeoffs require similar separation criteria, plus the verbal warning, "Caution, wake turbulence." You may delay taking off.

If you do suddenly find yourself caught by wake turbulence, act fast. Pilots who have lived through the experience are astounded at how quickly it happened. Prepare yourself mentally; if there is a possibility of wake turbulence, "predict" it to yourself. If your airplane is struck, use the ailerons and rudder immediately to roll level. Add full power and keep the airspeed up. It can definitely help to have had some aerobatic instruction and experience, if only to know what a roll feels like and to have familiarity with the sensations of being inverted and of recovering from that attitude.

When man took to the skies, he inherited the wind, its hazards, and its blessings. We have seen something of the dark side of this legacy. We have also seen how curiosity, intelligence, and skill can enable us to fly safely among the winds, including knowing when to leave bad enough alone.

Part Three
ICE

6
The Nature of Icing

Of all cockpit crises, icing is the most eerie. Its mysteries can be traumatic—and not only for low-time pilots. Highly experienced airmen, even veterans of deep-winter flying, have emerged trembling from encounters with ice, awed by what it can do to an airplane. Inevitably, some self-anointed experts have pushed their "ice wisdom" too far and have been destroyed, joining yet other pilots, who, because they were inexperienced, barely knew what had hit them. In fact, when icing leads to a crash, even trained investigators are all too often left wondering just what did happen. The details remain scanty, and, as these examples demonstrate, the bare, known facts only seem to add to the puzzle.

• During an instrument flight, the 4,200-hour commercial pilot of a Cessna 210 reported that he was "picking up a whole bunch of ice" and was cleared to fly to an alternate airport along his route. The pilot then informed ATC that he would have to reverse course and descend to a lower altitude. Shortly after the pilot reported the Cessna at 5,800 feet and "just about to stall," the aircraft crashed out of control.

• While flying a Piper Comanche 250 across Lake Michigan at 9,000 feet, a 267-hour private pilot reported that he was picking up ice. He was cleared to 11,000 feet but reported being unable to climb. He requested a descent to 7,000. ATC then lost communications and radar contact with the Comanche. Neither the pilot nor the airplane was ever found.

Two other cases show how icing troubles mount:

• A Piper Comanche 180 was flying VFR under an overcast when it began to snow. After picking up an IFR clearance for 12,000 feet, the pilot requested and was cleared down to 10,000. He then asked for a lower altitude, because the Comanche was "icing badly." ATC denied the request because the airplane was already at the minimum obstruction clearance altitude. The controller suggested a vector to reverse course over lower terrain. The pilot reported that he was turning but "losing altitude fast." The airplane crashed into trees. This private pilot had 1,096 hours.

• Another private pilot, with 250 hours, was flying VFR at 8,500 feet over high terrain in a Mooney M20F when he entered clouds with heavy rain and snow. A surviving passenger said that the pilot was attempting to climb out of the clouds when the engine "iced up and began running rough, and the airspeed indicator froze." The airplane crashed into trees.

What happens when icing strikes? How do normally careful pilots "get caught"? Is the pilot truly a nearly passive victim? What are the odds that the average pilot, VFR or instrument rated, will be added to the roster of those memorialized as having "flown into known icing conditions"?

Statistics indicate that structural icing is not a major cause of general aviation accidents. In a recent study, the National Transportation Safety Board found that icing was involved in only 1 percent of the accidents for a recent four-year period. However, as we shall see, icing casualties include dozens of passengers of airliners as well as occupants of light planes, and, as the board also noted, the incidence of icing accidents may be higher than the statistics suggest, since the evidence can melt before investigators reach the crash site.

While ice tends to be associated primarily with instrument meteorological conditions, one-third of the icing accidents covered by the NTSB report involved pilots flying under VFR. Some of those pilots may have encountered freezing precipitation, a particularly hazardous cause of structural ice, but many of the accidents resulted from VFR pilots' inadvertently flying into icey clouds.

An Icing Scenario

What are those pilots likely to have found in there? Let us say that you are flying in the middle of a postfrontal stratus deck and that you blunder into an icing encounter.

The deck is 5,000 feet thick. You know that from having learned from pilot reports that the cloud tops are at 11,000 feet and from having noted, on the way up, that the ceiling was at 6,000 feet. The sequence reports from stations along your route indicate surface temperatures of around 7 degrees C (45 degrees F). Pilot reports, area forecasts, and Airmets have also indicated the presence of "light-to-moderate rime ice." The outside air temperature at your cruising altitude of 9,000 feet is −5 degrees C (23 degrees F).

Having set up your airplane for cruise, after a few minutes you look up at the OAT gauge to check that the temperature is in fact −5 degrees C. It is, but there is more to see.

The forward-facing surface of the OAT probe is coated with a light frosting, though no other parts of the airplane show any evidence of ice. A few more minutes pass, and now the corners of the windshield have developed ice accumulations. The OAT probe now has an eighth of an inch of ice, and the leading edges of the wings are showing a milky, pencil-thin line. The windshield rapidly becomes opaque, and the ice on the wings builds to a quarter of an inch.

Your cruise airspeed, meanwhile, has dropped by 10 knots. To compensate, you advance the power. The wings now show half an inch of ice. You need even more power to hold airspeed.

A bad vibration starts, caused by an uneven load of ice on the propellers. The spinners grow weird spikes of ice from their centers. More and more ice builds on the cowlings and edges toward the propeller arcs.

Noises caused by changed airflows come from the air vents and antennas.

As the ice on the wings surpasses 1 inch, the airspeed falls toward 100 knots. It is taking all the power you have just to maintain altitude.

You hear a *bang,* and the radios go silent. An ice-coated antenna has broken off.

In your fear, you instinctively exert back pressure to hold altitude, and the airspeed decreases.

After a few more minutes, you feel prestall buffeting. . . .

Uncertain, Unheeded Forecasts

Thunderstorms, fog, and ice are the most hazardous weather phenomena that confront pilots of light aircraft. Of the three, ice is the most difficult to forecast accurately.

While atmospheric probes and weather radar observations of precipitation and freezing levels give the meteorologist something to work with, there is still not enough information for making precise forecasts. Therefore, the meteorologist opts on the side of safety by forecasting icing conditions wherever there is moisture at or near the freezing level. With metronomic frequency, the winter forecasts caution: ''Light-to-moderate icing can be expected above the freezing level in clouds and precipitation.'' Pilots are familiar with these words.

That warning is so common, it often ceases to impress pilots who have flown into areas of forecast icing and have found no ice. These pilots frequently base their go/no-go decisions on reports from other pilots flying their proposed routes. If no pireps are available, they go up for a look, which is not inherently unsafe as long as the pilot has the knowledge, experience, and discipline to select the proper escape plan if icing occurs. It should be remembered, nonetheless, that the FAA, in its prohibition against flying into known icing conditions—unless the aircraft is equipped and certificated for it—interprets "known" to mean both reported *and forecast* ice.

There is wisdom in that stern policy, although it may take an awesome experience for a nonchalant pilot to see the light. One pilot, Chuck Filippi, recalls how *he* saw the light—which lay at the end of a terrifying, icy tunnel:

Cherokee Arrow 4308 Xray was cleared as filed, Chattanooga Two departure, climb and maintain 6,000, squawk 0300, Departure on 119.2. ETA for Aurora, Illinois, was 8:30 P.M. CST. The reports from Flight Service were carbons of each other, except for a recent warning of moderate-to-heavy icing in clouds, but that was not unusual for February. I thought about some hangar talk I'd heard recently, when someone had said, "If you believed everything those guys at Flight Service told you, you'd never fly!"

In fact, along V-171, Terre Haute to Danville, the weather was much better than forecast. There were snow showers, but there were also comforting clusters of light below. The rest of the trip looked to be a piece of cake. No ice.

I knew, because Jim, my passenger, though not a pilot, had learned during many trips with me how to check for ice.

But then, Flight Service discouraged our trying to land in Aurora. My filed alternate, DuPage County Airport, was still reporting 400 overcast, ¾-mile visibility and snow mixed with freezing rain. As I was contacting ATC to change my destination to DuPage, Jim nudged me to look out through his flashlight's tunnel of light—to an alarming collection of rime ice.

I immediately requested the weather at Chicago Midway and reported to ATC that things up here were getting icey and hairy. The controller cleared me to Midway, 39 miles away, for landing. As the ice and my worries piled up, things were all at once becoming very busy.

Jim was used to relaxed flights, but now his frightened stare became ever more intense as he continued to point his beam of light at the mounting ice.

The iced-up prop was now out of balance, and its vibrations were becoming nerve-racking. The airspeed indicator and altimeter registered the aircraft's unwanted responses.

Midway could no longer be considered. My repeated pleas for someplace to land *right now* became more demanding.

An airliner just off O'Hare reported tops at 8,000. ATC gave us a clearance—if we could climb. Our attempt produced nothing but frustration. To compound things, the windshield was completely covered with ice, and the defrosters were blowing only cold air.

ATC now said that I was 10 miles northeast of Kankakee Airport, gave me the frequency, and cleared me for the approach. The controller also requested that the airliner try to contact Kankakee Unicom for the weather, since ATC was unable to reach them by telephone.

As I made a heading change to 200 degrees, the airspeed read 95 knots with full power, and the altimeter read 2,800 feet.

The airliner reported back to ATC that the visibility reported from Kankakee was about 1 mile, with freezing rain and no reports on the ceiling.

Frantically, I asked ATC to call the distance from the VOR while Jim flipped through the charts for the approach plate. ATC's transmissions began to break up. Bits and pieces of talk between the controller and the airliner still came through, but barely. The last readable information was that my position was 7 miles northeast of Kankakee. As the controller's calm, reassuring voice broke apart, I nearly became hysterical.

The VOR needle began to slide off center, indicating that we were passing over the field. I looked down, but there was nothing!

I was now only 400 feet above the ground. Perspiration burned my eyes. I could hear the airliner attempting to find out my progress so that he could pass it back to ATC. As I began to hyperventilate, I broadcast that I had seen nothing going over Kankakee and that I wanted something to the east or southeast. Instantly, I was cleared through the airliner to Lafayette, but had I tried to make it there, it would only have been a token effort. I was now sure that we were trapped and that all would soon be finished.

I had to go back to the VOR, because there I would at least know where I was. I began a turn to the right, and the engine gulped—several times.

My heart was actually pounding, and my ears rang. Things were happening simultaneously, and flashes of crash stories raced through my mind—those transcribed conversations from the tapes. This, too, would be seen as "pilot error: flying into known icing conditions."

I was coming to the VOR again. The needle began to move uneasily. A full deflection now. I tried one last look. There! Two strobe lights! My eyes darted back and forth. I almost didn't believe it. Then I suddenly knew that somehow I was going to make it. I continued an instant longer and could see crossing runway lights below, but it was too late to land. I was right over the runway on a left base.

Petrified that I wouldn't be able to maintain visual contact, I slowly circled to the left. I dared not lose sight of the strobes, for there would be no second chance. After making the final turn, I lined up for Runway 34, fearing now that the finale could be a stall, especially as I lowered the gear.

I've made better landings, but straining in at 80 knots under full power, with visual references only from the side, I was grateful for *any* survivable arrival I could manage.

The waiting lineman looked at us in disbelief. He recounted the moments before we got down—how ATC had reached him by telephone and explained the emergency, how the runway lights had been turned up and then turned back down the first time we had crossed over, and how he had turned them up again when he heard us the second time. Under the circumstances, he felt we would never get in.

Ice hung from everything on the Arrow. I then realized that as the outside air intake had been closing with ice, causing the engine to falter, it hadn't even occurred to me to open the alternate air source.

The Flight Service people were anxious to talk about our near-fatal "event." They ended by asking, "Are you a believer now?"

Arrayed in this true story are the basic ingredients of an icing battle. First, there was the lingering skepticism that many pilots have about icing, especially if they have flown untroubled over many hours in conditions for which icing was predicted. When the ice appeared, its buildup and influence were astonishingly rapid. The ice attacked on two fronts, wrecking the aerodynamic efficiency of the airplane at the same time that it added weight. As this happened, the two most valuable possessions the pilot had—airspeed and altitude—were wasting away, in part, due to diminishing thrust.

Then the airplane began to lose its "senses." As the pilot groped through cloud, frightened and coping with an enormous workload, normal communications collapsed. The windscreen became opaque, leaving him nearly blind, even after breaking out of the clouds on the approach. Growing panic and a sense of isolation accompanied the blinding and near deafening and muting of the Arrow. The pilot was nearly overwhelmed by the icing's mounting effects and by the horror that this actually was happening to *him*. As circumstances removed airport after airport as landing possibilities, the pilot had to confront ever-narrowing, ugly options. Nearly overloaded by strain, depression, and a sense of guilt, the pilot even forgot such a critical detail as turning on the alternate air source to maintain power. In fact, he could have lost the engine altogether.

At length, there was the saving power—it could easily have been an absence—of luck. Good fortune was with him in the presence of a helpful airliner, the fortuitous spotting of the runway lights, the help of a second set of eyes and hands in the right seat, and the outside-chance turning-on of Kankakee's bright lights at just the right moment by someone who had almost given the pilot up for lost.

Those hangar jockeys did have a point, of course. Forecasts of icing do *seem* to offer little solid guidance at times, especially for pilots who do not know how and why icing occurs. When to go or not to go is the question, both belief and disbelief have to be based on careful judgment.

Icing and Impact

Structural icing can occur whenever an aircraft enters visible moisture at outside air temperatures near or below freezing. Its probability and severity are determined by many factors.

Water droplets are supercooled at temperatures ranging from 2 degrees C to −20 degrees C and freeze on contact with a moving aircraft. Below −20 degrees C, moisture usually occurs as ice crystals, which will not adhere to an aircraft. In addition, the formation of structural ice is affected by the size of the water droplets, the size and shape of the aircraft, and, of course, how long the airplane is exposed.

The amount and rate of ice accumulation are proportional to the size of the water droplet. Small droplets tend to follow the airflow around the leading edges of the wings, propeller blades, and other components, so relatively few droplets impinge on the leading edge. By contrast, because momentum increases with mass, large droplets cannot readily make the turn with the airflow as it separates above and below the leading edge. Consequently, most of the droplets hit the leading edge and splatter back along the component's surfaces.

Any object moving through the air pushes a thin wall of air, called a pressure wave, before it. The larger the object, the larger the preceding pressure wave. Since water droplets are deflected somewhat by the pressure wave, ice accumulates more readily on small, thin objects than on large bulbous ones. Therefore, the pilot will spot ice forming on the OAT probe and tail surfaces before he sees it on the wing. By the same principle, a small single-engine airplane will pick up more ice more quickly than, say, a Douglas DC-3. That is important to keep in mind when analyzing pireps. A DC-3 pilot may report light ice, but the pilot of a light single flying alongside might well report the ice as moderate to severe.

Types of Icing

Depending on the temperature and the size of the droplets that strike the aircraft, there are four kinds of icing:

• *Rime* ice is associated with stratiform clouds in which the temperature is between 2 degrees and − 20 degrees Celsius. Stratus clouds typically have smaller water droplets and are less dense than cumulus. The small, supercooled water droplets in this type of cloud remain liquid until they strike the surfaces of the airplane. Then, almost instantaneously, they freeze, trapping minute air bubbles. This gives rime ice its milky appearance. The ice formations characteristically look like streamlined forward extensions into the relative wind (FIGURE 12).

• *Clear* ice creates far more severe problems. Transparent in appearance, it accretes by conforming to the shape of the airfoil. This is the kind of accumulation that nonpilots associate with the surface effects of a passing "ice storm." Clear ice readily

FIGURE 12 Rime ice can distort the leading edge of an airfoil into something grotesque. Note the forward projections of ice. Minute air bubbles trapped in the ice create the milky appearance.

occurs in cumuliform clouds when the OAT is between 2 degrees and −10 degrees C. Cumulus clouds have larger water droplets than do stratus, and their vertical currents can produce heavy concentrations of moisture. This combination of large-diameter droplets and high liquid-water content induces the droplets to run back as liquid for a short while after they have made initial contact with the airplane until they freeze into a quickly formed, heavy and slick ice coating.

Freezing rain is actually a form of clear ice; it represents such an extreme threat that it is often identified according to the weather condition that causes it. The speed at which it accumulates makes immediate diversionary action mandatory, regardless of the airplane or the capabilities of its ice-protection equipment. We will discuss freezing rain in more detail later in this chapter.

Clear ice occurs only about a third as often as rime ice, but its dangers are immediately more pressing.

• *Mixed* icing is a simultaneous buildup of rime and clear ice. It is usually found in stratiform clouds, where conditions are conducive to the formation of large and small droplets.

Under certain conditions, a double-horn ice shape can form on an airplane's leading edges and protrusions when the OAT is just a few degrees below freezing. The droplets hit the surface and splatter, forming a ridge of ice just behind the point of impact. As more droplets hit, the ridges enlarge, while the area of direct impact accretes ice at a lower rate. The result is a cusp-shaped formation that severely disrupts the airflow and causes a huge increase in drag.

• *Frost* is caused by moisture condensing from a vapor to a solid through contact with an airplane's cold surfaces. Unlike the other forms of icing, frost accumulations do not change the basic aerodynamic shape of a wing or other surfaces, but its roughness can slow the air as it flows over an airfoil. This, in turn, causes an early airflow separation over the wing and a loss of lift. For this reason, frost must be removed from all lifting surfaces prior to takeoff. Frost often forms at ground level in stable air and light winds. It also occurs in flight when a cold airplane descends into warm air with high relative humidity.

The aerodynamic effects of any form of accumulated ice are pronounced. Lift decreases while weight increases. Thrust is reduced—the propeller is an airfoil, too, and it collects ice like a wing—and drag rises sharply. The stall speed of the airplane increases, and the rate of climb severely falls. The power required for level flight becomes greater, and V_y (best-rate-of-climb speed) slowly decreases, until it converges with the increased stall speed. Half an inch of ice can reduce lift and increase drag by 50 percent. The loss of thrust can stem from propellers being rendered inefficient, from vibrations due to propeller imbalance, and from ice clogging the air intake. The engine may well overheat and certainly will consume more fuel.

The Range of Intensities

For locating areas of icing and gauging its severity, the best intelligence comes from fresh and accurate reports from pilots in the midst of it. Pireps may not tell the whole story, but they at least substitute direct observation for mere prediction. A pilot report should contain the basic information that other pilots need to evaluate conditions: the identification, type, and indicated airspeed of the aircraft, the location, altitude, and Zulu time of the icing encounter, and the intensity of the icing. There is a system used both in pireps and in forecasts for describing intensities:

• *Trace*. The ice is perceptible, and the accumulation rate is slightly greater than the rate of sublimation (when ice turns directly into water vapor). In this intensity, the ice is not hazardous, even if deicing and/or antiicing equipment is not used, unless it continues for more than an hour.

• *Light*. The rate of accumulation is more likely to be a danger if flight is prolonged in these conditions for more than an hour. However, occasional use of deicing and/or antiicing equipment can remove or prevent such an accumulation.

• *Moderate*. The rate of accumulation is such that even short encounters become potentially hazardous. The use of deicing and/or antiicing equipment or diversion is necessary. "Moderate" may sound benign and acceptable, but it isn't.

• *Severe*. This rate of accumulation is so great that deicing and/or antiicing equipment fails to reduce or even control the hazard. Immediate diversion is necessary.

A pirep is a valuable indication that icing conditions have been encountered, but it is not a guarantee that another pilot will find the same conditions in the same area. An icing pirep can quickly become obsolete, so be sure to catch the time reported. The absence of a pirep for an area is, of course, no sure sign that icing won't occur when you arrive there. Always be wary of ice when you fly in moist air at freezing temperatures or when you fly under a frontal inversion.

Frontal Hazards

When air masses with different moisture and temperature levels clash, there is far more *vertical* cloud development and precipitation than are found in winter air-mass clouds. Pilots often seek to climb to air that is so cold that the moisture there forms into harmless ice crystals. When there is a frontal clash, however, a climb could be precluded by a rising of the upper boundary of the icing area. We shall discuss escape tactics in the following chapter.

The most unpredictable icing situations accompany occluded fronts. An occlusion occurs when a cold front overtakes a warm front. The process begins at the center of a low-pressure system, where the cold and warm frontal zones meet. When the cold air behind the cold front is warmer than the air ahead of the warm front, there will be a warm front occlusion: a warm front at the surface and a second—cold—front aloft. A cold front occlusion is just the opposite: a cold front at the surface and a warm front aloft. In either case, the pilot must deal with the effects of two fronts.

An occlusion is slow moving and wet. Especially troublesome is the northeast corner of an occlusion, because this is where the upper front frequently is found. There is plenty of moisture all through an occluded front, but the northeast corner will be the wettest.

Perversely, occlusions often contain every type of cloud, along with a wide range of precipitation—rain, snow, freezing rain, the works. The icing conditions can extend far, both vertically and horizontally. Climbing or descending to evade ice may do little good during a traverse of an occluded front; be prepared instead for a prompt 180.

In such a conglomeration of clouds and weather, there are indicators as to what kind of cloud you may have entered. A *bumpy* ride signals the instability that produces cumulus. A good deal of water will run back along the windshield. Here, the primary danger is clear ice. A *smooth* ride and small drops on the windshield indicate stratus clouds and the probability of rime ice. In some situations, however, as we have pointed out, stratus clouds may yield a mixture of rime and clear ice—or even the double-horn variety of clear ice.

Clouds undergo internal cycles, and as they do, their liquid water concentrations change. Depending on the phase they are in, icing may or may not take place, even though all the right forecast elements are present. Pockets of ice may wander through an area.

Freezing rain is especially hard to forecast reliably, though not impossible. The conditions that precipitate freezing rain and drizzle are known and can to some extent be charted. And not every pilot who has been "caught" by such icing has been a victim of the unfathomable. One pilot, A. C. Grimes, has documented how a pilot can victimize himself.

On a trip from Mobile to Houston, this 150-hour VFR pilot had been plagued by days of waiting on the ground for IFR conditions to clear. Once on his way in a rented Piper Arrow, he immediately found himself struggling to avoid television towers and to keep from getting lost as he maneuvered below a lowering ceiling in wretched visibility. At length, in a near-panic and having seriously considered an off-airport landing, he made it into Baton Rouge.

After landing, I went to the FSS to check the weather again and to see if my legs would still carry me. Again I was told that the weather should continue to improve the farther west I flew. I decided to press on. After I crossed the Mississippi River, the weather did improve—a little. The ceiling was about 1,500 feet, the visibility was close to 2 miles, and the air was a little calmer.

My next stop was Lake Charles, Louisiana, where I was told that an ice storm was moving down from the north. If I left immediately, the FSS said, I "should be able to make Houston" before it got there.

"My God," I thought, "an ice storm. That's all I need." I did not know much about ice storms, but I knew that I did not want to be caught in one. My next stop was supposed to be Beaumont, Texas, but by the time I arrived there, the ceiling had improved to approximately 3,000 feet, and the visibility was about 5 miles. Why waste time stopping at Beaumont when Houston was only 45 minutes away? I had taken on fuel at Baton Rouge, so that was no problem. I told Beaumont I would be passing through their control zone en route to Houston. If there was anything bad up the road, surely they would tell me.

Approximately 4 miles past the Beaumont airport, my heart nearly stopped. All of a sudden, it sounded as though I had run up behind a gravel truck, which was now dumping its whole load on my airplane. Within seconds, the entire windshield was obscured. The side windows were still clear—and what I saw out there was *ice*. The wings were covered with it! What do I do now? I was 2,500 feet above Beaumont with nowhere to land, my forward vision was blocked, and the airplane was already feeling mushy from all that ice.

Beaumont, meanwhile, was asking my position and intentions. Unsure of both, I answered as calmly as I could bring myself to do that I believed I was on the edge of their control zone and would return for landing. No emergency, I said to them, as I said to myself, "You dummy, you got yourself into this, now get yourself out."

The controller's reply was almost enough reason to make me lose that little control I still had: I was cleared to land on Runway 36, but a DC-9 was descending from 18,000 feet, also cleared to land on 36. Beaumont believed I'd be down before the DC-9 arrived.

So now, I was covered with ice, blind, ignorant of my distance to the airport, and as invisible to the DC-9 because of the clouds as he was to me because of the ice.

Fortunately, the VOR was on the airport. I flew toward it for a few minutes and then turned about 90 degrees to look out the side. The defroster was wide open but had opened a hole in front of me only about 6 inches in diameter. Another turn, and there, at last, was the airport. I wasn't lined up with Runway 36, but I would take what runway I could find. The airplane was becoming extremely mushy, and I doubted it could fly much longer. I stuck my nose up to that 6-inch hole to stay lined up with the runway. At last, finally and shakily, I touched down. As I was rolling out, I saw from out the side window the DC-9, also just touching down—on Runway 36.

In this case, the setup for catastrophe was nearly perfect, and the pilot had failed to recognize it. He had been living with a sky full of moisture for days—waiting on the ground for it to go away and then coping with it in the air. He had been told that things were improving to the west, which indicated the approach of a front, and to cap the situation, according to the pilot, Flight Service had told him that "if I left immediately, I should be able to make Houston before it got there." *It* was an ice storm created by cold air driving in to wedge beneath warmer moist air.

In any preflight briefing, "should" must never be taken as being more reliable than *maybe*. The slight lifting of the ceiling to 3,000 and the improvement of the visibility to 5 miles—just VFR—was a sucker trap, for the real problem remained the odds of flying into precipitation. This pilot had reached into an ice machine and, predictably, had found ice.

Anatomy of an Ice Machine

The intensity of structural icing caused by freezing rain is almost always categorized as severe. The ice can build up so fast and is so tenacious that antiicing and deicing equipment are ineffective to prevent it. (In fact, manufacturers of airplanes equipped with antiice and deice systems are not required to demonstrate that the equipment can handle a bout with freezing rain. Even an airworthiness certificate for flight into known icing conditions means nothing when such icing is concerned.) Immediate diversion is the only recourse, and due to the nature of the beast, freezing rain can leave the pilot with very limited options for diversion. Sometimes, none at all.

As we have pointed out, not only the wings but the tail and the propeller blades are deformed by such ice. Furthermore, for each ½ inch of accumulated ice, about 300 pounds is added to the airplane's total weight. There are accounts of clear ice buildups of up to 1 inch per minute in freezing rain. The buildup deforms the aerodynamic contour of the airfoil; in effect, it sculpts its own airfoil—one that will stall at a lower angle of attack and at a higher airspeed. How much higher is a mystery.

Engine performance can be significantly impaired by ice accumulation in the carburetor or induction system; radio communication can be interfered with by buildups on the antennas or be lost entirely if the antennas break off; flight instrument indications can go haywire from a plugged pitot-static system.

Freezing rain can occur anywhere there is warm, moist air aloft with cold air below (FIGURE 13). Occluded fronts are prime candidates. When water vapor condenses in the warm air and

FIGURE 13   The potential for an encounter with freezing rain should be recognized anywhere there is warm, moist air aloft with cold air below, such as in the warm front depicted above. Be particularly careful in the vicinity of occluded fronts.

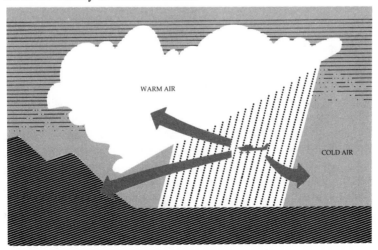

falls as large water droplets into the colder air below, the droplets remain liquid even though they are cooled to below freezing. These supercooled water droplets are very unstable, and if they are disturbed by a moving airplane, for instance, they can easily turn to ice. The droplets freeze slowly on contact with the airplane, which allows air between the droplets to escape as the water freezes. That is why the ice is clear and smooth enough to take a shape very similar to that of the underlying surface.

Getting the Most from Forecasts

At present, freezing rain is difficult to forecast, but meteorologists believe that Doppler weather radar systems now under development will provide better information on such factors as temperature variations with altitude and the size of water droplets. Today, fortunately, some warning is available if it is received with caution.

The words *freezing precipitation* in area forecasts and the abbreviations ZR (freezing rain) and ZL (freezing drizzle) in surface observations and terminal forecasts should trigger a warning in your mind. Stay clear of these conditions. Even a "look-see" can lead to trouble. Scrutinize all weather reports for clues of possible freezing precipitation.

One pilot of a piston twin, so reports the NTSB, was cleared for a localizer approach and given a surface weather observation that read, in part: "Estimated 800 overcast, 3 miles visibility, light drizzle and fog, temperature 34 degrees, dew point missing. . . ." Visible precipitation and a temperature near freezing should have warned him. The pilot elected to make the approach. He missed it and requested another but did not get a second chance. Shortly after he received his clearance to try again, the pilot requested a climb "to get on top to unload some [ice]. The plane is getting heavy right now." He then declared an emergency and asked for vectors to the airport. His last transmission was that he had the runway in sight.

The airplane stalled and spun to a crash about half a mile short of the runway. The accident report noted that a charter pilot who landed at a nearby airport at about the same time picked up 2 inches of ice during the approach.

An inadvertent encounter with freezing rain is one thing; sauntering into it with eyes wide open is quite another, and a few pilots do that every winter: for instance, a 45-year-old, very-low-time pilot, who just had to fly to his destination, even though everything, including his fixed-gear single on the ramp, was already coated with a thick layer of clear ice and the freezing rain had not abated. An airport employee had done everything he could to dissuade him except tie him up. His suggestion that the pilot drive the trip was refused because, the airman said, the highways were iced over. When the pilot was asked what he would do about an ice buildup, he shrugged and, ignoring the employee's fervent warnings, went to his airplane, scraped the ice off the windshield, and took off. The wreckage was found 5 days later. The airplane had stalled and crashed into a mountain shortly after departing the airport.

Experienced pilots have done the same thing. All too often, what we, as detached observers, see clearly as a stupid decision is the seemingly rational product of overconfidence and pressures that should have nothing to do with flying when hazards loom. Many such cases can be cited, including the following:

When a newly rated instrument pilot "gets his ticket wet," that is, takes on hard IFR alone for the first time, it is a time of special pride. As pilot Paul A. Mickey relates, it may not be a cause for celebration when the ticket gets both wet and frozen.

ROANOKE APPROACH: Cessna 2868Q, you are currently 25 miles northwest of the Roanoke Vortac. Radar service terminated. Resume normal navigation. Contact Charleston Approach 119.2. If unable, try again in ten minutes.

It was early November, and the sunny midafternoon sky carried an ominous cast. The winds aloft forecast obtained from the Raleigh Flight Service briefer showed winds 310 degrees at 29 knots at 6,000 feet and 320 degrees at 42 knots at 9,000 feet; broken clouds at 6,000 feet; overcast, 10,000 feet. The forecast for my route of flight from Durham, North Carolina, Skypark to Kanawha Airport, Charleston, West Virginia, included light rain at Beckley, West Virginia, and widely scattered showers northward ino south central Ohio, with a freezing level at 8,000 feet, lowering to 6,000 feet at Port Columbus Airport.

This late-afternoon flight was my first real outing as a newly rated instrument pilot. Accompanying me was a friend, who had taken his precautionary dosage of Dramamine. En route to the Roanoke Vortac, I requested 7,000 feet to stay on top of broken clouds and grant my companion a more comfortable and scenic ride. Eventually, our Cessna 172 fought its way through a 40-knot headwind along Victor 258 to Zooms Intersection. The sun was setting, and an overcast was sliding over the southern reaches of the Blue Ridge Mountains.

I rechecked the navcom for the airway centerline and dialed in the Pulaski Vortac to verify and monitor my progress on V-258. My efforts to reach Charleston Approach failed. Deep darkness fell, joined by the initial pelting of rain against the windshield. The OAT hovered at 35 degrees F; a gradual drop in rpm called for carb heat.

A flashlight check revealed rime and clear ice collecting on the struts and leading edges. The airspeed began to dissipate from 75 to 70 knots.

I quickly abandoned hope for Charleston, and Raleigh seemed equally distant. Roanoke told me to call Indianapolis Center, but the reception was too poor. I needed to descend to 6,000 feet. Suddenly, I saw the airspeed indicator drop to zero, but we were still flying. No pitot heat! I turned it on. The ice kept building. Reason dictated that we return to Roanoke, which was VFR, but I had a dinner engagement in Columbus, Ohio, that evening, so press on.

The airspeed indicator was functioning again: 70 knots indicated, but there was a 40-knot headwind, and clear ice was accumulating. Our groundspeed was 30 knots. When I was finally able to contact Indianapolis Center, I was told that a Piedmont propjet had just executed a missed approach at Beckley and had been cleared to 6,000 feet, direct Roanoke. My descent clearance would not be issued until it could be established that the propjet was clear. Radar coverage at lower altitudes in that sector was unreliable.

My airspeed continued to wither: 65 knots. Anticipating a stall, I was afraid to try to maintain 7,000 feet. My passenger, however, seemed reassuringly comfortable, and I hoped he wouldn't sense the panic that was spreading from my stomach to my voice; my mouth was so dry, I could hardly form words.

Finally, I radioed the Piedmont aircraft that I could no longer hold 7,000 feet. I gave my fix from Pulaski and Roanoke and asked if he thought we would clear—I had to get down. Cool, calm, professional, the Piedmont pilot said he would swing to the north and would relay my plight back to Center and to Charleston Approach. Down to 6,000 feet, we were finally able to communicate with Charleston Approach by listening to the Beckley Vortac. We still had no radar contact.

The airspeed temporarily stabilized, but ice continued to collect; carb heat was costing precious power. The sluggish controls were now grueling to manage. A cross-check showed our position to be 20 miles northeast of Beckley. We had been flying three hours on a two-hour flight plan. Then the airspeed began to decay again. I was exhausted and scared to death.

In an effort to fathom the situation, I thought about advice on icing I had read, then I double-checked my procedures and began to relax a little. I was doing all I could. But the 172 could not maintain 6,000 feet—the minimum en route altitude. Explaining to Charleston my need to go lower, I began a gradual descent to 5,000. I remembered from numerous VFR flights along this route that the ground reached up to 4,500. I also knew about downdrafts and began to anticipate a crash landing—in the mountains, at night, in freezing rain, and carrying clear ice in an airplane that was barely controllable.

Still 15 miles from Beckley, I was unable to cling even to 5,000 feet. As the controller confirmed my position, I again declared that I needed to go lower.

Now, down to 4,000 feet, I suddenly heard a sharp cracking and banging along the sides of the airplane. This was it! We were skimming the tree tops—and I couldn't see a thing.

But gradually, ever so slowly, the aircraft became more stable. The airspeed began to edge upward. The engine regained a healthy sound. The outside air temperature was up to 36 degrees F. The terrible racket was not from tree tops but from ice fracturing and striking the aircraft as it broke away.

The fuel level was low, and my fatigue level was high. Nevertheless, advised by an instructor who assured me that I could safely land a 172 on a 5,000-foot runway with a 30-knot tailwind, I completed an abbreviated, low, VOR approach to Beckley in a surface wind of 28 gusting to 35.

As I wobbled away from the plane on my jelly legs, ice still clung to the antenna wires. My fuel bill confirmed how few minutes of flying time I'd had left. At our hotel, I started talking with the proprietor. He was just out of a lower body cast. He had lost first one and then the other engine of his new twin and had made a forced landing in those same mountains while trying to reach Roanoke.

The instrument rating makes one a better and more flexible pilot, yet there may be times when not having the rating would be safer, for that would block the temptation to penetrate ice-bearing clouds. This pilot wisely sought to remain atop a broken deck, but his caution could protect him only if nothing changed for the worse in that frozen atmosphere. It changed, and he soon found himself sandwiched between layers, in freezing rain. By then, his situation could only degrade further, and it soon did.

His—and his passenger's—prospects for survival were diminishing steadily just so the pilot could try to make a dinner engagement. He could have turned around, as he had contemplated doing. With a strong tailwind replacing the headwind and pushing him toward better weather, lower terrain, and more inviting airports, he would have had a genuine reason to relax.

When getting an IFR briefing, it is smart to ask where the nearest VFR is likely to be along your route. This can help not only if the route is invaded by ice-laden clouds but if thunderstorms loom or other emergencies occur. It can't always be determined with precision, but it can be a lifesaver to know even approximately where the clouds end and, at each stage of the flight, the ground begins.

When diverting could mean survival, pressing on is often a matter of self-deception, a delusion that things miraculously will get better. It's like drafting Providence to undo one's mistakes.

7
Escape Routes

Now that we have anatomized icing, we can turn to the options the pilot has in coping with the beast. Perhaps the most important thing to remember is that the enemy is not only ice itself but the *threat* of it. Perceiving menace in the "chance" of icing can lead to taking steps to avoid icing before it shows up and to making sure that the aircraft is in the best condition to handle it if it appears.

Such steps begin on the ground. As the following case demonstrates, when icing conditions are in the offing, make it a rule to slow down and take even more care than usual with all the duties of the preflight before setting off.

The Super King Air landed at Arapahoe County Airport, near Denver, at 10:17 A.M. Snow had begun falling there about an hour before the airplane arrived and continued until early afternoon. The aircraft was piloted by an experienced crew. The captain, a 52-year-old ATP, had a total of 10,225 hours, including 9,225 hours in this particular Beech, N456L. The first officer, 42, was a commercial pilot and an airframe and powerplant mechanic. He had logged 5,600 total hours, including 4,000 in twins and 200 hours in N456L.

After shutdown, the first officer requested that Arapahoe line personnel fill the outboard fuel tanks and put 25 gallons of fuel into each inboard tank. During the refueling, the captain asked the linemen how much fuel the first officer had ordered. Upon learning the amount, he said, "Do not put a drop more than that in."

At about 10:20 A.M., the captain contacted the Denver FSS

for a weather briefing for N456L's return flight to Lufkin, Texas, scheduled for 1:30 P.M. He filed an IFR flight plan and told the briefer that he would check weather again before departure. At 1:30 P.M., after lunch, the captain and first officer watched as a lineman brushed snow off the King Air's wings and tail surfaces. The lineman later said the snow had come off easily, leaving a beaded film of water on the aircraft. However, he said, between 1 and 2 inches of wet snow had remained on top of the fuselage. His offer to spray the King Air with deicing solution was declined by the crew.

As eight passengers began boarding the aircraft at 2:10 P.M., the captain told the first officer that they would "have to burn off 10 to 15 gallons of fuel during the taxi." The first officer concurred.

N456L took off at 2:34 P.M. Ten minutes later, when the aircraft was at 12,700 feet MSL and about 14 miles southeast of the airport, the first officer made the following transmission to Denver Departure Control: "Okay, we would like to go back to Arapahoe County. We're getting a little too much ice up here." He then amended the request, asking for vectors to Denver's Stapleton International Airport, which was about 25 miles northwest of the aircraft.

The following is a transcript of pertinent transmissions between the King Air's flight crew (N456L), Denver Departure Control (DDC), and Denver Approach Control (DAC), beginning at 2:44 P.M.:

1444:59—*DDC:* 56L, maintain 11,000 and turn left to a heading of 040.
1445:06—*N456L:* 11,000, 040.
1445:34—*DDC:* 56L, proceed direct to the Kiowa VOR. Cleared to the Kiowa VOR. Maintain 11,000. Contact Denver Approach control, 120.8. They will have further clearance for you.
1445:44—*N456L:* Direct Kiowa; 20.8.
1446:41—*N456L:* Hello, Colorado Springs. King Air 45 . . . ah, Denver, 456L.

1446:46—*DAC:* 456L, fly heading 030. Be vectors for an ILS Runway 26L, at Stapleton.

1446:56—*N456L:* Okay, what's the weather at Colorado Springs?

[Colorado Springs Airport is about 33 miles southwest of the Kiowa VOR.]

1447:00—*DAC:* Well, I'll get it when I get a chance, sir. Denver altimeter, 29.82.

1448:18—*DAC:* 56L, the Springs weather: sky partially obscured; measured ceiling overcast; visibility 2.5 miles; and light snow showers and fog. Over.

1448:39—*N456L:* Okay, we were asking below 11,000. We can't hold it here at eleven.

1448:44—*DAC:* 56L, do you need to come into Stapleton?

1448:47—*N456L:* Affirmative. Anything we can get there.

1448:50—*DAC:* Understand, 56L. Descend and maintain 10,000. That's the best I can do right now. Unless I have to vector you eastbound, just stay on the heading. There's traffic off your left. Ten o'clock and eight eastbound at eight-five.

1449:03—*N456L:* Okay, we'll declare emergency, if necessary. Just get us straight to the runway.

1449:08—*DAC:* I understand, 56L. Do what you have to do . . . stay on the heading.

1449:20—*DAC:* 56L, descend and maintain 8,000.

1449:23—*N456L:* 'Kay, coming down to eight.

1449:43—*DAC:* 56L, turn left, heading 340 vector final approach course. We'll take you right into a base leg from there.

1449:49—*N456L:* 340, roger.

1449:53—*N456L:* 56L's gonna be descending all the way.

1450:05—*DAC:* Say again?

1450:07—*N456L:* 6L gotta come right on down. You better get us to the nearest airport.

1450:11—*DAC:* 56L, you're 21 southeast of Stapleton. Are you gonna be able to make that, or what?

1450:19—*N456L:* Naw, get us to the nearest airport. We gotta come on down.

1450:51—*DAC:* 56L, turn left, heading 310. Try and hold the altitude as best you can, because you still got 10 miles to go to Buckley. That is the closest airport from your position.

The controller was trying to vector the aircraft to Buckley Air National Guard Base, where a ground-controlled approach would have been available. But no further transmissions were received from the King Air. The aircraft crashed and burned in an open field about 14 miles southeast of Buckley, 15 miles east of Arapahoe County Airport and 22 miles southeast of Stapleton. The elevation of the accident site is 6,280 feet. There were no survivors.

The NTSB determined the probable cause of the crash to be a rapid accumulation of ice on the bottom of the wings and behind the deicing boots, which "destroyed the aircraft's ability to maintain level flight." That situation stemmed, said the board, from the crew's failing to obtain a current weather briefing before takeoff and to make a timely decision to discontinue the climb and return to Arapahoe, and from its operating the "over-gross-weight" aircraft at high angles of attack in severe icing conditions. Had the crew obtained a briefing after the one received four hours before takeoff, the board continued, they would have been given a Sigmet and several pilot reports of moderate and severe icing conditions. That Sigmet had actually been issued in Kansas City only minutes before the King Air captain's briefing but had arrived at the Denver FSS too late to be relayed to him.

Weight in the Balance

The Super King Air's operating manual advises maintaining a minimum airspeed of 140 knots in sustained icing conditions, to prevent ice from accumulating on unprotected surfaces of the wing. This ensures that the aircraft, at gross weight, will not exceed a wing angle of attack of 4 degrees. Icing certification tests of the Super King Air had revealed that at higher angles of attack, ice can build up on the bottom of the wing, behind the boots. A careful recreation of N456L's flight indicated that the flight crew had maintained the normal climb speed of 160 knots through 8,000 feet and then had reduced the airspeed to near, and briefly below, the minimum of 140 knots. The NTSB believes that the decrease was due either to an attempt to maintain normal climb speed with an increase in pitch or to an effort to expedite the climb through icing conditions by seeking a higher rate of climb. Whatever the reason, the reduction led to decreased climb performance and an increase in wing angle of attack above 4 degrees.

Why did the angle of attack exceed 4 degrees if the crew did not let the airspeed decay below 140 knots? According to the board, the King Air was about 600 pounds above maximum gross weight on takeoff. "The higher angles of attack at 140 KIAS," reported the board, "were a direct function of the aircraft's high gross weight, because for a maximum gross weight in unaccelerated flight, a 4-degree angle of attack would occur near 140 KIAS."

The flight crew's explicit refueling instructions and their discussion of a necessary fuel burn before takeoff are evidence that they knew they had a weight-and-balance problem on their hands. Considering the weather conditions, the problem of ice buildup should have become obvious shortly after takeoff. Yet, so said the board, the crew "failed to realize the significance of the higher angle of attack in these conditions, and also they failed to recognize in a timely manner the substantial performance decrease that was occurring."

Significantly, about five minutes after the crash, another Super King Air landed at Arapahoe County, having picked up moderate ice while cruising at 11,000 feet and while descending through 9,000. Its deicing equipment shed the ice. This King Air had penetrated the icing conditions at about 180 KIAS, and consequently at a very low angle of attack. It had thus taken on ice at about the same rate as N456L, but the ice had remained on or very near the deicing boots, so that the boots removed it.

The first sign of performance loss in an icing situation should be viewed as a loaded and cocked pistol pointed at the pilot's head, whether the aircraft is a cabin-class twin with full deicing gear or an unprotected, low-power single. The decision to take the quickest and safest way out of icing conditions must be made before the hammer falls. N456L was airborne for only about 10 minutes before the flight crew decided to return to the airport. By then, it was too late. Before losing radar contact with the King Air, ATC saw it descending at a rate in excess of 2,000 feet per minute.

Failure to deal with weight and balance, to heed the advice of the manual, to get what turned out to be an invaluable, updated briefing—details such as these can get you if you neglect them.

Impatience is often the culprit in ground-borne winter accidents. Pilot Harlan R. Davis describes an event shared by many airmen. With the mercury at 5 degrees, the 100-hour private pilot arrived at 8:30 one morning to find himself alone at the airport. He began to prepare his rented Cessna 172 for flight.

I opened the airplane, put the flaps down (battery okay), checked the fuel and controls, and performed a complete walkaround. I pulled the prop through once or twice to limber the oil. I knew that I should preheat the engine for an easier start, but a 100-hour pilot is impatient and inexperienced.

I climbed into the left seat, primed the engine, and turned the key. The prop turned over, but the engine did not fire—the battery refused to drive it any further. It occurred to me that I had pulled the prop through only once or twice and that a few more manual pulls might do the trick. I got out, positioned myself up front of the prop and pulled. The engine fired . . . and started to rev up! For a split second, I could not believe the engine was running, but the airplane started to move, and I was in the way. I lurched to the passenger side of the airplane, slipped, fell, pulled my feet up so they would not get chopped off. The engine was now running at about 1,700 rpm, and the airplane was picking up speed.

As the right wheel rolled by, I grabbed it, hoping to hold the airplane, and then realized that, on the hard packed snow, I could not hold it and would only deflect it off the taxiway onto the runway. Dead ahead were a snowbank and a parked aircraft. I let go of the tire.

The 172 whizzed across 20 feet of taxiway and embedded itself in the snowbank. The prop threw quite a bit of snow in my face as I scrambled to the passenger side. The door was locked. I slid under the fuselage, opened the door and turned off the key. *Turned off the key?* Why had the key been left *on?* In my big rush to get the prop pulled through, I had turned off the master switch but had left the magneto switch on Both, and, of course, the mags were hot.

No damage was evident, either to the aircraft or to me, although I had come close to becoming human hamburger.

Leaving the key in the ignition was a careless error, equal to leaving your car with the engine running and the selector in Drive. My mistake had been one of impatience. Had I moved a bit slower, I would have turned the key off and *taken it with me.* Pulling the engine through is a good procedure, especially in cold weather, to limber the gooey oil. But do not leave the key in the ignition. Put it in your pocket when you leave the pilot's seat, and leave the tail tied down, so that, if there is a broken ground wire, the airplane will stay put.

I have heard gruesome stories about propellers. I was very lucky.

Benign Neglect in Washington

An airport doesn't have to be small and deserted for a pilot, in his eagerness to depart, to forget to check all the details. A few years ago, at a major terminal, with a small army of ground crew and an array of equipment, sensible procedures, and regulations to help them, a professional flight crew lulled themselves into a disaster in the snow. In a time of rush-hour hurry up and wait, the ground crew also contributed to the making of grim history. By means of their Boeing 737's cockpit recorder, we know how the pilot and first officer spent their time while waiting to begin their fatal takeoff run. They misspent it. They neglected signs and steps created to prevent what happened. As a result of that and the ground crew's errors, seventy-four people aboard Air Florida Flight 90, including the crew, and four people at the crash site were killed.

On January 31, 1982, the 737 was scheduled to make a return flight to Fort Lauderdale, Florida, from Washington (D.C.) National Airport. The airliner had arrived a short time earlier from Fort Lauderdale in snow, which had increased from moderate to heavy. When the captain asked the ground crew, which was on contract from American Airlines to handle the job for Air Florida, to deice the airplane in anticipation of an imminent pushback clearance, the 737 was covered by about half an inch of wet snow. The crew lacked specific deicing instructions for the 737 and instead followed their *General Maintenance Manual* procedures. They sprayed the aircraft with a mixture of ethylene glycol and heated water in various proportions. As the airport closed because of the snow and then reopened, the deicing was started and stopped and restarted. As they sprayed, the crew failed to notice that the standard spray nozzle had been replaced with a nonstandard—and defective—one that was releasing a weaker mixture than had been dialed into it. Furthermore, the crew *sprayed* the airliner's left side instead of removing snow from the wings and empennage with brooms. The 737 maintenance manual stipulates that brooms be used, since snow melted by deicing fluid can refreeze.

The crew also critically failed to install engine inlet covers, although Air Florida's maintenance manual called for installing them "for even short periods" of exposure to heavy snow or ice.

When the pushback clearance finally came, the ground tug could not move the airplane through the snow. For about a minute, the captain tried to move it with reverse thrust from the engines. Not only did he fail, he also violated a Boeing operations bulletin's prohibition against doing so. The heat from the engines, the bulletin points out, could lead to a melting and refreezing of the ice and snow on the leading edges of the wings. An American Airlines mechanic later stated that he had found no evidence of water or slush on the wings. In contradiction, an Air Florida official, who had been inside the terminal, said that he had seen a light coating of snow on the upper fuselage and left wing, as a second tug, equipped with tire chains, pushed the airplane back.

Snow continued to fall as the airliner began taxiing toward Runway 36 behind nine other airliners and seven general aviation airplanes. The weather at the time: ceiling indefinite, 200 feet obscured; visibility ½ mile; moderate snow; temperature 24 degrees F, dewpoint 24 degrees F; wind 010 degrees at 11 knots; Runway 36 visual range 2,800 feet, variable 3,500 feet. The length of Runway 36/18 is 6,869 feet.

The crew went through the pretakeoff checklist. At 3:38 P.M., the first officer queried the captain on the status of the engine antiice equipment. "Off," was the captain's reply. This was a crucial item. The Boeing 737 flight manual specifies that the engine inlet antiice must be on when icing conditions exist, meaning a dry-bulb temperature below 46.4 degrees F, a wet-bulb temperature below 39.2 degrees F, and a presence of visible moisture, such as fog, rain, or wet snow. If a turbojet's compressor inlet pressure sensor (the Pt2 probe, in turbine jargon) is iced, erroneous thrust indications will show on the airplane's engine pressure ratio (EPR) indicators. *For the Boeing 737, the EPR gauge is the primary instrument for setting thrust.* The Pt2 probe needs to be warmed by the antiicing system to prevent ice blockage.

At 3:40, as Flight 90 was still taxiing, the captain suggested that it might be a good idea to "go over and get deiced." "Yeah, definitely," said the first officer, "it's been a while since we've been deiced."

Air Florida 90 was now in line behind a New York Air DC-9. To the NTSB, it appears that the captain taxied the airplane extremely close to the DC-9's exhaust flow so as to melt the 737's rapidly accumulating snow. Again, a Boeing operations manual states that greater-than-normal distances should be maintained between airplanes when taxiing over ice or snow, since snow on the aircraft's surfaces can melt and become ice if a nearby engine's exhaust is directed onto it. "Tell you what, my windshield will be deiced; don't know about my wing," the captain said. The first officer answered, "Well, all we need is the upside of the wing, anyway. The wingtips are gonna speed up on 80, anyway. They'll shuck all that other stuff." Then, apparently referring to the right wing, he added, "This one's got a quarter to a half-inch on it all the way." "Gonna get your wing now," the captain said. Soon after, apparently responding to a shift in New York Air's position, the captain said over the ground control frequency, "Don't do that, Apple, I need to get the other wing done."

Then came the first indication that the first officer was suspicious of the EPR gauge indications: "See this difference in the left engine and right one?" "Yeah," said the captain. "I don't know why that's different," the first officer went on, " 'less it's hot air going into that right one. That must be it—from his exhaust—it was doing that at the chocks a while ago." The NTSB later reasoned that what the first officer may have observed were fluctuations of the EPR gauge, a symptom of Pt2 probe ice contamination. Still, the thought of using engine antiice apparently never occurred to either crewman.

At 3:53, the first officer was still concerned about the snow and ice accumulations. He said, "Boy, this is a losing battle here on trying to deice those things. It gives you a false sense of security, that's all it does." "That, ah, satisfies the Feds," the captain replied and then added, "Right here is where the icing truck, they oughta have two of them, you pull right, like cattle, right between those things and then . . ."

Four minutes later, the crew ran through the last of the pretakeoff checklist. The EPR setting for takeoff thrust was determined to be 2.04. The airplane was to rotate at 140 knots, and takeoff safety speed was to be 144 knots. The first officer would perform the takeoff. The captain would adjust the thrust levers to the takeoff EPR settings before reaching 80 knots on the takeoff roll, monitor the engine instruments, call out V_1 and the command "rotate" at V_r, continue to monitor the instruments, and raise the gear once a positive rate of climb was established.

Just before they were cleared for takeoff, the first officer sought advice from the captain: "Slush runway. Do you want me to do anything special for this or just go for it?" The captain was noncommittal: "Unless you got anything special you'd like to do." The crew could have used what the Boeing manual calls the "Improved Climb" procedure, which is essentially a liftoff and climbout at a higher-than-normal airspeed.

The Boeing 737's takeoff behavior with ice-contaminated wings had already been well-documented. Boeing had issued three operations manual bulletins since 1974, when it first concluded that the 737 could pitch up or roll off on one wing immediately after liftoff (there had been twenty-two known cases). All of Air Florida's 737 flight manuals carried this information.

Expediting though in Doubt

The tower cleared Flight 90 for takeoff at 3:59 P.M., adding, "No delay on departure, if you will. Traffic's two-and-half out for the runway." The crew replied, "Okay." Eastern Airlines Flight 1451 was cleared to land on Runway 36 at 4:00 P.M.

The 737's cockpit recorder detected the sound of the engines spooling up, but the sound frequency on the tape did not match the frequency that an EPR setting of 2.04 would produce. After a series of tests of blocked 737 engine inlet probes, it was learned that this 737 was only developing an EPR of 1.70. The 2.04 reading in the cockpit was the result of the ice-blocked probe sensing the lower-pressure air at the vent port of the engine inlet nosecone, instead of at the probe's inlet orifice. Instead of having a 2.04 EPR takeoff power value of 29,000 pounds of thrust, Flight 90 took off with only 21,500 pounds.

The significance of the few terse comments in the moments during and after the takeoff are open to speculation, but experts have reached an unofficial consensus. After the sound of engine spool-up, the captain's remark, "Cold, real cold," and the first officer's "God, look at that thing. That don't seem right, does it?" are construed as observations of an EPR overshoot as the thrust levers were first set. Two seconds later, during the takeoff roll, the first officer again expressed concern, referring perhaps to the poor acceleration, the EPR readings, the airspeed, or the fuel-flow indications. Tests showed that the only quick clues that the engines were not developing the proper power were the fuel-flow gauges. All the gauges would have read as normal with an ice-blocked inlet probe except the fuel-flow gauges, which would have been lower than normal. "That's not right," the first officer said. The captain, who by Air Florida policy, had sole authority to abort the takeoff, said, "Yes, it is, there's 80." "Naw, I don't think that's right," said the first officer. Then, after a pause—perhaps in deference to the captain's authority and experience—he said, "Ah, maybe it is."

The captain called out "120" as the airspeed increased, and the first officer again expressed doubt: "I don't know."

The captain called out V_1 and two seconds later, after the first officer lifted the nosewheel, said, "Easy." The NTSB interpreted this as a warning. The flight data recorder showed that the 737 did pitch up abruptly after rotation, which apparently startled the captain, and also that the initial rate of climb was approximately 1,000 feet per minute. However, once it was out of ground effect, the airliner could not maintain a positive rate of climb.

Two seconds after Flight 90 lifted off and reached V_2 (takeoff safety speed—in this case, 144 knots), the stickshaker, a stall warning device, activated and started to vibrate the control column. The captain said, "Forward, forward," which has been interpreted as an instruction to exert nosedown pressure on the control column. This and his following statements indicate that he was concerned about pitch control. His comment, "We only want 500," is taken as a reaction to the rate of climb. Probably having seen the airspeed and rate of climb first sharply increase and then degrade as the 737 left ground effect, the captain was telling his first officer that they needed a climb rate of only 500 feet per minute.

Preoccupied wth the pitch, the crew left the thrust levers at the inaccurate 2.04 setting. However, witnesses on the bridge the aircraft eventually struck said that they had heard the engines speed up just before impact. A transient frequency, possibly associated with increased engine rotational speed, was detected on the cockpit tape sixteen seconds after stickshaker activation, but the crew had waited too long to apply more power.

The airplane climbed only 300 feet before stalling and crashing onto a bridge that is approximately 0.8 mile beyond the departure end of Runway 36. After striking the bridge, the 737 broke into four large pieces and sank back into the Potomac River.

The NTSB believes that the accident could have been avoided by the crew's immediately adding thrust. Simulator tests showed that the 737 could have climbed out had the thrust levers been advanced to maximum power. Instead, said the board, the crew, in response to the stickshaker, "probably reduced nose attitude at first but later increased it to prevent descent into the ground." The board added that crews should be trained not to respect engine paramater limitations to the point where "they will withhold the use of available thrust until it is too late to correct a developing loss of control."

Applications to Lightplane Operations

The winds of error that contributed to the crash apply to all kinds of flying, from air carrier to sport. The probable causes of the accident, said the NTSB, were the crew's failure to use antiice during ground operations and takeoff, their decision to take off with snow and ice on the airfoil surfaces, and the captain's failure to reject the takeoff during the early phase, when his attention was called to anomalous engine instrument readings.

Contributing factors were Flight 90's prolonged wait, in continuous precipitation, between deicing and receipt of their clearance, and the known inherent pitch-up characteristics of the 737 when the leading edges of the wings are contaminated with even small amounts of snow and ice. The safety board also mentioned the crew's limited experience in jet transport winter operations. In his 1,100 hours since upgrading from first officer, the captain had conducted only eight arrivals or departures in icing-conducive weather; in his 1,000 hours as co-pilot on 737s, the first officer had conducted only two ground operations in ice-prone weather.

The NTSB made several recommendations, among them the development of ways to expedite traffic in such weather conditions and improved use of antiice equipment on the ground.

For *general aviation pilots,* the most significant finding was that the crew had violated a simple regulation, FAR 121.629 (b), which prohibits taking off when snow, frost, or ice is on an airplane's wings, control surfaces, or propellers. Other cautions for lightplane pilots are:

• Do not fixate on any one instrument; keep your scan up to speed and cross-check all instrument indications.

• Do not hesitate to abort a takeoff if you feel that all the instrument indications or takeoff sensations are not right.

• When flying with another pilot, never substitute concern for his approval for your own good judgment.

• Be sure that you know the recommendations and warnings about flying your aircraft under winter conditions that have been published by the manufacturer or are in the FARs.

• Handle every inspection and procedural detail scrupulously, and don't downplay poor or worsening conditions.

Neither the ground crew nor the air crew was sufficiently punctilious about or familiar with the safety measures various bulletins and manuals contained. Overlooking the faulty spray nozzle, casually accepting the suspect EPR reading, warming the 737 in the heat of the preceding DC-9, the fixating of both pilots on the control column—these and other oversights froze Flight 90 into an avoidable catastrophe.

Decisions at Departure

As we have suggested, the first line of defense against icing is evasion, which can mean not going, at least until conditions are right. For example, many experienced IFR pilots, knowing that icing in frontal weather can be particularly severe, will wait for a front to pass before attempting a flight in wintertime instrument conditions. Similarly, a pilot's virtually having to ice-skate out to the aircraft through precipitation should be enough to persuade him to cancel or at least postpone the departure. A report of moderate or severe ice or freezing precipitation is a firm basis for a no-go decision. A look-see in an area in which trace or light ice has been reported should be attempted only by an experienced and cautious pilot flying an aircraft certificated and equipped for known icing conditions.

If the freezing level is at the surface and there are low ceilings and high cloud tops along the route, postpone the flight. But if you can cruise at an altitude below the freezing level or descend safely to VFR conditions should ice begin to collect, you might take a look.

In winter, cloud tops do not often build very high, so it may be possible to climb through the clouds and cruise in the sunshine. However, before committing yourself to such a course, carefully and candidly consider the performance of your aircraft. Even under the best conditions, for instance, a normally aspirated single that climbs like a bat at sea level may behave like a sick bird at high altitude. Add a load of ice, and the airplane may require full power just to maintain its best glide speed.

A twin with marginal single-engine performance calls for the most rigidly conservative evaluation.

Likewise, one should not lightly accept an instruction from ATC that can lead to prolonged flight in or a premature descent into an area of potential icing. When en route, it would be better to request a safer altitude or even a slightly different routing; when nearing the approach, it makes sense to negotiate for a hold, if necessary, so that you may descend into the questionable air at a higher-than-normal airspeed when you can be cleared for the approach. If the pireps and forecasts indicate that over-the-top is the only way to go, ask for a clearance to climb to cruise altitude in a holding pattern over the departure airport. A holding descent may similarly be requested for the destination airport. This type of procedure will ensure that an airport will be within reach should your aircraft pick up too much ice on climbout or descent.

When stratiform clouds dominate the scene—they are associated with warm frontal activity—evade icing by flying above or below the icing zones in the clouds or between layers. Cumulus clouds, which are usually associated with cold fronts, have thicker icing zones but generally cover smaller areas than do stratiform. They are repositories of clear ice, so that even though a flight through cumulus may be much shorter than through stratus, clear ice can accumulate very quickly on the aircraft and will be more difficult to shed than rime. Therefore, if the terrain and minimum navaid reception heights permit, plan to fly below cumulus clouds or at an altitude below the freezing level. Flight into cumulus clouds that loom over mountain ridges should be avoided. Severe icing zones can tower as high as 5,000 feet above the ridges, as moist air is forced aloft.

In all cases, if you wish to take the low road, be wary of a frontal inversion, which occurs when warm, moist air is forced to rise over a mass of colder air. A pilot flying under an inversion can encounter that worst cause of structural ice, freezing precipitation.

First Things First

What are the options a pilot carries with him into an icing encounter, especially in an airplane not equipped for ice? Just as important, what should his mind-set be if the encounter builds into a crisis?

Above all, remember the golden rule of winter flying: Take action to escape as soon as ice starts to accumulate. Do not sit there with your fingers crossed, hoping that conditions will improve. More than likely, the situation will snowball. Ice and complacency form a killing combination.

Watch for the first signs of ice on small components, such as the OAT probe, the corners of the windshield, or the leading edges of the horizontal tail. At the first sign of ice, prepare to climb, descend, or turn back. Immediately tell ATC what is happening, what you need, and what you are doing or are going to do if you are forced by circumstances right then to deviate from your clearance. Be willing to cooperate with the controller, certainly, but also be ready to assert your authority as pilot-in-command if safety demands.

Complacency is one creator of cockpit crises, panic is another. An aircraft that has been allowed to accumulate a hefty load of ice can become an unfamiliar and unfriendly mount that can betray any pilot who fails to stay calm and concentrate on flying. An ice-laden aircraft requires a delicate touch. Handle the flight and power controls smoothly and cautiously, since the margin between flying and stalling the airplane will have been reduced to an unknown quantity.

Over the years, some rules of thumb have emerged, such as "climb in freezing rain." *Generally,* this is a good tactic, the idea being to reach the warmer layer of air from which the rain is falling. Yet unless you begin to climb immediately, and unless your airplane is capable of performing a good, healthy, sustained rate of climb (turbocharging is almost essential), the accumulations you may endure on the way up could make things worse. As we have seen in the Super King Air crash, when climbing in icing conditions, it is important to maintain a relatively high airspeed. A slow climb at a high angle of attack will allow ice to form on the underside of the wing, further upsetting the flow around the wing and more rapidly diminishing lift. Similarly, other adages, such as "climb in a cold front and descend in a warm front," are not to be applied in all situations.

It should be mentioned here that once the OAT probe has iced up, it will continue to show the temperature that existed when the ice formed. Unless you remember that, you may be misled as you climb or descend in search of a colder or warmer air mass. Correct indications can come only from an ice-free OAT probe.

Descending out of the clouds or into warmer air is a logical tactic, and it could turn out to be the only one available. Needless to say, it is vital that you know where the terrain begins and what the temperatures and visibilities nearer the surface are likely to be. Descend slowly, keeping to where the MEA or MOCA gives you protection. Again, it is extremely helpful to know where the closest VFR is likely to be, so that, if necessary, you can run to improving weather or an approachable airport.

Climbing Out of Freezing Rain

Conventional wisdom used to hold that the best way out of freezing rain is to climb into the warmer air from which the rain is falling. Experience has shown, sometimes the hard way, that, if followed blindly, that rule is likely to prove simplistic and can be dangerous.

As a case in point, a turbocharged single flew into freezing rain at an altitude of 11,000 feet. The pilot requested clearance to climb to a higher altitude and immediately was assigned 13,000 feet. Radio communication with the airplane was then lost. The controller working the airplane said that his radar showed that it had climbed only 300 feet before descending out of radar contact. The aircraft had crashed into a mountain. A piston twin was flying at 11,000 feet in the same area at about the same time. After encountering the freezing rain, this pilot turned on his deicing equipment, descended to 10,000 feet, and flew safely to his destination.

Warmer air may exist within a couple thousand feet above your altitude, but even under the best conditions, the climb speeds of most singles and many light twins at altitude are glacial.

Equally important is the question of whether warmer air will be where you expect or hope to climb to it. As we have seen, a warm front is a flow of usually moist air over cooler air. As this warmer air is lifted over the cooler, it, too, cools; its pressure lowers and its moisture condenses to form clouds. Usually, the overriding air remains warmer than the air below it, creating a temperature inversion. However, the extensiveness of the areas where this condition will exist may vary with conditions affected by the wind and ambient temperatures. As a result, while an airplane may pick up ice at point *A*—at which an inversion exists—it may not necessarily be climbing into significantly warmer air as it heads for point *B,* since point *B* may not only be thousands of feet higher but miles removed from the warm air that lay over point *A.* After all, the climb path will most likely be an upwardly slanting, not a vertical, line. To be sure of climbing into warmer air, one would have to plan carefully on the basis of up-to-date temperature and winds aloft measurements and other information, using charts generally not consulted by pilots during the usual weather briefing.

When *Plan A* Doesn't Work

Descent may therefore be the best bet if the pilot knows that the air temperature at a lower altitude is either above freezing or cold enough to change the freezing rain into sleet. A firm knowledge of terrain features in the area is also clearly important. Clear ice can build quickly upon the windshield and is relatively immune to the best efforts of defrosters. A VFR pilot caught in freezing rain may thus find his visibility limited to peeking out the side window, as was illustrated by some of the case histories we have cited. Likewise, an IFR pilot may have to descend below the minimum vectoring altitude to get to a suitable lower level.

Many experts now recommend an immediate 180-degree turn, together with a climb or descent, as the best course of action. Freezing rain can occur in a widespread area, so if you are encountering it for the first time along your route of flight, it makes sense to head back that way when the stuff appears.

Though it is all well and good to consider the options while sitting comfortably with a good book on the subject, we must realize that a bout with freezing rain may leave us with but one recourse for escape.

One pilot was flying a Navy Grumman Trader utility transport, an airplane equipped with full deicing equipment and two 1,525-horsepower Wright engines. The effectiveness of the deicing equipment became nil once the ice began to build up. The ice turned his Grumman "into a glazed doughnut just like *that*," he later recounted. Navy pilots go by the book, and the manual said to climb. With the engines screaming at maximum-except-takeoff power, the Trader actually began to *descend* at 200 feet per minute. There were mountains below, but fortunately, the aircraft was flying along a nearby coastline. The pilot headed out to sea, where, over the water, he found warmer air. "ATC told me I could not do that," the pilot recalls, "and I told him that I not only could but *was* doing that."

A pointer to be learned from that experience is that freezing rain will not give you the time to try to make *Plan A* work, against all evidence that it won't. Another lesson is that if you are in such a situation, don't linger while seeking and awaiting an amended clearance. If the controller can't clear you right away and your airplane is weakening, begin your escape and tell ATC what you are doing—as soon as possible. The wrath of an ATC facility supervisor and some paperwork are nothing compared to the potential consequences of hesitation. That could also apply to rime or mixed ice, if you let the buildup go too long. At the first sign of such ice, let ATC know about it and have a request in mind. Be ready to take independent command action if your condition is approaching the can't-wait point.

It does often occur that, if a climb is begun immediately, the aircraft will be able to top the offending cloud layer or reach an altitude with temperatures so cold that any moisture is frozen as ice crystals, which will not adhere to an airplane. If you decide to climb, determine to climb *all the way* out of the clouds. The uppermost levels of stratus clouds contain the worst icing conditions, so it does not make sense to linger near the tops.

The Antiice Arsenal

The best route of escape from ice is "out of there," but there is an assortment of equipment that can give a pilot more leverage and time in dealing with icing. This arsenal must be handled with care. Although the National Weather Service asserts that no airplane—not even a sophisticated airliner or warplane—can safely penetrate severe icing, an airplane's certification by the FAA for flight into known icing allows a pilot to fly legally in the worst conditions. Realistically, such a certification should be thought of as a comfort while flying out of icing, not as a license to disregard icing reports, the nature of icing, and common sense. As we have seen, enough of an accumulation can cause any airplane to stop flying, regardless of its equipment.

What is "known" icing? In 1974, the NTSB ruled that "known" signifies that icing conditions are being reported or forecast in reports which are known to a pilot or of which he should reasonably have been aware. Strictly interpreted, this means that, if a pilot flies into an area forecast to produce ice, he can be penalized for violating FAR 91.9 (careless operation) or, if the airplane is not certificated for icing, for violating FAR 91.31 (a) (noncompliance with operating limitations).

There is reason to believe that some pilots assume that if their airplanes have supplemental type certificated (STCed) deice boots, propeller antiice, and windshield alcohol systems, they are equipped as adequately for flight into icing as if they were properly certificated for it. In fact, an icing certification is the result of testing, however limited it may be, a *package* of equipment.

A properly equipped airplane usually carries these items, as required:

• *Propeller antiice.* Electrically heated boots that are activated before icing conditions are entered, to prevent ice from forming. Old systems use slingers, which disperse alcohol to the props, but this is seldom seen today.

• *Deice boots.* Pressure from the airplane's vacuum system inflates rubber boots on the leading edges, breaking ice loose. One quarter to ¾ inch of ice should be allowed to build up before activating the boots. This is a *deice* system, designed to remove ice. Continuous operation will not prevent ice formation but rather will form an air cavity under an accumulating ice formation, so that the ice will not break off. The ice should be allowed to build periodically to ½ inch or so between activations. In clear icing, boots can be useless, because the accumulations on the lifting surfaces behind the deiced leading edges remain unaffected by inflation/deflation.

• *Electrically heated windshield.* Alcohol antiice often cannot do the job on serious accumulations. Even when it does work, it can distort forward vision and cloud the windshield as the liquid runs over the surface. That is why instruction manuals often recommend turning the alcohol off on approach. The electrical antiice windshield, with its embedded heating elements, is much better. (Not the removable kind: These heated panels, which rest on the windshield, can permit moisture to accumulate between the windshield and the heated plate.) Most icing-certificated airplanes have heating elements incorporated within the windshield proper. Heated windshields are usually considered to be antiic-ing. The windshield heat is turned on before icing is encoun-tered to prevent ice from forming. Some windshields, however, are designed as deicers, capable of removing ice once it has ac-cumulated. The operating instructions should be checked for procedures.

• *Pitot heat* keeps the airspeed indicator from blockage by ice. Most airlines require that pitot heat be on whenever their air-planes enter *any* cloud. Not a bad practice for general aviation either. Certainly, it should be on before entering any ice cloud.

• *Heated stall-warning vane.* An especially helpful device for low-speed flight in turbulent conditions and clear-ice.

• *Heated fuel vents.* These devices prevent fuel starvation caused by ice plugging the fuel vents. Whether they are needed or not depends on the location of the vents.

• *Ice detector light.* This is simply a light that shines a beam at one of the leading edges to observe ice accretions at night or in poor visibility.

• *Alternate engine-air source.* For use in case induction icing blocks the normal filtered air inlet. Some alternate air doors op-erate manually and some open automatically.

Fly an airplane into icing with only a partial complement of this equipment, and you are asking for trouble. Matters can be-come grim enough even with a certified package of equipment, let alone a few untested elements.

Problems on Landing

Many icing-related accidents occur when iced aircraft stall on approach to landing. To avoid stalling or mushing, keep the power well on, as needed, and make a steep approach at a higher-than-normal airspeed. The first notch of flaps may provide some lift, but further deployment would aggravate the already exces-

sive drag. Lower the gear only when you are sure the aircraft
will reach the runway. Land in a relatively flat attitude and be
willing to accept an overrun. You should also act on the premise
that any attempt to go around could be disastrous.

It seems terribly unjust, but it is true that a pilot doesn't necessarily conquer ice as the wheels touch. Under some conditions, the villain still will pursue him. And as pilot Tom Eggleston
learned one winter as a passenger aboard an Aztec at the conclusion of a flight to upstate New York, the enemy may be lying
in wait on the ground.

At 1,500 feet MSL, we broke through the clouds and began pilotage to our destination. After thanking Albany for their assistance, we
again contacted Unicom at our destination. "Braking is nil," we were
advised. After a short pause, we noted that the OAT was 45 degrees
F and began the landing checklist.

While on downwind, we discussed the Unicom advisory, noting
the frequency of similar conditions due to freezing rain. We took a
close look at the runway for ice glare but could not make a judgment
due to the low ceiling. Our final call to Unicom went unanswered, because the FBO's occupants had all gone outside to watch our landing.
Checking the temperature again, we set up for final, lowered the gear,
and began our approach. The air was so smooth that our final was ef-
fortless. Until the mains touched. Yes, braking was nil.

We had but 3,200 feet in which to produce some fast remedies and
no time for feeling helpless. The strip's hard surface was only 20 feet
wide, and our first move was onto the grass shoulder, which provided
some braking. Next, the flaps were brought up so as to put full weight
on the mains. This allowed more braking, but we were still skidding
badly. As we tried a slight crab for more friction, the Aztec began to
slow up, but the end of the runway had now appeared.

Our last chance lay in a plowed snowbank. We grazed it with a
wingtip, and that proved to be the right touch—we now had control of
our groundspeed, with about 75 feet of runway to spare.

Not until we tied down did the full nature of the ground conditions
hit us. Walking off the apron was nearly impossible. Although the air
temperature was warm, the ground was still frozen. The runway was
a massive hockey rink.

Disregarding a statement like "braking is nil" can quickly make young pilots old.

With so little runway length and width available, the landing should not, of course, have been attempted, however smooth the air or confident the pilot. Finding a more congenial runway at another airport was clearly indicated. However, the pilot's handling of the crisis is instructive, for he managed to get the Aztec under control and stopped with a minimum of damage to men and metal by applying sound principles. He did his best to plant the airplane's weight on the mains and tried to avoid the ice on the runway enough to obtain some slowing friction. Finally, with a crackup looming at the nearing end of the runway, he accepted the necessity for some slowing contact and went about making the best of it. Nothing heroic, just safe.

Such sensible conservatism is the mark of the safe winter pilot, although the best winter pilots usually opt for prevention over self-rescue. In pursuit of survival, from flight planning to tying down, they maintain hard-nosed discipline.

Prescriptions for Winter Protection

Cold-weather operations call for a check of the ignition system, a change to thinner oil, and installation of any special winter equipment—the oil cooler and air intake baffles, for instance. The exhaust/heater system should be inspected for any cracks or poor joints that could allow carbon monoxide to enter the cabin.

As we have seen, be it an Aeronca or an airliner, the airplane must be cleared of ice, snow, or frost, especially the wings, tail surfaces, cowlings, propellers, landing gear, antennas, and windshield. A broom can take off the snow; a warm hangar, covers, or deicing fluid can handle the ice, but be sure to wipe any residual moisture away, lest it refreeze. (Deicing fluid is toxic, so follow the manufacturer's instructions and warnings.)

Check drain holes, air scoops, and control surfaces for ice.

Covers over recessed fuel caps and the pitot tube can prevent moisture from freezing in hard-to-reach crevices. Once more, if you don't see ice but do see water, remember that the liquid can freeze at altitude and create major difficulties.

Preflights in bitter cold carry many temptations to be careless. The best antidote is warm clothing, including comfortable and pliant gloves. Bundle up so that you can conduct the preflight as unhurriedly as if it were a spring day.

When temperatures are at or below freezing, it is wise to preheat the aircraft. A further aid to starting a cold engine is to rotate the prop by hand, which can help to loosen congealed oil. Never handprop unless you are absolutely sure that the key is not in the ignition, the brakes are set, the wheels are chocked or the tail is tied down, the master switch is off, the magnetos are off, the throttle and mixture controls are all back, and no one but you is near the prop. If these measures seem extreme in their redundancy, they are meant to cover the various ways in which airplanes seem to have taken on lives of their own just because someone moved the prop.

Be thoroughly familiar with the manufacturer's cold-weather starting procedure for the type aircraft you are going to fly. What is correct for one engine may not be correct for another.

Once the engine is running, closely watch the oil pressure gauge, keeping in mind that it will probably take longer to reflect a pressure rise than it does in warmer seasons. However, if there is no pressure response after one minute, shut the engine down. The engine may be lacking lubrication.

Taxiing over snow and ice demands a slow speed and a judicious use of the brakes. Steer clear of puddles, to prevent slush from accumulating on the underside of the airplane and interfering with the landing gear or antennas.

Fixed-gear aircraft with wheel fairings are vulnerable to slush accumulating in the housings and freezing there, hindering movement on the ground. Also, the wheels could freeze in flight, leading to trouble on the landing. Many manufacturers recommend removing the wheelpants if slush promises to be a problem. During the preflight, be sure to poke around inside the pants to remove any ice that may be hidden or stuck there. Even if the airplane is preheated, such probing can still find stubborn pieces.

Just as one should be careful taxiing on loose gravel, be wary of taxiing to the runway with a large aircraft close ahead. Prop-blast or jet-blast can blow hard-packed snow or ice into a propeller and damage it.

Check the carburetor heat and alternate air during the runup and always apply *full* carb heat when you check or use it.

During the takeoff run, try to stay in the clearest section of the runway. If there are snowbanks at the sides of the runway, remember that those harmless looking piles can be concrete-hard. They also may mask stiff crosswinds that can surprise you on climbout.

After takeoff, cycle and recycle retractable gear to prevent slush from being trapped in the system and freezing the gear in the wheel wells.

Some experts suggest that during the en route portion of the flight, the pilot should vary the pitch of each constant speed propeller by a few hundred rpm every half hour or so, in order to keep warm oil in the hub.

Because vents are usually kept closed during winter, keep alert for carbon monoxide fumes, which are odorless and colorless. Telltale signs of incipient poisoning are nausea and headache. If these symptoms appear, cross-ventilate the cabin immediately. Periodic cross-ventilation is always advisable.

Plan your landings so that power can be maintained during the descent to keep the engine reasonably warm. Power-off descents in cold weather shorten engine life. So that engine power may be maintained, descend with the landing gear and flaps deployed.

Observe the same caution during the touchdown and rollout as during taxi and takeoff, with special care for icey runway surfaces, snow banks, slush pools, and tricks of the wind.

Try to keep your aircraft hangared overnight, wherever you

may be keeping it. If it can't be sheltered, leave the airplane with the trim controls at the takeoff positions. Furthermore, to prevent a frozen lock from barring you from your own airplane, keep the door unlocked, if circumstances permit.

In olden lore, winter was a time of strange and harmful forces, when the winds did howl and the wolves grew bold, and overnight was best spent near hearth and home. Pilots who fly far in winter understand that. Strange doings still ride on the chilling winds, and in the skies, there can be predators aplenty, as this story by Terence A. Brock illustrates.

That February morning began early for us. It was the last day of a busy East Coast trip, and our aircraft, a cabin-class turboprop, had sat on the ramp in steady rain and near-freezing temperatures every night. We noticed no ice on the airplane during our careful but chilly preflight that morning and departed on schedule for a short hop to Petersburg, Virginia. The aircraft sat on the ramp at Petersburg, enduring the continuing drizzle, until our mid-afternoon departure. No ice was visible during our secondary preflight, so we took off for Norfolk, picked up additional passengers, and started our final leg to Kansas.

The takeoff and climb out of Norfolk were uneventful, although we did pick up some rime before leveling off at our approved altitude of 20,000 feet. We were in the soup immediately after takeoff. Surmising correctly that we would not change altitude for the next four hours, we set the autopilot/flight director to the altitude hold mode and settled back for the long flight home. I recall remarking how smooth the ride was . . . nary a bump or jostle.

About four hours later, 60 miles east of Kansas City, we were ready to start down. Still in the soup, we were instructed by ATC to "descend to and maintain 10,000." I was flying right seat, so I repeated the clearance while observing that the pilot used the pitch control thumbwheel to lower the nose the usual 2 degrees and thus initiate our descent. But the nose did not lower. Instead, the airplane droned on. Inside the cockpit, in rapid succession, the elevator trim wheel spun full nose down, the trim fail warning light glared bright red, and the autopilot promptly kicked off. All the controls were freed except the elevator. It would not budge.

We both suspected that the autopilot's altitude hold mode had failed to release itself, despite the fact that the disconnect light was glowing amber on the panel, so we proceeded to remove all power going to the autopilot. We were certain that our analysis of the problem was correct. The elevator would not simply freeze on us up here at FL 200, at night, in the soup! So we methodically pushed red release buttons, flipped switches, pulled circuit breakers, and disconnected cannon plugs, but the elevator remained immobile. Then we checked for objects that might be lodged, blocking the free travel of the control columns. But we found none. Finally, for want of a better idea, we pushed and pulled on the control wheels with considerable force, but that elevator was unyielding. If we were going to change the pitch attitude of the airplane, it would not be done in the usual way.

Our operator's manual does not say much about flight control malfunctions, but neither do most. Fortunately, the pilot knew his aerodynamics well, and I recalled some wisdom in an article on the subject. He and I decided upon a course of action.

The ATIS reported partial obscuration, a measured 600 overcast, 1 mile in fog, and an OAT of 37 degrees—below minimums for our destination airfield. That should have bothered us, but it did not. We were looking for a much longer runway than the 6,000 feet at home, anyway. I declared an emergency and requested vectors to a long final for the ILS Runway 19 at Kansas City International. ATC's response was prompt, courteous, and efficient.

As we had planned, power reduction gave us a nice pitch-down attitude, and a combination of added power and full up on the elevator trim wheel would level the aircraft. However, we could not raise the nose much above a level attitude even with lots of power. Pulling off all the power caused a significant pitch down, and we did not want to hit the runway nose first—if we found the runway—at the end of our approach. More thinking was clearly needed if we were going to have a successful roundout.

We then decided to use a no-flap approach to facilitate a go-around and to minimize pitch changes. We had decided that, over the numbers, the pilot would pull off power and roll the elevator trim wheel full nose up while I popped out the flaps to the approach position, which should slow our descent and speed while pitching the nose up. We dropped the gear, slowing us to below 160 knots as we lined up on the localizer. A power reduction put us on the glidescope, and the pilot kept us there. I strained my eyes searching the murk for something resembling a runway.

Approach cleared us to land as we neared decision height. The controller had been calling out the changing visibility all during our approach; it was now a quarter mile in fog. Just then, a faint glow of blurry light came into focus. Those flashing lights never looked so good. Over the numbers, we pulled off power and popped out approach flaps. That airplane sat down on the mains so very, very softly that it belied our true predicament to the spectators in the emergency vehicles at the runway's edge.

After clearing the active, we both breathed huge sighs of relief. Then something strange caught our attention. We watched in amazement as the control wheels crept slowly forward until they hit the stops. Somehow, the elevator had released itself, but not until after we had sweated through that no-elevator landing.

After off-loading our passengers and talking to the FAA, we inspected the aircraft. The FAA, the manufacturer, and our own mechanics all examined the aircraft carefully. An inspection of the closed-cable bellcrank system did not reveal the cause of the stuck elevator, but a large chunk of ice fell from the aft access compartment when we opened the door, and standing water was found just below the elevator control horn. An opinion emerged that something, perhaps ice, had held the control cables immobile. The stretch available in the cold cables must have allowed for the limited elevator travel that occurred when we moved the elevator trim handwheel. According to the manufacturer, no other explanation made sense.

Later, I pored over the operator's manual, searching for reassurance that we had done everything by the book to prevent the occurrence of that situation. I came upon this sentence: "During flight, trim tabs and controls should also be exercised periodically to prevent freezing." I showed it to the pilot, confessing that I had never really noticed it before. Neither had he. We mentioned to the manufacturer that the sentence seemed a very significant one and warranted bold print, preceded by the word *Warning*. They disagreed, saying that the sentence was a mistake and did not belong in the operator's manual at all. The aircraft, we were assured, had sufficient drain holes properly placed to eliminate water that might later freeze internal flight control cables. The matter ended at an impasse.

I could not help blaming myself, in retrospect, for not noticing such a potentially significant statement and complying with it. Had we moved the controls occasionally during the climb and long cruise portion of our flight, perhaps the elevator control would have functioned normally; perhaps we would not have put our passengers' lives and our expensive aircraft in jeopardy, and perhaps we would have been spared those long, anxious moments from FL 200 to the runway. Just because it is not in bold print does not mean it is not important.

We began this section on ice with the assertion that of all the hazardous phenomena pilots must face, icing is the most eerie. Like a science fiction alien, ice can creep into the most unlikely places and suddenly strike with telling effect. Even when the pilot is safe by hearth or Holiday Inn, water and cold—like prowling wolves—may conspire to waylay him on the aerial road. Then the pilot will have to use all his ingenuity and knowledge to survive. The pilots of this cold-locked plane did just that and triumphed. Others might not have been so successful.

The battle against ice need not end in defeat. It need not even contain surprises that many pilots have experienced. As we have seen, while not everything about ice—its whereabouts, especially—can be predicted with certainty, the crisis-conscious pilot does have enough forecasting capabilities, ice-combatting equipment, and routes of evasion and escape to improve his odds considerably. As we have also seen, all the antiicing weapons in the world won't save pilots who neglect what they have to know or who literally fly in the face of good sense.

Part Four
SYSTEMS
FAILURES

8
Thrust Busters

The crises we have confronted thus far strike from outside the airplane in clouds and darkness, winds and ice. But there are dangers that threaten like traitors within the walls. They cripple basic systems by which we fly, such as the powerplant, the instruments, and communications. The most immediately demanding is the complex of problems that cause engine failure.

Impact Ice Again

Structural ice can creep into an engine and strangle it. It can build on the leading surfaces of the upper and lower cowling and form, for instance, on the inside of the induction air box, in the first bend aft of the filter, and in the second bend prior to entering the induction manifold runners (FIGURE 14). To many pilots, this process and the terminology that describes it may be mysterious, but the eventual result is a thrust-destroying restriction of the air that reaches the cylinders.

The more familiar air filter can ice over, but because its filtering materials are porous, moisture-laden air normally passes through it rather than solidifying on contact. However, sudden contact with the cold, nonporous metal surfaces of the air box easily causes ice to accumulate. To prevent this, installations, like those shown in Figure 14, nearly always incorporate an in-

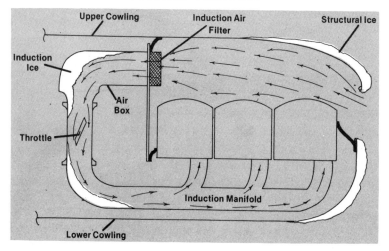

FIGURE 14

duction heat source. On some installations, induction heat is triggered automatically if the air filter is iced over. Some aircraft equipped with an automatic alternate air source also have a manual control. The application of alternate air may create effects similar to those of carburetor heat. If so, the mixture should be leaned enough to restore smooth engine operation and reduce power loss.

Induction icing is rare in fuel-injected and supercharged engines. The compression process of the supercharger heats the air passing through the compressor considerably. However, it is possible to encounter structural, or atmospheric, icing at the induction airscoop and the air filter prior to the compressor. Supercharged installations are therefore usually fitted with an alternate, or heated, air source.

Alternate air should be used with respect, for, with few exceptions, it bypasses the induction filter to enter the induction system. Heating unfiltered air increases the density altitude and thus reduces the power, which, in turn, calls for leaning the mixture.

Ice-Blue Sky

All pilots are aware of carburetor ice, but fatal accidents due
to it still occur with regularity. In training, we are led to believe
that carburetor ice is simply handled, but is it? Pilot Steve Widmer opens some room for doubt:

On this mid-February morning, I planned to fly my Citabria from
Bethel, Alaska, to Mountain Village, on the lower Yukon River. My
passenger, a 14-year-old friend, and I were excited, because for once
the winds were calm and the sky was CAVU. Our takeoff was normal,
and as I climbed into the blue air, I opened my flight plan.

On reaching my cruise altitude of 3,000 feet, I noticed thin fog
patches stretching around the area. I turned northwest. The temperature, which was below zero on the ground, rose to 31 degrees F at
3,000, which I maintained to assist cabin heating, for higher and lower
altitudes offered colder OATs. I could make out the river winding past
the scrub line where the trees gave way to scrub and then to tundra
vegetation.

At about this time, the fog seemed to dissipate below us. I suddenly noticed a slightly different odor in the cabin. It reminded me of
the smell that always occurred when my rear seat heater was initially
opened. As I realized that the rear heater control was already open,
things began to happen fast and furiously. I reached for the carb heat
and checked the controls and instruments. Simultaneously, the engine
sputtered, and the power dropped to 1,200 rpm. The carb heat control
seemed frozen: It reluctantly moved, but as more power was lost, I
returned it to its off stop and began to set up my emergency glide speed.

My altitude began to dwindle surprisingly fast. I worked with the
throttle to get a maximum of 1,500 rpm. I switched the radio through
the frequencies, including 121.5, finally raising the Bethel FSS. I an-
nounced my Mayday, gave my approximate position as 40 miles south
of Mountain Village and, when asked by the FSS, supplied my former
heading. I searched the tundra for a possible landing spot, but the
windblown "potholes" normally seen all over the terrain were nowhere to be found. I chose a frozen bog that seemed long enough to

land in, though I knew that the tires could dig into the snow and flip us.

I was so occupied that when I turned around to announce my landing intentions and instruct my passenger to get his head down between his legs, I was surprised to see tears in his eyes. I realized that his fears were magnified by the cold, wilderness landscape. His tears made me shudder as my responsibility for him hit me like a hammer.

I started to swing out toward an uncoordinated final, again announcing my intentions into the blind, so that *anyone* listening would know we were down. To my surprise, the voice of a local charter service pilot came over the headset. He was somewhere over the tundra. I heard him relay my plans to the FSS, which was out of my reception range, as I glided to 500 feet, about 300 feet above the ground.

I pulled on flaps, putting on the last notch as we neared my target. The vibration from the engine was frightening. I noticed, however, that I seemed to be able to maintain straight-and-level flight at 60 mph indicated. As I balked at what to do next, my situation seemed more tenuous when my passenger pleaded, ''We can make it back.'' I had my doubts, as the engine now fluctuated between 1,200 and 1,700 rpm. At 400 feet, I turned toward a heading that I hoped would take us to the Bethel airport. My turn was shallow to avoid a stall. For the first time, I looked around the plane, and I saw the wing struts shaking mightily under the engine's unknown ailment. Now I broadcast my new hope to ''fly her home.''

My return heading took me directly toward the fog banks I had passed before, only now they were directly in my flight path. I strained upward to 700 feet, passing over the tops with feet to spare. In what seemed an eternity, at 1,000 feet, I saw the old White Alice radar site near Bethel on the horizon.

The vibration was so severe that it was causing the mixture control to slip out. On a hunch, I eased the control to a leaner setting—and as quickly as the power had dropped, the leaning (or something) caused it to rebuild. My joy was overwhelmed by the fear of a recurrence, but the power continued steadily as I hastily began a climb to get all the altitude possible. The instruments were all normal except for a lower cylinder head temperature. I could now prepare for what proved to be a normal landing at Bethel.

What had caused the trouble? Everything seemed to point to carb ice—the 31-degree-F moisture-laden sky would have been perfect for such a condition. With the sky so blue that day, it would have been hard for me to believe such a thing, despite so much instruction warning me about it. Later, I realized how hesitant I had been to apply carb heat at the initial power loss. It turned out that I also had magneto problems, but which factor caused the loss remains unclear. One thing I did learn was that the mere 800 hours in my log may have been enough to prevent panic but not enough to induce me to follow the proper procedure and use carb heat, however blue the sky.

Widmer found one way in which carb heat can sneak up on a pilot. It can also happen to an airplane waiting in moist air to take off. Even when the OAT is in the 60s, the inrushing air can be cooled to below freezing and ice up during takeoff. Even flying in warm climes is no guarantee of protection.

Of Ice and Heat

When sufficiently moist air enters the Venturi section of a normally aspirated engine's carburetor, vaporization causes cooling, and that, along with the accelerated, lower-pressure air at the Venturi tube (a narrowed passage in the carburetor throat), promotes ice formation that can cut the air supply.

Float-type carburetors have the worst icing potential, because fuel is injected ahead of the Venturi, and ice forming downstream of the vaporization area tends to adhere at the worst places for accumulation—the Venturi and the throttle's butterfly valve. Pressure carburetors, in contrast, inject fuel downstream of the Venturi and therefore away from this refrigerated area, lessening the likelihood of icing.

The range of conditions that cause carburetor ice is very wide. Ice can form when OATs range from 10 degrees to 100 degrees F, dewpoints range from 10 degrees to 82 degrees F, and relative humidities are greater than 20 percent. With the right combination of variables, the large temperature drop within the carburetor (as much as 70 degrees F) will cause ice to form.

Note, in FIGURE 15, how ice forms on the throttle valve and carburetor throat below the Venturi. If this continues, power will be lost. The illustration does not depict any ice on the fuel-discharge nozzle or the upper area of the Venturi but shows only the effects of refrigeration-type icing from fuel vaporization. However, ice can accumulate on the discharge nozzle and upper Venturi area, because they are also chilled by the Venturi and vaporization actions. While you can expect carburetor throat temperatures of 60 degrees to 70 degrees below ambient for float-type carburetors operating at cruise power and above, the temperature drop for the pressure-injection carburetor is only about half this amount, as a result of the location of the fuel-discharge nozzle.

Theoretically, the worst icing potential should be under takeoff conditions, and yet *most* ice attacks have been at cruise power

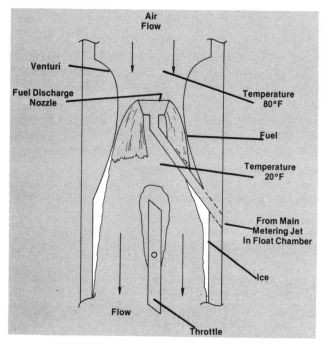

FIGURE 15

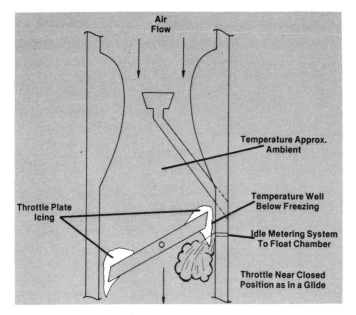

Figure 16

or on glides to landings. Takeoff power is used briefly, and carburetor ice resulting from invisible moisture does not build as rapidly as visible or impact ice. Substantial ice forming from the mechanical process during takeoff usually shows up during climbs. Humidity is the key factor in mechanical or refrigeration icing; damp days of spring, early summer, and fall are the most critical times, because cool, damp air contains more moisture per volume than warm, damp air. Of course, once the OAT descends to 20 degrees F, the chance of mechanical icing from nonvisible moisture falls rapidly.

If sufficient moisture (70 percent or more) is present, ice will form upon contact with the cold throttle plate. This type of carburetor ice—throttle-plate ice—can be very hazardous. From Figure 16, you can see that not much ice is needed to bridge the gap quickly between the throttle valve and the throat walls. Such a condition can freeze the throttle valve to the carburetor throat. When the unwary pilot attempts to open the throttle, it doesn't budge. Using force is more likely to damage the throttle linkage before it breaks the weldlike grip of the ice.

This is the type of icing we are taught to prevent through carb heat and gently gunning the engine during a glide. Like the other forms of mechanical icing, throttle-plate icing is at its maximum potential during cool, damp days. The potential for mechanical icing with carburetor-equipped aircraft is present in ambient temperatures from about 65 degrees to 20 degrees F, for pressure-type carburetors, and 100 degrees to 20 degrees F for float-type.

You should be able to prevent a power failure from carburetor ice if you remember that the temperature drop in pressure carburetors will seldom, if ever, exceed 30 degrees, while it can be as much as 70 degrees for float types, and if you have a reasonably accurate OAT gauge and you are aware of the ambient humidity.

Symptoms and Cures

For fixed-pitch propeller aircraft, the initial symptom is a gradual loss of rpm and airspeed. The second notice usually is increasing engine roughness until the power plant stops firing. The rest is silence.

For constant-speed-prop planes, the governor will keep the rpm constant, but watch for a gradual reduction in the airspeed and MP, followed by worsening roughness and then just the whistling of passing air as you descend.

At the first warning, apply *full* carb heat and lean the mixture, which eliminates heat-induced roughness. A gradual increase of airspeed (and, for fixed-pitch propellers, rpm) will confirm icing. After giving the heat a few minutes to clear the ice, you can verify matters (with constant-speed propellers) by returning the carb heat to full off, reenriching the mixture, and observing a rebuilding MP. Just watching the MP while the carb heat is on is not always accurate for verifying ice. Various carb heat systems have different effects on MP, depending on how much temperature rise and how much ram effect the alternate source negated.

Engine roughness occurs immediately upon heat application, if considerable ice has built, due to extreme mixture changes caused by the heated air and pieces of ice passing into the engine. It can be unnerving suddenly to face roughness before applying heat and still more after. However, don't turn off the heat, lest you do damage. You can kill the engine if you let *partially* melted ice refreeze. Be very careful about using partial heat ever. Significantly, Lycoming advises not using partial heat at all unless your equipment includes a certified carburetor air temperature gauge. Go full hot or cold, so that the ice crystals in dry snow, ice, or ice fog will not melt just enough to *prevent* their flowing harmlessly through the carburetor. Melted ice can refreeze inside the discharge-nozzle area.

Heat must be applied very quickly to prevent the carb heat valve from freezing in the off position, assuring engine failure. Furthermore, carb heat comes from a heat exchanger mounted on the exhaust system. If the engine quits, no heat will be available to help an attempt to restart.

Because the application of heat brings a lighter, less dense flow of air into the engine, you can lean the mixture to raise the engine temperature, and thus the carb heat temperature, for more melting power. Increasing the power setting also will provide more heat. When the initial bout with the ice is over, it is wise to increase the power and lean the mixture in conjunction with carb heat, to forestall another ice buildup. Be cautious, for overleaning can stop the engine, cool the heat, and thus prevent a restart.

Always check the carb heat during run-up, looking for an rpm drop with the heat full on; if there is no drop, investigate. Except in arctic conditions, carb heat should not be used with takeoff or high-power (above 75 percent) settings, because the increase in inducted air temperature erodes the detonation margin designed into the engine and can deplete 15 percent of its power. If you are going to apply carb heat for a long time, as in cruise, lean enough to eliminate overrich-engine roughness; this will also restore much of the power loss caused by the heat. When carb heat is called for in glides to landings and other maneuvers, apply the heat before reducing the power (turning it on when the engine is idling and cooling is pointless); during long glides with the heat on, gun the engine periodically to clear the combustion chambers of the overrich effects of the heat and to generate heat to prevent throttle-plate icing.

If the engine doesn't respond to carb heat, try inducing a backfire with the mixture control. Do this with the carb heat *off* to avoid an engine fire. Retard the mixture until backfiring occurs. If it works, you will be rewarded with a surge of power as the ice is blown out the carburetor.

If you have to go around, apply power before removing carb heat, to eliminate any ice left in the carburetor with combined high power and heat.

Freeze and Refreeze

That ice is like a mischievous *poltergeist* that assumes a multitude of states, pilot David Bielefeld reaffirms:

When Rapid City Tower cleared me for takeoff, I lined up on the centerline, eased in the throttle, and, in good time, lifted off. But somewhere less than 200 feet off the ground, with the end of the runway about to pass beneath me, I began to lose power. The tach needle was below 2,000 rpm.

I was a new pilot then, with 125 hours, and had purchased my Grumman-American Traveler only six months before. I had been flying, and at times delaying, legs of my trip in snow-affected conditions, heading for Billings, Montana, on my way home to Great Falls. The night before my takeoff from Rapid City, a blizzard had passed through, with temperatures down to −25 degrees F and much blowing snow.

By eight the next morning, the air had warmed to a brisk 8 or 10 below. I had done my walk-around while waiting for the line crew to preheat my engine. The storm had blown snow inside the cowling and air intake area, and I had brushed a reasonable amount of it off, knowing that what was left would melt during the preheating.

After the hot-air machine had warmed it, the engine started readily. The oil pressure was okay. I should have been more attentive during the run-up: One or both of the mags dropped well below normal during the check, but after I repeated the check a few times, things looked all right. By the time I realized that I was in trouble, I was out of runway, with no chance to put it down the easy way.

I checked the carburetor heat, fuel tank, and auxiliary pump and searched the panel, trying to think of what else might work. Finally, about half a mile from the end of the runway, I called the tower: "Five-Two-Lima is losing power, returning to land. Can I do a 180 and land on 32?" I didn't think that I could hold altitude through the whole pattern, and the wind was light enough to permit a downwind landing. Besides, a hot landing was the least of my worries.

The tower cleared me. I didn't actually declare an emergency; like so many pilots, I didn't fully accept that this could happen to me. In fact, I think I was too busy to realize then that I was in serious trouble. I desperately continued checking the carb heat and anything else I could think of. I turned the plane around and headed for the runway, but I was losing altitude. The fence posts in the pasture that sloped downhill from the end of the runway looked awfully close. I could even see the barbed wire—an unfriendly place to land.

In fighting to keep the nose up and save precious altitude, I had slowed down. I was getting closer to the end of the blacktop runway, but it seemed to be taking a long time. About 200 yards out, the stall buzzer blared and kept playing—it seemed like the only sound I could hear. I had not been very frightened before, but the buzzer was now doing a job on my nerves.

At last, with 10 or 15 feet of altitude, I reached the end of the blacktop. Then the buzzer delivered on its threat, and I stalled about 10 feet up into a rough landing—but I was down in one piece, and the damned buzzer had finally stopped.

Afterwards the dealer asked me if there had been much snow inside the cowling. Yes, but I had gotten some of it out. The preheat machine was then used to blow hot air into the air intake scoop. Water soon was dripping out. The snow that I had neglected to clear completely from the inside cowling had melted during the preheating, but the water had collected on the air intake screen and frozen. The engine wasn't getting enough air. (Later, the annual inspection showed enough dirt in the screen to add to the problem.) Now, during my preflights, I give the screen special attention.

Any moisture, in whatever form, that is attached to an airplane in very cold air must give the pilot pause.

Under Fire

In the early days of flying, engine fires were commonplace, but today, due to improved technologies and certification standards, we are more fortunate. However, in spite of many built-in precautions that manufacturers take to prevent and confine engine fires, there is an average of fifteen such accidents per year, the bulk of them caused by loose or disconnected fuel lines, catastrophic engine failure, or electrical arcing. The NTSB typically blames "improper maintenance or inspection" for these fires, most of which end with an uncontrolled crash. Approximately one-fourth of all engine-fire accidents are fatal.

• An Aztec's right engine had been overhauled in October, but the airplane was not used until February 3, when the pilot (commercial, instrument, multi-engine rated), accompanied by one passenger, took off from Tamiami Airport, Florida. Ten minutes after takeoff, he told Miami Departure, "Zero-Eight-Yankee's gonna return to Tamiami for a moment. . . . I shut down my right engine for a few minutes—see how that goes—seems like we've got a small fire in there." Four minutes later, the pilot stated that "the fire seems to be out now, but we'd still like to go ahead and land."

Shortly after this conversation, the pilot switched frequencies to the Tamiami FSS Airport Advisory Service, announcing that there had been a fire in the right engine, that it was out, and that he intended to make a single-engine landing. He first asked for Runway 9L but then changed to Runway 27R. Soon after, at 11:49 P.M., the pilot said, "We've got the right side started; we're going to maintain position over the airport."

An FSS employee saw the airplane pass directly over the airport at about 150 feet with a "significant amount" of gray smoke coming from the right engine. At 11:53 P.M., the pilot reported inbound to land on Runway 27R.

A witness saw the airplane in a shallow, descending bank: "The airplane continued its turn and impacted the ground in a left-wing-low configuration. . . . Upon impact, the aircraft came to a dead stop . . . against sand and rubbish piles that had been dumped in the construction area. There was a loud crack (not an explosion), and fire was observed on the extreme right side of the aircraft." He added that within seconds of impact, an explosion occurred on the right side of the airplane, followed by one on the left.

The airplane was destroyed, and both occupants were killed by smoke and carbon monoxide inhalation. The investigation disclosed a maintenance-related cause. The oil line running from the accessory section to the turbocharger centershaft housing is supposed to be secured by a *B* nut, a type of locking nut. This nut was screwed on only finger tight. Since this line carries full engine oil pressure, the loose connection allowed oil to escape from the line and be ignited by the engine's heat. The NTSB cited improper maintenance and inspection, an under-torqued oil line fitting, and the pilot's improper inflight decisions or planning as probable causes.

Fire Fighting

Inflight engine fire procedures are simple and vary little from plane to plane. Check your operating manual for details about your aircraft. *At the first indication* of an engine fire:

• Turn the fuel-selector valve to *Off*, to prevent the flow of fuel beyond the fire wall.

• Move the mixture control to idle cutoff, to stop the flow of fuel to the cylinders (which operate between 200 degrees and 450 degrees F) and shut down the engine.

Some manuals advise reversing this sequence, so check your airplane's specific procedures. After these two steps, there should be little, if any, fuel in the engine compartment.

• Fully retard the throttle.
• Turn all fuel boost pumps off.
• In a multi-engine airplane, feather the propeller, then reconfigure for single-engine flight. In a single, move the propeller control to the low-rpm position, to improve glide performance.
• Turn the magnetos off, to eliminate sparks generated by the magnetos and spark plugs (that is, properly grounded ones).
• Turn the generator or alternator switch off, to prevent the generator or alternator from producing electricity (assuming that these units are properly grounded).
• Turn the cabin heat off. With the cabin-heat valves open, flames can travel through the heating ducts to the cabin. Closing the valves also helps to prevent smoke and toxic fumes from entering the cabin. For dealing with in-cockpit smoke, check the operator's handbook. Essentially, there are two approaches to handling smoke. One holds that fresh-air vents and windows should be opened to allow smoke to escape. The other maintains that opening the windows and vents may intensify a fire in or near the cockpit. Your choice.
• Assess the situation. Is the fire out? If so, *do not attempt a restart,* lest what caused the fire resume action. This is a cardinal rule.
• *If the fire is still burning,* dive to an airspeed, recommended by the manual, to blow the flames out. Diving presents a bitter situation if you are already at a relatively low altitude. You need height to set up a stable forced landing, but *the first priority is*

to put out the fire, so if there is altitude to do so, dive. If necessary, sideslip to direct the flames away from the cabin.

• If you can, transmit Mayday over 121.5 or your current ATC frequency, saying your position, heading, altitude, and intentions, and squawk 7700. Activate your ELT, if possible.

• Look for the best available landing site, but don't be so picky you deprive yourself of the altitude and time to set up a controlled landing. Pilots often become preoccupied with the fire and neglect the forced landing. An engine fire is *two* crises: the fire and getting down—and out—whole.

Among preventive measures, the most worthwhile is maintenance quality control *by the pilot.* If you have any doubts, speak up; have a supervisor make a final check of the engine before you start it. If you still suspect something, get an opinion from another mechanic. When you preflight the engine compartment, don't stop with checking the oil and draining the gascolator. Remove the cowling, if necessary, to check inside for signs of a previous fire or an abnormal concentration of heat. Look for oil and fuel leaks. Check the security of all the fuel-line connections to each cylinder and see if all electrical wiring is properly secured and in good condition. If you do not know what to look for or how to look, ask a mechanic.

Failure to Firewall

You draw back on the power or mixture control to make an adjustment—and it comes out of the panel. This is a crisis such as movie comedies are made of—and pilots' nightmares. In one recent two-year period, fifty-six pilots lived through crises in which throttle assemblies became disconnected. In forty-two of them, the engines went to idle power; in five, to *full* power; in the rest, the throttles froze in an intermediate position. A disturbing number stemmed from broken mixture cables.

• After twenty-five minutes of cruising in his Cessna 150J, a pilot returned to his home field and performed a touch-and-go. The plane handled normally. On a second touch-and-go, when the pilot reduced power at pattern altitude, the throttle control completely left the panel and the power froze at 1,500 rpm. The pilot replaced the control in its housing, and the power went to full 2,650 rpm. The pilot orbited the field at 2,000 for 10 minutes and then descended by applying carburetor heat and leaning the mixture. He entered downwind, but on his attempt to reduce power with the mixture control, the engine began to run rough on base and then quit. He turned straight for the field and tried twice to restart, but the airplane glided into trees about 200 yards short of the runway and was badly damaged. The pilot suffered only minor injuries. Investigators found that the throttle cable had broken inside its housing just forward of the solid rod portion of the throttle control. The broken cable was not deemed detectable by normal inspections.

Military and most high-performance airplanes have safety springs or other restraining devices on their power control assemblies. If a throttle cable fails, they automatically set the power to around 55 percent, enough to maintain level flight and enable a landing. Instead of facing an immediate forced landing, the pilot has only to determine how to reduce the power—as a light-plane pilot must do if the power freezes at an intermediate setting due to a failed throttle.

Carburetor heat can be used to reduce the power, as can the alternate engine-air source. Fly such approaches at a higher-than-normal initial attitude and declare an emergency. When you reach an altitude that assures a good chance of a safe dead-stick landing, you can further reduce the power by alternately killing and restarting the engine with the mixture control (assuming it is still functioning). Remember that once the propeller has stopped windmilling, you will be unable to restart solely with the mixture control; you must move the mixture to full rich and engage the starter. Stay high and delay extending the landing gear or full flaps so that too high a sink rate will not force you to restart at such a critical time.

Turning off the ignition is another way to ready the airplane for a dead-stick landing. Again, if the prop stops windmilling, you will have to engage the starter to attempt a restart and arrest the loss of altitude.

Confusion, Guilt, and Engine Failure

We come now to the problems of engine failure, starting with singles. Pilots, not mechanical problems, are responsible for the majority of power plant failures, with inadequate preflight preparation first on the list, especially when leading to fuel exhaustion. Fuel mismanagement and improper operation of the engine and its controls account for nearly half the engine-out fatalities. Rushed or incomplete preflights wreak havoc, because fuel quantities and contents are not checked, gas caps are not secured, oil levels are overlooked, loose wires and leaks go undetected or unfixed, and run-ups are rushed or not done, so that rough magnetos, abnormal gauge readings, strange noises, or improper tank selections dog the airplane as it careens down the runway. In addition, hurrying pilots make short, intersection takeoffs, which deprive them of runway if they must abort. Too often, the pilot does not know the terrain and obstructions that lie beyond the runway. Many pilots have no abort plan at all.

• A Bonanza made an intersection takeoff, leaving half the available 8,500-foot runway unused behind him. Moments after liftoff, the engine quit. The tower cleared the pilot to turn and land in the reciprocal direction. The aircraft was in a left turn when the nose suddenly dropped, and it crashed in a slightly nose-down, right-wing-down attitude. Fire consumed the airplane, and the three occupants died. Among the causes cited by the NTSB was the pilot's failure "to obtain/maintain flying speed" and that in an "improper emergency procedure," he "attempted a 180 turn back to the airport."

Had this pilot taken the time to use the full runway, he might have had as much as 4,000 feet of it for setting down. Had he thought out a plan, he would have avoided the speed and altitude loss accompanying the steep turn. Rolling off a runway is safer than an uncontrolled crash. If you are going to run off the end, turn the magnetos, fuel, and master switches off and try to steer clear of obstructions, ground looping if you must.

To gain maximum altitude over a short distance, climbouts from short fields or toward obstacles should be at the best-angle-of-climb speed (V_x). Where conditions permit, climbing out at best-*rate* (V_y) offers a higher airspeed and a smaller pitch-down adjustment if the engine dies. Retract the gear as soon as an on-runway landing becomes impossible, for extended gear increases drag and usually reduces the rate of climb.

It is not certain that the engine is more likely to stop if the power is changed on climbout. Pilots have slain their steeds, however, by pulling back on the wrong engine controls. It is prudent to climb at least 500 feet before coming back from takeoff power.

The "There-It-Goes" Plan

When an engine falls, you can lose valuable time in disbelief. Always expect engine failure as you head for liftoff and climbout. If the engine dies, your responsive "there it goes" should reflexively trigger the right action.

If your single engine stops on takeoff or early climbout, do not be tempted to restart; you have too many other tasks to handle to fantasize about that. You will be low and slow, with no reserve of airspeed except what lowering the nose can provide. You will have a very limited distance in which to find a safe touchdown point and little time and few hands to do everything. The fatality rate for low-altitude engine failures is generally high, though it is lower for singles pilots, essentially because single-engine failure forces a simpler response—to land immediately.

Immediate action means, first, lowering the nose to fly the best-glide speed, which you must know from your operator's manual. (In a pinch, go for the normal flaps-up approach speed.) Quickly trim for that speed and select a place to touch down. Knowing from your manual the best-glide-speed distances, judge prudently and head for a clear spot you can reach. The straighter your glide the better. In a 180 back to the runway without power and at low altitude, you will have to gain airspeed, which means giving up altitude. Stretching the glide while turning is begging for a stall/spin. It is possible that the ace of the base, after having often practiced such a maneuver (at a safe altitude), could pull off a gliding return, but is that *really* you? Do you want to bet lives proving it?

Unless you have grossly misjudged the obstacles or the terrain, or a school bus pops into your selected spot, or a better, *closer* spot appears, don't change your mind. Pilots die from abandoning *controlled* landings on acceptable or poor terrain only to crash while reaching for greener pastures. Make your approach high, if possible, to avoid undershooting and hitting low-lying obstacles, *but don't try to grab for altitude or stretch the glide by lifting the nose.* You will only *accelerate your descent* while draining precious airspeed. If you are too high near the spot, slip down or use full flaps.

Since flaps may improve slow-speed maneuverability and lower the stall speed, using one, maybe two notches can help, but remember that flaps also increase drag and decrease gliding distance. A clean airplane is better with a relatively long distance to glide; one or two notches can help if you are on short final; full flaps help a descent and/or quick slow-down. Again, consult the manual or an instructor for the best configuration(s).

An NTSB study offers up and down arguments as to where retractable gear should be on touchdown. Up, because extended gear can collapse into and rupture a fuel tank on impact or roll-out, and retracted gear can make a landing on level, soft terrain, across the furrows in a plowed field, or onto water less damaging, with a reduced chance of a flip-over. Down, because lowered gear may allow a safe rollout over relatively smooth, firm ground, or it can cushion the impact onto rugged ground or trees.

Gear up or down, *fly* the plane all the way onto the ground and along it until it stops. Steer as long as you can, relying mainly on the rudder. While highways and roads can make tempting "runways," consider the dangerous presence of vehicles, road signs, poles, and powerlines as you decide. If you must come down among trees, rocks, poles, or other firm entities, aim between the objects so that the wings will take the impact, not the engine and cabin. Saving the cockpit area is your primary objective. Landing *on* thick vegetation, small trees, or crops can cushion the impact. The wings, gear, belly, and aft fuselage are expendable aids to absorbing the shock. Flare before touching down, but avoid flaring drastically when too high and stalling into a nose-in crash. If the gear is down and you are heading toward a threatening object, immediately retract the wheels or groundloop.

If you can, open the cabin door before touchdown and keep it ajar with a seat belt, Jepp book, manual, bag, or whatever, to prevent its jamming shut if the cabin frame bends. However, do this only if you can also retain full control of the aircraft.

Controls to Fix, Switches to Move

Obviously, once your engine stops, your plate is full and everything must be done swiftly, efficiently, and economically. In an on-takeoff failure, switching tanks and applying carburetor heat probably will be the only restart measures you will have time to apply before concentrating entirely on landing. (If failure occurs high on climbout or in cruise, you still must act quickly, but you will have more recourses for a restart.)

• *Airspeed*: Lower the nose to the best-glide speed, roughly 1.3 times the clean stall speed, for fixed gear, and 1.4 V_{si} for retractables. Set the prop control to low rpm. (If the engine dies while you are *cruising,* you may need to apply a slight back pressure as the nose naturally lowers, in order to slow to best-glide speed and possibly gain a dividend of a hundred or so feet of valuable altitude.)

• *Carburetor heat*: Apply full heat. If structural icing may have caused the failure, select alternate air. The main problem here is that a dead engine soon cools, rendering carb heat ineffective.

• *Fuel selector valve*: If your fuel system draws from one tank at a time, switch to another tank; if you can draw from both tanks, select *Both.* Remember that in banks or uncoordinated flight, fuel tanks that are less than one-third full are apt to unport and cause surging or power loss or both.

• *Auxiliary fuel pump*: On, if you have one. If the stoppage was caused by a failed engine-driven pump, this can restore the flow. You will also have to use the auxiliary pump for a fuel-injected engine any time the fuel flow has been interrupted for a significant period.

• *Mixture*: Full rich. If the mixture was too lean, or if there was a problem in the fuel-metering system, a rich mixture may help a restart.

• *Magnetos*: Try all positions. Ignition in one of the single-magneto switch positions may be better than in *Both*—that is, if the propeller is still windmilling. If the prop has stopped, move the switch to *Start,* to make it rotate; then try the other switch positions.

• *Primer*: In and locked. An engine can stop or become rough if the primer comes out of its locked position, because then the engine draws fuel through the primer instead of through the fuel pumps.

In some designs, it may be possible to use the primer as a crude backup fuel pump, if both the engine-driven and auxiliary, electric pump have failed. That is rare, but in such a case, you could obtain momentary shots of power by pumping the primer manually; on every pump, the engine would start and then die until the next shot of prime. Consult your manual or a mechanic who knows your system to see if this applies.

All this time, at whatever altitude the failure occurs, most of your attention must be on maintaining your best-glide speed and setting up to land. If you are descending from cruise, be diligent in selecting your spot so that you can reach it quickly, preferably with enough altitude (time) to spiral down over it, gauging the wind and setting up your approach as you do. You should have time to announce your emergency over the ATC frequency or 121.5. After you call Mayday-Mayday-Mayday and your number, give your position, aircraft type, and intentions. Squawk 7700 and activate your ELT.

Don't overestimate the benefits of altitude. If you see a distant airfield or particularly desirable landing spot, be conservative in estimating if you can glide that far and set up a safe approach. Consider what you might descend into if you fall short. A nearer, rougher site with a clearer path to it could be a smarter choice.

On short final, along with steering the airplane and avoiding a stall, your objectives are to avoid a postcrash fire and evacuate the plane:

- Check that the seatbelts and shoulder harnesses of all occupants have been put on and secured. If shoulder harnesses lamentably are not available, have your passengers grab their ankles or at least hunch forward.
- Mixture to idle cut off.
- Fuel selector *Off*.
- Magnetos *Off*.
- Unlatch and jam open a cabin door or the canopy, *if you safely can.*

- Master and alternator switches *Off*.
- *Evacuate the aircraft* immediately upon its coming to a stop. Don't pause to retrieve *anything,* and do get well clear, even if no fire is evident.

Turning the mixture and fuel selector off prevents fuel from getting forward of the firewall. With the ignition off, the magnetos will not be able to generate sparks. A master switch that is off will stop the flow of any other electricity through the airplane's systems. The only remaining potential fire sources are sparks from the impact, postimpact sliding, shearing between parts of the plane as they are torn away, or residual heat from the engine. Hence, immediately get everyone away from the plane.

Suddenly Single

Light twins can be described as single-engine aircraft with the power divided between two packages, the loss of one of which removes more than 50 percent of the aircraft's capabilities, while the dead engine becomes an unwanted load and a drag. That can happen with astounding swiftness at the least expected time, as pilot Frank P. Bacci relates:

My 1974 Pressurized Navajo, N7325L, was scheduled for a 6 A.M. departure. The evening before, I went to check on her: She was sparkling. In fact, as I went out the air-stair door, the Navajo's ready-to-fly condition sparked an irresistible urge to go up. My perfunctory, if not lackadaisical, walk-around was followed by a routine start-up. The big Lycoming TIGOs instantly roared to life.

"Palo Alto Tower, Navajo 7325 Lima, taxi, VFR, with the numbers, main ramp, pattern."

"Roger, 25 Lima, taxi Runway 30, altimeter 30.10, expect close right-hand traffic."

As I taxied out to 30, my mind was not really on flying but mainly on business problems. Even as I waited for the engine oil temperature to reach the required 150 degrees before run-up, I wasn't thinking flying.

The run-up was routine. Checklist complete. "Two-Five-Lima, taxi into position and hold." Before I could acknowledge even with a click of the mike, I heard, "Two-Five-Lima, cleared for takeoff, right-hand traffic, straight out to Cooley Landing before crosswind turn, please."

With no real mental preparation, and having gone only through the physical motions, I opened the throttles and thundered down the runway. Unconsciously, I was saying, "What's to worry—I flew her yesterday for four hours, everything A-OK—today's CAVU, 15 knots right down the runway, half fuel, light weight. What could go wrong?"

After liftoff, my mind was still only partially on flying, but something told me all was not right. The usually spectacular climb of the "P" was now less than awesome; a slight ripple in the airframe was a new sensation. Yet my complacent mind had still not grasped the obvious—it wasn't seeking the unexpected as the tower broke in: "Two-Five-Lima, you have smoke and debris trailing from your right engine. What are your conditions and intentions?"

Now I was fully pumped up. At 800 feet, the right engine emitted a loud crackle; black oil sprayed all over the right cockpit window; the oil pressure went instantly to zero; the engine locked up. Everything forward, all up, identify, feather, fuel shut off. I could clearly see flames flare up and then die down along the inside cowling.

Even with everything clean, full power on the left, and all shut down on the right, I knew I was behind the airplane. Apparently, the prop gears had rapidly ground themselves up with the loss of engine oil, so the right engine was not feathering. Light or not, 25 Lima did not want to fly with a big three-bladed prop flat-pitched and not feathering.

"Equipment on the way, 25 Lima. Smoke but no fire showing. Intentions, please?" "I'm straight in for Moffett now and will decide on a turn in to Palo Alto opposite the numbers." My altitude was now 600 feet, my airspeed was at blue line but deteriorating, and I had full power on the left engine. I could not risk gear or flap extension.

Over the cool bay, the airspeed finally settled at the blue line, and I initiated a slow, careful turn toward 2,500-foot Runway 30 at Palo Alto. At about a ¾-mile final, I dropped the gear and immediately regretted it as the airspeed fell rapidly and the yaw became excessive. As I quickly retracted the gear, the tower came on with "Twenty-Five-Lima, check gear, appears to be cycling."

For some reason, at about a quarter-mile final and 200 feet of altitude, the failed engine suddenly feathered. From that point, I had excess power, and the landing was assured.

A catastrophic engine failure can happen at any time. Even the confusing delay in the feathering of the failed engine is less significant than my complacency and unpreparedness for an emergency. Had it been heavy IFR, or had there been any other negative factor, the results could have been fatal. Now, on every takeoff, my last checklist item is a question: "What do I do *when* one goes?" I also now have a reminder printed on my lap board: "Complacency can kill."

A point to notice is that the Navajo's performance improved as the plane passed over a cool bay. For light twins generally, an engine failure in high-density altitude is particularly tricky; if the airplane is heavy, the challenge can become unbeatable. At the heart of the light twin's inherent risks are two elements: poor or nonexistent engine-out climb performance and potential control problems under asymmetric thrust. If the airspeed decays to V_{mc} (minimum control speed with critical engine inoperative), the airplane will begin an uncontrolled turn into the dead engine, even with full rudder deflection opposing the turn. Allow the airspeed to fall below V_{mc} in this asymmetric condition, and in the resultant stall, the airplane will roll inverted. At altitude, a recovery can be initiated by closing the throttle of the good engine and using standard spin-recovery techniques, but this can consume 2,000 feet or more of altitude.

Ignore these factors, and you are asking to be caught unawares by the light twin's ugly aspects. Safe handling of twin-engine emergencies needs keen proficiency and timely, precise decisions throughout the crisis. Let's take a light twin through each of the major phases of a flight, asking, What would you do if an engine failed?

Low-Altitude Recoveries

• *What if an engine fails on the takeoff roll, before you are airborne?*

Retard both throttles immediately and stop straight ahead. You should already have worked out your accelerate/stop distance and determined that you can really stop safely within the length of the runway. Even if you haven't done this vital homework, close the throttles and stop.

• *If an engine quits when you are airborne after V_{mc} plus five knots (or V_{sse}, if your airplane is newer and uses this "safe single-engine" speed), accelerating to V_{yse} with the gear down, and less than 50 feet up?*

Retard both throttles immediately and land straight ahead. Even if you have determined that a climb would be *possible* (under the best circumstances; that is, in a lightly loaded airplane, flying into a headwind with density altitude no factor as you take off over an obstacle-free path), you would be climbing against heavy odds. The altitude loss that comes from retracting the gear and acclerating to V_{xse} (best-single-engine-angle-of-climb speed) or V_{yse} will put you at or near ground level at a high airspeed. Accepting that the airplane probably will be demolished, *you* are more likely to survive if you cut all power and steer to as safe a landing as you can manage. Your choice is between a controlled and a probably uncontrolled crash. Again, adopt the "there-it-goes" approach, expecting a failure and knowing reflexively that instead or risking a stall at great height, you will switch off the ignition, pull the mixtures to idle cutoff, and put the fuel selectors to *Off* as you near touchdown.

• *What would you do if an engine fails as you are climbing and accelerating through V_{xse} or V_{yse}, the gear is in transit or up, and you are reaching 50 feet of altitude?*

It's close-judgment time, when high proficiency is crucial. If your reactions are fast and accurate, you should be able to climb away with little loss of airspeed or altitude as you transition to single-engine climb. This assumes that conditions will allow a single-engine climb. You must know *already* what those conditions are and if your airplane can handle them. If what you know says no, cut the power and head for a landing site. Similarly, if your airspeed control is poor or you take too long to feather the dead engine, you will not climb at all but will descend at about 300 fpm with a windmilling propeller. Since you will be covering about 170 feet of ground per second as you near obstructions or the ground at 90 knots, a poor execution of this procedure will be highly dangerous. The level of your *current* proficiency is thus a critical go-or-no condition.

In calculating the acclerate/go distance for clearing a 50-foot obstacle with a feathered engine after takeoff, the airplane's manufacturer makes the enormous and, in your case, possibly false assumption that you will identify and feather the dead engine as soon as the problem occurs and will then fly the rest of the procedure flawlessly. One flaw, for instance, would be trying even briefly to climb with a windmilling propeller.

Here is an illustration of what can happen if a pilot isn't up to dealing with such a crisis:

• The pilot of this Cessna 421 had 3,000 hours total time, including 600 in multi-engine aircraft and 110 in the 421. His takeoff run was normal, and after liftoff, he retracted the gear. At this time, the left engine began to surge. The pilot attempted a 180 to return to the airport. He did not maintain airspeed and crashed into a field. He later said that he had panicked, had not even tried to identify the cause of the surge, and had not feathered the affected prop, leaned the mixture, or moved the boost pump switch. He single-mindedly tried to get back to the airport. In the attempt, he said, he had allowed the airspeed twice to fall below V_{mc} and was lucky to level the wings before impact. Presumably, with his experience, he could have performed better. As he began his takeoff run, he probably presumed so, too.

Let us say that you have reason to be confident in your present sharpness and that an engine stops about 50 feet up. To obtain the best single-engine climb performance, make sure that, after correcting for the yaw caused by asymmetric thrust by applying generous opposite rudder and identifying, verifying, and feathering the dead engine, you establish a 5-degree bank into the good engine. The rudder ball will lean toward the good engine, but you must resist the urge to kick it all the way back to center. Press just enough rudder to place the ball a quarter of the way into the central area (leave three-quarters of the ball out of center) and leaning toward the good engine. Only by using this "zero-sideslip" technique can you get the single-engine climb performance the manufacturer promised.

Recoveries with an Altitude Cushion

• *What if the engine fails as you are climbing out at* V_{yse}, *the gear is up, and you have more than 50 feet of altitude?*

Correct for the yaw, identify the dead engine (the rudder you are pushing is on the "good engine" side—hence dead foot/dead engine), and verify that it is dead by retarding the suspect engine's throttle. If there is no change in the sound of the engine or in the rudder forces, you have retarded the dead throttle. Now feather the dead prop and bank 5 degrees into the good engine. If you *know* that the conditions are right for it, continue climbing to a safe maneuvering altitude and return to the airport to land. Tell the tower or Unicom what you are doing so as to clear the pattern and obtain assistance on the ground.

At such a time and height, engine failure is not as critical or as potentially dangerous as engine failures earlier and lower, though, again, low proficiency can render you ineffective enough to increase your danger.

• *What about an engine failure en route?*

First, advance both mixtures, both props, *and then* both throttles. The primary thing is to maintain airspeed and altitude. At altitude, you have a cushion on which to troubleshoot the failure, since you don't have to sweat an immediate climb or a heading or yaw problem near the ground at low speed. Switch tanks, turn on the boost pumps, and check the magnetos. Look outside for any sign of fire or escaping oil. If you see smoke or flames, or the bad engine resists resuscitation, immediately feather its prop and secure the powerplant. Pull the mixture to idle cut-off, turn the fuel selector to *Off*, turn off the boost pump, and move the ignition and generator or alternator switch to *Off*. Close the dead engine's cowl flaps.

Running with but one engine, you have one generator or alternator and you must not overload them. Turn off all nonessential electrical equipment and save the system for the landing, including operating the gear and flaps. See chapter 9 for details about electrical conservation.

Baby the good engine, keeping the mixture on the rich side and using only as much power as you need to hold altitude. If the cylinder head temperature edges toward redline, open the cowl flaps. As soon as you can, tell ATC about the problem and head for the nearest airport with a runway long enough to allow some overshoot. If you are IFR and at or near the MEA, be aware of any approaching mandated climbs to avoid terrain or obstructions. Such a consideration takes on special poignancy if the engine failure takes place over terrain that reaches near to your airplane's single-engine service ceiling. If climbing or even maintaining altitude on one engine is impossible or even unlikely, be prepared to make a forced landing.

Back to the Ground

· *How will you handle an engine-out landing in a twin?*

As you would handle an angry grizzly—with care. Unless you are on final, hold altitude by advancing the mixtures, the props, and the throttles. If the engine quits on downwind, identify, verify, feather, and secure the laggard motor and remain at pattern altitude, keeping your pattern close to the runway. Promptly report your problem to the tower or Unicom.

When to lower the gear depends on your airplane's system. If you have a hydraulic-type gear-extension system that runs off one of the engines and that engine has failed, advance the power on the good engine to hold altitude. Then break out of the pattern so that you can pump the gear down manually with only that and maintaining altitude to worry about. It is doubtful that you will be able to pump the emergency handle or turn the crank those thirty to fifty times while safely flying the remaining legs of a single-engine approach. Only desperate need should induce you to try.

For other types of gear-extension systems, you can either lower the gear at your normal downwind gear-extension point or delay lowering the gear until on base. Proponents of extending on downwind argue that by following normal gear-extension procedures, you will be less apt to forget. Others advocate a base-leg extension as allowing conservation of altitude. One takes one's pick. However, the benefits of increasing the drag substantially later, on a leg with only one turn for the runway remaining, are obvious. That assumes, of course, that the pilot is disciplined always to check the gear before turning final.

Maintain blueline airspeed and make your first flap extension only when you are established on final. Keeping your pattern in close and delaying gear and flap extension should help you to make a high, fast, steep approach. Avoid a low, slow, dragged-in approach, because in the landing configuration, a light twin with an inoperative engine will not maintain altitude.

When it looks as though you may touch down at the runway midpoint, put down full flaps and slowly reduce the power on the good engine. If you have put in any rudder trim to counteract the yaw from the dead engine, the rudder pressures will change at this point—expect it. In this configuration, you should land in the normal touchdown zone.

One dictum: Once you have selected full flaps, you are *committed* to land. Let us say that for some reason you come in too high and it looks like you will land on the last third of the runway. In a single-engine landing, your twin will float longer than it ordinarily would when you are near the runway. A feathered prop drags less, hence more float, which can take you off the end of the runway after too high an approach. So be it. You will not be able to go around. It will be much safer to hit the trees at 40 knots than to risk a crash at blueline while you wait for a climb that will not come. The point is that there is no hope for an attempted go-around with full flaps, gear down, and an engine out. Even if you have a single increment of flaps and the gear down, if you push a go-around early, with a hopeful cushion of altitude, you have only a marginal chance of success.

Should you forget to put down the gear, land anyway. The lesser drag of a smooth belly will not be enough to enable a go-around. As you settle in, make sure that both mixtures, the fuel selectors, and the ignition switches are all off—you must hurry. Fortunately, a gear-up landing after engine failure is statistically not a high-fatality accident. In fact, it is pretty common. Again, *you and your passengers* are the objects of survival. As for your aerial steed, if it must scrape on a runway, well, good-bye old paint.

If an engine fails on base, immediately turn toward the runway as you perform the engine-out procedures. Your goal is to arrive at a "key position," halfway down your final approach path, that *may seem* high. As in the previous situation, delay your final flap application and then aim for your normal touchdown point.

The good news accompanying the bad news of a failure on final is that you were intending to descend anyway and are at least heading toward a runway, although that still doesn't make the event fun. Again, run the engine-out procedures, if there is time, but your main job is to stabilize the approach: Maintain directional control and airspeed; make sure that the fuel selector to the affected engine has been shut off in preparation for the landing.

If you are accustomed to making high, steep, blueline approaches, you now can realize why this is a good practice—you are better assured of making the runway, even though the gear and flaps are extended.

There are many reasons why engines fail. Contaminated fuel, misfueling, and reliance on broken or inaccurate fuel gauges are some of several we have not discussed. The main point here is that there are enough causes to justify regarding a ''there-it-goes'' way of thinking as a way of preserving your life.

Simple, prideful neglect causes not only engine failure but other losses as well. We conclude this chapter with a candid and valuable personal revelation by pilot Jerry D. Sanders, who is unusual not in erring but for his willingness to describe his errors to help others to avoid such mistakes:

Two Are Better than One

Sanders and his law partner had purchased a 1965 Cessna Super Skymaster that was in less than mint condition but offered in-line engine-out safety plus fuel economy. On the evening of this flight, Sanders was a new instrument and multi-engine pilot. He and his wife, whom he was to drop off at her father's home in Tallahassee . . .

. . . arrived at the airport. I slipped the precoded plastic cardboard into the slot; the system worked flawlessly. That was the last thing that went right that night. I immediately noticed that the aircraft had not been placed back in its hangar but was still tied down near the radio shop, where technicians were to have worked on it. The radio shop personnel also had not repaired the number-one radio (which was inoperative), and the main tanks had not been refueled after the previous flight. I had used some fuel from the auxiliary tanks, and both main tanks registered slightly over three-quarters full. I knew that our flight from Columbus, Georgia, to Tallahassee would be less than one hour, and from Tallahassee to Pensacola one and a half hours, so I calculated that with over three-quarters in each tank I had ample fuel to make the flight and still have a considerable reserve. At 60-percent power, the Skymaster will go 5.1 hours at 5,000 feet on the main tanks. As it was already getting late and we were behind schedule, I elected not to have the main tanks topped off; I would refuel in Tallahassee.

The weather had been predicted to be marginal VFR from Columbus to Tallahassee, with IFR from there to Pensacola. I had already filed an IFR plan. As we taxied out, the number-two radio seemed to be working adequately; with the weather forecast not too bad, I chose to go.

On climbout, the gear lever refused to go up. It wasn't that the gear failed to retract after I lifted the handle—the handle would not go up. The Skymaster has an electric-over hydraulic system, and the gear handle requires about 3 inches of movement in order to properly indent for the retraction cycle.

After the airplane climbed to about 2,500 feet AGL with the gear still down, the visibility was better than 10 miles, and scattered stratocumulus layers were all that separated the ground from the sky. I noticed that the airspeed had deteriorated only about 15 knots from what it ordinarily would have been at 65-percent power.

I thought about retracting the gear manually, for I had read in the book that it could be done by pumping the gear handle or something. My decision to leave the gear down took about a tenth of a second as I realized our predicament if the gear retracted and then refused to extend. I chose to sacrifice the 15 knots.

After landing at Tallahassee, I taxied innocently to the gas pump to top off the mains and avoid concern during the leg to Pensacola. I had also decided that I would have the gear problem looked into at Pensacola, since gear-down flying had posed no problem. Over the pumps was a sign, "We close at 10 P.M." Although the field operator appeared to live adjacent to the FBO office, no one could be aroused.

My father-in-law greeted us and was watching my preflight for Pensacola. An old Navy aviator, he was interested in these new "modern" airplanes. He remarked that I appeared to have an oil leak on the front engine, and, sure enough, in checking the dip stick, I found I had only slightly over seven quarts in that engine. However, there was no one at the FBO to sell me oil and (naturally) I had none in the plane. We usually flew at eight quarts anyway, and it was a short flight to Pensacola, so I was not particularly concerned. (Looking back, I realize that I was less concerned with the condition of the aircraft because I had no passengers—a ridiculous consideration, for the airplane has to be just as good carrying me alone.)

I elected to take off. I wasn't about to turn back to face a ribbing by my father-in-law. I could just hear him say, "A little oil leak never stopped us in the old days, son." I did notice that the oil pressure on the front engine was a little low during run-up, but it was still in the green, and I was anxious to continue.

I climbed toward my assigned altitude of 8,000 feet. As I passed through 5,000, I saw that the oil pressure on the number-one engine, which I began to monitor very closely, was dropping out of the green. As I reached 6,000, it was out of the green but not at the red line. I began to think, Have I done something wrong? I could now smell the distinctive odor of burning oil, which I assumed to be crankcase oil dripping or splashing on the exhaust manifold.

Deciding that I had better climb no higher, I obtained approval to remain level at 6,000. When I pulled back on the power, the oil pressure seemed to stabilize briefly but then plunged to zero.

I figured that I had two choices: I could continue flying with the oil pressure below the red until something happened to the engine (I foolishly hoped that the trouble was only a malfunctioning oil pressure gauge), or I could feather the front prop. The decision required about one second, for I had heard stories about what occurs when engines freeze in flight due to lack of oil: Pistons go flying through firewalls, and other bad things.

Although I had practiced the engine-out and feathering maneuver several times in a 310, I had never feathered an engine in flight in my Skymaster. The disturbing question was whether it would feather at all, this being such an old bird. I went through the drill of identifying the affected engine and then feathering the propeller. Much to my surprise and pleasure, the front prop immediately stopped, like two butter knives sticking into the wind at a 45-degree angle across my field of vision. I closed the mixture control and bumped the starter until the prop was horizontal. I then turned off the mags and other electrical connections to the front engine.

I immediately noticed a decay in my airspeed and found that an ever higher angle of attack was required to maintain 6,000 feet. I had thought this aircraft was supposed to fly well on either engine! I quickly looked up the single-engine service ceiling; it was 7,500. Was that for either engine? I should have been able to maintain a reasonable cruise speed at that altitude. What was wrong? I suddenly realized that I had three additional pieces of drag sticking into the wind besides the front prop: the malfunctioning landing gear.

As the airspeed decayed and I was unable to hold 6,000, even with 25 inches and 2,500 rpm, I was thinking that nothing could be worse, when the air around me—already quite black—became a sea of ink. I had entered solid IFR. At least Florida is very flat, so I could probably descend without hitting anything. Jacksonville Center cleared me down to 4,000, which would have happened anyway, and I slowly descended with 25 inches and 2,600 rpm. For an instant, I considered declaring an emergency and diverting to a closer field, but the thought of ridicule and embarrassment again impelled me to continue the flight.

As I closely monitored the engine instruments, I noticed that the rear engine was consuming a lot of fuel and that the right main tank, which supplies the rear engine, was below the one-quarter mark. Now I realized that with such a high power setting and so much drag, the rear engine would use much more fuel. I recalled the crossfeed technique, immediately crossfed the left main tank to the rear engine, and then began repeating, ''Check the fuel,'' to remind myself to switch back to the right main for landing.

After being handed off to Pensacola Approach, I was informed on my only good radio that the weather had deteriorated to a ceiling of 200 overcast, with ½ mile in rain and fog, and that I would receive vectors to the ILS approach course. I had previously shot the ILS to minimums at Pensacola in a 182, so I was not unfamiliar with it. This was the only bright spot of the entire evening.

Over the outer marker, I instinctively reached to lower the gear to reduce the airspeed, and I quietly laughed to myself that that would not be necessary. Everything went smoothly through the touchdown.

This bland conclusion to the flight masks a sinister ''might-have-been'': a fatal crash. The loss of an engine can cause so much else to fall below safe operating margins that any multi-engine pilot expecting to be in IFR or darkness should make it a no-compromise rule that all systems must be go or no flight. That may sound wimpish to macho types steeped in ''the daring of the old days,'' but even the deepest drawl can lift an octave or two when its owner is clung to by cloud or is drenched in darkness, and is lugging an engine that won't pull any weight at all. Add dragging gear or other ''preposterous,'' preventable, and prevailing problems, and that controlled basso profundo can rise to a fearful soprano. ''All-go or no-go'' is not the pontification of the purist, it is the spirit of the survivor.

9
Deaf, Dumb, and Partial

The golden rule of instrument flying is, "Trust your instruments as you would have your instruments be faithful unto you." Yet instruments do not always keep the faith. An airplane, after all, is a wonderful combination of technological capabilities flying in formation—but it is, therefore, also a gaggle of glitches capable of anarchy when you most need them:

• A cold front that was running on a northeast-southwest line was situated off the Oregon and northern California coasts, spreading marginal VFR and IFR ceilings and visibilities deep into the coastal mountains. A Sigmet was in effect for occasional moderate turbulence and moderate icing in clouds and precipitation. This corporate pilot (ATP, CFI, with multi-engine, Learjet 23 and 24 ratings; age 28; 6,500 hours total time, 500 in type) and co-pilot of a PA-34 200T Seneca departed the North Bend, Oregon, Municipal Airport at 5:06 P.M. on an IFR flight plan for Hood River, Oregon. Two minutes after takeoff, Seattle Center advised the pilots of a report of moderate rime icing at 11,000 feet (their requested altitude) along their route. The Seneca acknowledged and requested 12,000. At 5:30 P.M., the Seneca had leveled at 12,000, but the pilot reported picking up light rime ice. He immediately requested and was granted clearance to 10,000. Shortly thereafter, the flight was handed off to Portland Approach.

Portland asked the pilot his heading. Fifteen seconds later, the pilot responded, "Ah, Portland, be advised we just lost our gyro, ah, both gyros." Approach asked if he wanted to continue on his route. The pilot said that he did. Three minutes later, Portland asked, "Did you just make a turn to the right?" "Ah, probably. I'm not really sure here. I gotta hold her steady for a second, [then] I'll tell you what the heading is."

The pilot was subsequently given no-gyro turns to avoid the high terrain near Mount Hood. The pilot requested no-gyro vectors to The Dalles, Oregon, and a clearance to the lowest permissible altitude. He was cleared to 7,000 feet—the minimum vectoring altitude—and was expecting to shoot an instrument approach to The Dalles Airport.

The controller advised that "the Flight Service Station is closed now. You can shoot the approach if you want; however, they do not have an altimeter setting for you from The Dalles, and the present weather is a measured ceiling 1,900 overcast." The pilot replied that he would continue to the original destination. At 6:01 P.M., though, he requested no-gyro vectors to the ILS 10 Right approach at Portland, where the weather was a measured ceiling of 1,600 overcast, visibility 4 miles in light rain and fog. While issuing vectors, Approach asked if the airplane was experiencing any problems besides the gyro loss. The pilot answered, "We can't get the ice off the wings."

As the Seneca drew nearer to the ILS approach course, Approach cleared a descent to 6,000 feet. The pilot immediately reported severe turbulence and requested lower, but was refused due to high terrain. A minute later, all contact was lost with the aircraft approximately 22 miles northeast of the airport.

The wreckage was found two days later. The airplane had crashed on the side of a ridge in a near-vertical, nose-down attitude. Both pilots had been killed on impact. While examination of the right-engine vacuum pump was impossible, investigation revealed that the drive shaft of the left-engine pump had sheared off. The NTSB cited failure of the vacuum system as one of the probable accident causes, with accumulation of airframe ice, as well as low ceilings, rain, and turbulence, contributing factors.

Flying against such adversaries, these pilots must constantly have been trying to catch up with the situation. Reading a swirling magnetic compass while trying to hold the airplane steady in turbulence and in the blind could in itself have been a nearly impossible task. This accident illustrates why gyro failures, while they are *relatively* rare statistically, are among the most lethal crises an IFR pilot may face.

We will examine this problem along with two related ones: loss of altimeter and airspeed indications when the pitot-static system is lost, and the loss of communications and other aids through electrical failure.

Partial Preparation for Partial-Panel

What to do when the instrument panel becomes a mere shadow of its former self is only briefly touched upon in instrument training. Partial-panel drill time averages two hours, and many IFR students fly not a single partial-panel approach or recovery from unusual attitudes. Pilots consequently have become over-dependent on their pneumatic systems for heading and attitude information. Spoiled by the gyro instruments' accuracy, we tend to become awkward, sluggish, or even confused by forced, sole reliance on other instruments and "old-fashioned" basics of instrument flight—needle, ball, and airspeed. For instance, studies of scan patterns show that novices and veterans alike spend as much as 70 percent of their scan time on the attitude indicator or DG. When the air pumps that drive these instruments fail, inaccuracy, bewilderment, and even panic may ensue. In VFR, gyro loss does not pose much of a problem, but in IFR conditions, a lack of partial-panel proficiency can dangerously compound the pilot's already high work load. In one reported accident, a 22,000-hour airline pilot took off in a Cessna 182 one dark night, climbed to 500 feet, and then made a slow, power-on, descending turn into the Pacific Ocean, having obeyed his failed AI to impact.

A failed gyro instrument usually dies quietly, with no flags or lights, piling on deceptive information as the spinning wheel winds down from its normal operating speed of 24,000 rpm. Only by maintaining an adequate scan of the other instruments can you suspect what you are told by the AI and/or DG when that happens.

How They Work and Fail

Pneumatic systems come in two varieties: (1) Vacuum pumps move air by sucking it through the pneumatic plumbing; (2) pressure pumps move air by blowing it through the system. Most of the light singles we fly have vacuum pump systems. Vacuum pumps are light and cost relatively little to replace when traded in. Unfortunately, they are prone to failure. The two major vacuum pump manufacturers warrant them for one year or 1,000 hours, whichever comes first, but the evidence suggests that most pumps will last no longer than 500 hours. Pressure pumps have an even shorter life expectancy, 400 hours, because they work harder. They move air faster, which is why they are installed on singles and twins with deice boots and pressurized cabins requiring inflatable door seals. They usually are installed on airplanes designed for flight at higher altitudes. The higher it is, the thinner is the air. A pneumatic pump compensates for lower air density by pumping more air. You can increase the pumping capacity of a vacuum pump at altitude by increasing the rpm, but this overheats the pump and shortens its lifetime even more.

Even though many airplanes equipped with deice boots, hot props, and windshield heaters are not certificated for flight into known icing, pilots of multi-engine planes with dual pneumatic pumps and inflatable boots often are lulled into complacency by thoughts of system redundancy. An icing encounter in such a craft can be faced with some security options in searching for a way out of the ice—as long as things are working properly. However, a pneumatic system failure in icing conditions is a major hazard, for the same pumps supply air for the gyro instruments and for inflating the leading-edge boots. In fact, these dual demands can instigate failure as ice accumulation begins. The Seneca pilot's complaint that ''I can't get the ice off the wings'' reflects the consequences.

Failure Begins on the Ground

Do not undertake IFR flight if you lack complete confidence in your pneumatic system and gyro instruments as a result of these checks:

• You should know the maintenance history of your aircraft and its systems. If you are renting, look at the maintenance records to determine how long the pumps have been in service. If the vacuum pump is more than 500 hours old or the pressure pump more than 200, be wary. Determine also if the system's filters have been changed at the recommended intervals, and more often if you operate in a dusty or polluted environment. (Smoking should be prohibited in cockpits; tars contaminate gyro instruments badly.)

• Look for low vacuum- or pressure-gauge readings soon after you start the engine. Check the owner's manual for the acceptable range. During the flight, regularly monitor the gauge, for a pattern of consistently lower readings over a succession of flights can indicate a pump about to fail. During flight, at the first hint of erratic gyro instrument indications, look immediately to the gauge for signs of system illness.

• On the way to the active, beware of the AI's describing more than a 5-degree bank during taxi turns. There should be no instrument vibrations, and the AI should be fully erect after five minutes, for a vacuum gyro, and three for an electrically driven one. After engine start, set the DG by the magnetic compass and check for excessive precession—more than 3 degrees of error within fifteen minutes. During the run-up, check the DG again and reset it, if necessary. If the card keeps turning after you un-cage the gyro and turn the knob, consider the instrument to be in rebellion. When in position on the active, check that the DG corresponds closely to the runway heading.

Being Partial with Your Panel

If you have determined that the AI and DG have had it, you now must become completely partial to the other instruments. In fact, block out the gyro gauges with paper or other objects—rubber or sponge coasters work nicely. Where the AI has been your prime source on attitude, you must now look to the turn-and-bank (or turn-and-slip or turn coordinator) and the pitot-static instruments for close consultation.

Your panel analysis will now demand a close evaluation of *trends*. The ASI, altimeter, and VSI take a few seconds to fully react—they show changes that have been developing from control inputs, not what is immediately happening. Take that into account or you will soon futilely be chasing the needles. Your control inputs should be small and aimed at adjusting for unwanted trends. If, for example, your normal cruise speed is 150 knots but the ASI is nudging 200, do not haul back on the yoke until the needle returns to 150. Rearing back will cause a steep climb attitude and an accelerating *rate* of airspeed decrease, so that when the needle reaches 150, you could be much slower.

If the airspeed is increasing to, say, 200 knots, brink the yoke back gently and check the altimeter and VSI for further indications that you are leveling. Hold light back pressure as the airspeed needle slows to a stop and recheck the altimeter and VSI to confirm level flight. To return to your assigned altitude, pull the yoke lightly and, by the VSI, establish a shallow rate of climb, say 300 fpm tops, letting the airspeed bleed a bit, but not too much. If you must climb more than a few hundred feet, go to climb power and set up a 500-fpm rate of climb, and level by reference first to the altimeter and then the ASI to establish height and cruise airspeed.

To eliminate banking, coordinated light aileron and rudder pressures can center the turn-and-bank needle. Fine heading corrections can be made with light rudder. In fact, in most righting situations, the rudder is a better friend than the ailerons, unless the bank angle is large; then, coordinated aileron support will be needed. In the case of a spin—shown on a turn coordinator by the little airplane's banking (in truth, *yawing*), apply hard opposite rudder to stop the turn, with ailerons centered to level the wings. The point is, be a conservative investor in control inputs and *play the trends* by targeting sensible rates of acceleration, deceleration, climb, descent, roll, and turn.

Power Power

Many pilots recommend easing the aircraft into all climbs and descents by using the throttle and tachometer, disturbing the yoke as little as possible once you have trimmed for a normal cruising speed. Using this method, you can level at the desired altitude by resetting the power, which requires little change in trim and relieves the work load. This technique is efficient if you know specifically what power settings to use. It can magnify the load to descend partial-panel on an approach, experimenting with the pitch and power to obtain the right airspeed. On a VFR trip or during practice, work out the rpm or MP numbers for your airplane in various flight regimes, for the speeds you use in climb, cruise, and approach. This is as important as knowing your V_x, V_y, flap extension, gear operation, maneuvering speed, and other significant velocities.

If you lose an instrument, you must tell ATC as soon as possible. If you are in cloud, request special handling if you need it, and if you feel that you are in an emergency, declare it. If the ceilings are high enough and you are uncomfortable with partial panel, let ATC know that you wish to descend to VFR. Try to postpone vectoring until you are down to where you have an outside horizon.

No-Gyro Procedures

If all the airports within range are IFR, ask for clearance to the nearest one with an airport surveillance radar (ASR), or no-gyro, approach, during which Approach Control will monitor your flight path and provide you with headings and turns to the final approach course. If you don't have the ASR approach plate, the controller will provide the information, as well as your distance from the runway during the approach.

On a no-gyro approach, the controller will tell you when to start each turn (at standard rate), pause while you turn, and tell you when to stop turning. Once you are established on the final approach course, all turns should be at half standard rate (1½ degrees per second).

Some military installations can provide a gyroless pilot with a precision approach radar (PAR) procedure (once called a ground control approach, or GCA). This combines the features of an ASR with descent guidance along a radar-monitored glideslope. (ILS and PAR are the only precision approaches in the IFR repertory.) A PAR can take you down to Category II minimums (100 feet above the touchdown zone, with ¼-mile visibility), if the situation warrants. During a PAR approach, the controller continually will advise you of your azimuth and elevation. When you are established on the final approach course, you are expected to execute a missed approach if communication with the controller is lost for more than five seconds. By contrast, on the final segment of an ASR approach, you must fly the miss if you lose contact after 15 seconds.

With the DG lost, relying on the magnetic compass for turns and heading information is necessary. It is also potentially frustrating—because the magnetic compass, dominated by the earth's magnetic field, has curious habits. When you turn from a northerly heading, its response lags; when you turn from a southerly heading, the compass hurries past the target heading. On easterly and westerly headings, the compass remains accurate if the airspeed is constant. So if you are on partial panel, try to land on an east-west runway. As the Seneca crew experienced, in turbulence, a magnetic compass stubbornly swings about. To compensate, you can hold heading by keeping the turn-and-bank needle centered or the turn coordinator's wings level, with the ball in the middle as you average out the compass's fluctuations. Admittedly, it won't be easy.

Facing such handicaps, you will have to be coordinated, observant, and precise about details to succeed on partial panel. The turn-and-bank or turn coordinator will be your primary guide horizontally. Without the direct bank information of the AI, you must keep your turns coordinated by needle and ball. The turn needle displays the direction and rate of the *turn;* the turn coordinator indicates the rate of *roll;* remember that when you roll out of a turn, the turn indicator will suggest that you are banking in the opposite direction. That is why using the rudder for control and the ball for guidance is essential.

A standard-rate turn is made at 3 degrees per second. To turn to a new heading accurately, divide the difference between your present and target heading by three—that answer will be the number of seconds to spend turning, *at standard rate*. For instance, from 090 to 060 degrees is a turn of 30 degrees, which divided by 3 seconds equals 10 *seconds* of turning. Unless requested differently by ATC, always turn the shortest way; for directional and arithmetical help you can use the ADF or VOR compass rose.

No Alternate Static Source

If you are without gyros, the pitot-static system can well be your lifesaver. Your preflight must therefore include a thorough check of the pitot tube and the static-air port(s) for blockage (one pilot found his static port painted over) and for working pitot heat. Turn on the pitot heat when you are about to enter cloud. There are other considerations to keep in mind regarding this system. Why is related by pilot Robert T. Styer in his account of flying his Cessna 172 from Gastonia, North Carolina, IFR to Florida:

The first half of our trip was pleasant. The flight proceeded nicely. I reported leaving 2,000 for our assigned 4,000 feet. In another twenty minutes, I was thinking about how well I was remaining precisely at 4,000, but I was puzzled as to why my airspeed seemed to wander between 105 and 120 mph. A second clue that all was not well was my VSI's jumping up and down like a band leader's baton. The altimeter stayed still on 4,000 feet.

I quickly reviewed what I had learned about partial-panel work under the hood. This situation was quite different. During training, when my instructor would suddenly slap a piece of cardboard or a rubber sink stopper over one of my instruments, I immediately knew which gauge was supposed to be inoperative. It was easy to ignore the stopper and concentrate on the good instruments. Now several instruments were providing contradictory information.

"Charlotte Approach, this is 22L. I believe I have a small problem with my altimeter system. I'm not sure how serious it is, but my altimeter seems to be stuck on 4,000, and my vertical speed is jumping all over the place." "Roger, 22L, I'll advise Columbia Approach Control of your difficulty—contact Columbia now on 118.2."

"Columbia Approach, this is 22L, with you at 4,000." No answer. "Columbia Approach, this is 22L, radio check. I'm with you at 4,000, I think. . . ." I wasn't sure I was "with" anybody, and the 4,000 was rapidly becoming questionable. I looked at my wife, Judy. She was silent, white-knuckled, and detecting my mounting discomfort. I called again, with no results. Charlotte advised me to keep trying—I was probably still a little out of range.

Suddenly, "N122L, this is Piedmont 452. We're in contact with Columbia and can relay." "Thank you. I'm not sure I know my precise altitude. Please advise Columbia that I am probably close to 4,000 feet, but I wouldn't bet on it. Do you know where the top of this soup is?"

"Roger, Columbia understands your situation and is keeping traffic well clear of you. The cloud tops are at 17,000 feet. What's your aircraft type?" "Cessna 172." We both knew that escape was not up.

Then, with Columbia's concurrence through my relay, I attempted to break the altimeter loose by abrupt up and down maneuvers, primarily using my airspeed indicator and artificial horizon to guide me. Eventually the maneuvers broke the needle loose, but it then stuck at various altitudes. I had no idea how high I was above the ground. My fear was shared by Judy, who, I later learned, had interpreted my maneuvers to mean that I had lost control of the airplane.

My Piedmont friends suggested that if I didn't have an alternate static source (which I didn't), I should consider breaking the glass on my VSI for an alternate source of air pressure. Fortunately for Judy, I declined. She had not heard the suggestion and would have become convinced that I had lost my senses, were I to assault the panel with the blunt end of a screwdriver. I made a mental note to install an alternate source, if we were lucky enough to pull out of this mess.

We finally made contact with Columbia Approach, and, yes, we all agreed that the most important thing to do was to figure out a way to get us safely on the ground as soon as possible. Columbia consulted with some local Skyhawk owners and worked out a couple of beautiful plans to get us down. Their diagnosis was that water or dirt probably had entered the static system.

Plan A was to vector me to 10 miles from Columbia Metro Airport, put me on the localizer for an ILS, and then let me fly the localizer inbound until (we hoped) I would intercept the glideslope at a precalculated altitude ranging from 2,000 to 5,000 feet. If, during the approach, we should find more serious problems, I would fly a missed approach away from the airport area and move on to Plan B and the nearest Air Force Base to try a PAR approach. Both plans sounded great. *Anything* sounded great, especially those reassuring voices in the Columbia radar room. The thought of totally losing communications crossed my mind, but I tossed it out as unproductive.

The approach on the localizer, a lengthy and weary process, went smoothly. Columbia kept me on a discrete voice circuit, which eliminated extra cockpit work for my sweaty hands. Finally my glideslope needle came alive! I was obviously below the electronic glideslope, which matched a calculation that I was somewhere near 3,000 feet. As it turned out, the altimeter was indicating approximately 600 feet off at that altitude. We broke out of the overcast immediately before crossing the middle marker and uncomfortably close to decision height. With relief we spotted several rows of bright runway lights winking in the murk. I think I mumbled into the mike, "I love you guys."

Much of what this pilot did in conjunction with the advice of others should be known to a pilot prior to suffering a pitot-static problem. Of course, one kind of help that seems like a luxury but isn't would be a spare hand-held altimeter. These instruments are inexpensive and independent of the airplane's pitot-static system, have adjustable settings like those of panel-mounted instruments, and are accurate to within 100 feet or less.

If you are IFR, you must, by regulation, inform ATC of the loss of any required instrument. Don't try to fix the thing first to spare the controllers. They won't be relieved to discover that you've been wandering about IFR without knowing your altitude. Remember that the altitude encoder fails if the altimeter dies.

It was later established that Styer's system was contaminated. Yet a faulty instrument may be a lone problem. Altimeters, for instance, are generally kept "loose" by aircraft vibrations, but dirt or wear can cause a needle to stick or uselessly hang. If a needle sticks, try tapping firmly on the instrument face to jar it loose.

Especially if you fly IFR, to tolerate the lack of an alternate static air source is foolish. It is also senseless not to know how to work one you have. For owner or renter, ignorance is no excuse.

This pilot's unwillingness to break open the VSI for fear of further scaring his passenger violated the first rule of emergency survival: Get out of the emergency; fly the airplane. He had time to explain what he needed to do. In any case, he should have "attacked" the VSI, whatever his passenger's feelings, for a shaken *surviving* passenger is better than the alternative. Before doing that, nevertheless, determine that the remedy does not lie elsewhere, say, in removing ice blockage of a static source in the pitot tube, where such holes are often located. If the pitot heat is not on, activate it and give the heat a chance to remove the ice.

It is important to know the pitot-static instruments and how they go wrong. For example, the ASI responds differently under various circumstances. If its pitot tube is blocked, as an airplane climbs, the speed will *seem to increase;* a descent will *show* a slowing. Such confusion has led to one highly experienced flight crew's raising the nose of their jet airliner ever higher as they fixated on an accelerating-airspeed indication and the jet kept climbing. This continued through the ''surprising'' stall and crash.

If a static source is blocked, the ASI will become inaccurate or overly sensitive. If the pilot and static sources of information are both blocked, the system will ''freeze'' the ASI, altimeter, and VSI indications. The altimeter and VSI are not affected by pitot tube blockage, of course, but a loss of one or both static sources will lead to inaccuracy and supersensitivity in turbulence and a freezing of the instrument indications.

If the altimeter fails, keep in mind that your manifold pressure gauge (not the tachometer) is, in effect, a barometer. To use it that way, keep the prop pitch and power setting steady. Then, if you climb more than a minor amount, the MP will decrease; descent causes higher MP.

Speed Signs

If you lose the ASI, remember that power plus attitude equals performance. If the power is held at a cruise setting and the pitch is level, the aircraft will maintain its trim airspeed. Again, to prepare against an ASI emergency, know your plane's proper power settings for the various regimes of flight. If you still have your altimeter and VSI, all the better, but even if you lose them, if you retain the attitude and power indicators, you can work from what you know (power and attitude settings) to come safely close to what you cannot see (the airspeed).

In such a case, the VSI becomes especially useful for climbing and descending, even if you lack an altimeter. Set the power and attitude as your knowledge of the airplane dictates and check the rate of ascent or descent indicated on the VSI, allowing a few seconds for the rate to be established. (The VSI will immediately indicate *if* you are climbing or descending.) If you are descending a bit too rapidly, gradually bring the nose up until you obtain the rate you want. If you enter a spin or steep dive, quickly bring back *the power* before raising the nose. In a climb at full power, as is the case with most lightplanes climbing more than a few hundred feet, control the ascent *rate* by pitch. An excessive rate can induce a stall.

The airspeed affects the prop speed in fixed-pitch airplanes. The power setting may be constant, but a faster airspeed will increase the rpm, and slowing will decrease it.

What if you lose your ASI and The Great Murphy Upstairs also kills the engine of your single? The pitch setting then becomes critical. You should know where the nose dot rests on the AI and what the VSI shows when you are at best glide speed. Use the altimeter, if you still have it, but your best tactic is to set up the best-glide-speed attitude, keep pitch and bank adjustments slight and shallow, be ready to extend the flaps to lower the stall speed, and prepare for landing.

Gray Areas

We come now to another IFR crisis that plants fear in the hearts of pilots, again the work of The Great Murphy, electrical failure. A sample case:

Pilot Robert Harrison was making a routine IFR flight from

central Texas to Georgia. Because the nearest telephone was 20 miles from his noncontrolled home airport, he had to rush to get his clearance, drive to his airplane, and do his preflight to beat his looming clearance void time.

. . . Invariably on such occasions, my Debonaire makes an issue over starting. The battery had to be jumped, and by the time I taxied out, I was several minutes behind schedule. Nevertheless, as I rolled to the end of Runway 35 for takeoff, I performed what I thought was my customary IFR predeparture check. (As it turned out, I omitted one item.) Everything seemed in order as I released the brakes one minute before void time. It was ideal instrument weather—soft, wet clouds.

The first hint that all was not right came when the DME, an old windshield-wiper type, went hunting, as it periodically did. After some half-hearted attempts to lock it on, I switched it off. Good riddance, less battery drain. Fifteen minutes later, Houston Center called to say that my radar contact had been lost. This, too, was usual, for I was in an area of north central Texas where the remote facilities were widely separated and contact was often lost. I reset the transponder a few times, and we decided to let Fort Worth Center worry about it later. However, even after I came well within range, Fort Worth was not receiving my squawk, and now the CDI was waggling, as if a trifle unsure of itself. Then the flag began to *wave* at me.

Why hadn't I noticed before that I was in the grip of an electrical failure? There seemed to be a reasonable explanation for everything that was going on—or off—for it had all happened often before. Only much later would I look closely enough at the ammeter to observe that the needle was pointing straight up, rather than about a millimeter to the right, where it should have been.

Now, as I flew over northern Louisiana, I recognized the nature of the problem. I quickly turned off everything but one nav and one com and requested a diversion to Shreveport. I was immediately given a vector to the ILS course. Things now seemed moderately okay. This was, after all, only a generator problem that could quickly be set right on the ground. At this time, the nav receiver died. I tried the other. Dead. I shut them both down.

Thumbing rapidly through my approach plates, I found that Shreveport had surveillance radar, so I explained my difficulty to Approach, asked for an ASR, and declared an emergency. The controller promptly cleared me. His last words were "Fly heading 090; descend and maintain 3,000."

Time passed slowly and quietly. As I descended through 6,000, it struck me that these Louisiana controllers were laconic chaps, not given to idle chatter. After another minute, I decided to break radio silence. Nothing. Not even a transmit light on my com, nor, I now noticed, a gear or flap light to brighten the panel. At last I was tasting complete electrical failure.

I tried to remember what the *AIM* says about such a situation but could not recall the problem being touched upon. One thing was certain: I had no intention of burning off my fuel on a heading of 90 degrees at 3,000 feet when, according to the area summaries, eastern Oklahoma was still marginal VFR. So I leveled at 4,500 feet and took up a northwesterly heading, assuming that I would be least likely to meet another aircraft at a VFR westbound altitude, and began searching for a hole. The situation was still far from critical. I had almost three hours of fuel left at low cruise—enough to take me to Kansas, if need be.

The clouds grew brighter, and I came to a large hole through which the earth could be seen. I spiraled through it and leveled beneath the cloud bases at about 500 feet. The episode now went from high adventure to low comedy. Safely out of the IFR emergency and in full view of farms, roads, and houses, I suddenly found that I was lost. I knew that I was somewhere west of Shreveport, but I did not have a Sectional for the area. I had to revert to the original IFR—I followed rails from village to village until I came to a town with an airport. As a paved runway with "Atlanta" emblazoned on it appeared, I swung toward it, pulled down the gear handle, and simultaneously realized that if I lacked the electricity to light a bulb, I certainly didn't have enough to operate a gear motor.

The next minute or so was full of instruction. First, I learned that to fly a Debonaire straight and level while operating the emergency gear crank, which is located on the floor behind the front seats, one must have either the reach of a gibbon or the agility of a circus acrobat. To be fully appreciated, the feat must be performed while one is skimming beneath a ragged cloud deck at 400 feet above the ground, and it is best accomplished by diving for the gear handle, cranking furiously for a few seconds and then popping back up to see how the flight is progressing, before going below again. At length, I decided that the gear must be down and hauled myself upright. But the nose gear logo did not quite center in the window beneath the power quadrant. So it was back to the mine, find the strength for one more turn of the crank, and see the logo line up perfectly.

This took place on final. Somewhat uncertain about the status of the gear, I gingerly felt for the runway, like a fat lady settling onto a camp stool. Possibly because it had my complete, undivided attention, the touchdown was flawless but punctuated by a chirp, chirp, *bang*— the left main tire blowing out. Full right rudder kept me on the runway for a while, until near the end of the rollout, when I wandered off into the grass.

The final ignominy came the next morning. As I climbed into the cockpit, I saw behind my left shoulder my ELT, complete with microphone jack. I could have used it to inform Shreveport of my intentions when my transmitter failed, saving me from having to explain, after the landing, my deviation from my assigned clearance. I simply had not thought of it at the time.

The Silent Surprise

Pilots are often startled over electrical failures that have been hours in the making. Failure to scan the ammeter is common; remarkably, so is failure to notice a low-voltage light. A series of instrument or device failures is often regarded event-by-event instead of as a harbinger of total blackout. This is critically important in IFR, when a blackout leaves the airplane unable to hear, communicate, and navigate—deaf, dumb, and partially blind. Reducing an electronic crisis to workable proportions demands recognizing the problem, troubleshooting for its nature (alternator or generator failure? drained battery? something else?), and immediately reducing the drain on the battery by taking nonessential equipment off line. Yet that may not end the crisis. Knowing the quickest way to VFR may still be necessary.

A pilot who chooses or is forced to remain IFR in this condition needs even more knowledge. Pilot John V. Dean, a former naval aviator and a veteran of more than forty-five years and 6,800 hours of flying, lays bare what can happen when an electrical problem is slighted until it becomes a crisis:

Dean's airplane was a Cessna P337, on a trip to northern Missouri from Spokane, Washington. Departure was at 3 P.M. Over Colorado, one of Dean's two alternators failed, but he was concerned only about the loss of redundancy. The airport at Kansas City could only refuel him, so he planned to take care of the alternator in Chicago, but circumstances again dictated otherwise. On the morning of his flight back to Spokane

. . . the weather took a dramatic turn: a solid, low overcast, forecast to be layered to 25,000 feet. It was spitting snow locally, with heavier snow reported to the west and strong northwesterly winds. Not promising, but I surprisingly found calm air, with rare traces of ice.

At Great Falls, the situation worsened. Daylight was gone, and it was −13° F on the ground. The weather to the west was reported adverse, and headwinds were forecast for 60 knots at FL 180, the altitude required to get above the cloud deck from Great Falls to Mullan Pass. The tops were reported lower at Spokane; the forecast posed the possibility of moderate icing and occasional heavy, blowing snow. However, conditions were expected to improve by my ETA. Since I could proceed all the way on top, have a look, and use Great Falls as an alternate, I continued the trip.

The real headwind was 110 knots, my groundspeed less than 100. Still, after I passed the continental divide, my DME groundspeed readout picked up to about 130. While near the Mullan Pass VOR, I requested from Approach a pilot report by a United airliner going into Spokane International, 10 miles from my destination, Felts Field. International could become my alternate. United's report was heartening: He had had the city lights at 6,000 feet, and tops were at only 10,000, with but a trace of ice during the descent. Six thousand was well above the DH for most of the approaches, the outer marker was near the city, and the 4,000 feet of cloud I would penetrate would normally be of little consequence during the descent. As it turned out, the bases were variable. The tower later reported 300 feet broken-to-overcast.

The alternator was still out, and, perhaps, should have been a no-go item in that weather. Felts Field had two VOR approaches, the more commonly used being from the west, from over the VOR. I had that chart ready, but now my errors and problems began to compound. It had been a long, tiring flight under tough instrument conditions; the approach could be tight. Finally, Center made the turnover to Approach, who gave me an immediate clearance to descend to 9,000 and for the VOR-DME approach from the *east*. The Jepp book was open on the seat beside me, with the Spokane ILS chart on top. The chart for the Felts Field VOR Runway 3 (from the *west*) was on my kneepad.

Now, with this unexpected clearance, the manual got a quick shuffle. I got out the chart and set up to slither down the radial. This time, however, the radial was not to be had. The needle oscillated rapidly to full deflection from side to side; the identification was fine; the off/on flag was on. An investigation later showed that this could have been caused by drifted or heavy snow on the ground at the VOR.

Approach gave me a vector and clearance to continue, using DME distances for the descent points—sort of a modified ASR. At first, all went well—then the DME also became intermittent. A quick glance at the wing showed that there was more than a trace of ice developing. One by one, each of my planned "outs" was being left behind. Things were tight but not critical—yet.

Felts had an FSS that is used when the tower is not operational. Approach turned me over to it to get field conditions. Their report, the wild swings of the VOR needle, and the undependable DME forced an immediate change of plans. I aborted the approach to Felts and got a clearance for the Spokane International Runway 21 ILS. The outer marker was about 90 seconds away.

Up to that point, I had hand-flown the approach. Now that the ILS chart was needed, it was no longer readily available. I grabbed my flashlight. It would not work—not a glimmer! It had worked perfectly a few minutes before. No amount of shaking, whacking, or pounding could get it going. I turned on the autopilot to hold course and altitude while I reorganized. However, I inadvertently left it in the VOR-tracking mode. I turned on the overhead light long enough to sort out the manual and get the needed chart. The problems of the lights, my head movements, finding the chart, and weariness slowed the process.

The rapid swinging of the VOR signal caused the shear in the autopilot roll servo to do what it was designed to do—break. By the time flying the airplane got the attention it deserved, the Cessna had turned

180 degrees. It was in tight left bank, indicating about a two-needle-width rate. Luckily, the altitude hold had not been affected, or I might have come very close to a number of hills. I took the airplane under full control. The proper approach plate was now in place—and then the second alternator light began to flicker, indicating more serious electrical problems.

The electrical equipment would not last long just on the battery. Without a radio, getting down comfortably would be very doubtful. I shut down the heater, all exterior lights, the pitot heat, and the number-two radio. I would need the windshield deice. Ice was building faster now, although the accumulation on the airframe was not yet a problem. Other results of icing showed as the ASI dropped to about 40 and then to zero. It was to be attitude flying the rest of the way—my military training would be valuable.

About this time, I had occasional glimpses of the city lights through the muck. With passage of the outer marker, the ADF could be dispensed with. The electric flaps and landing gear would have to wait until a landing was assured, and then, if power was not available, I would have to go in on the belly. There would be no time to pump the gear. Plenty of airspeed on final was in order. The tower had mentioned that my turn had been observed, and now they asked if the crash wagons were needed.

Runway 21 has CAT II lighting, a beautiful sight—a landing was assured.

The next day, I found that the alternators were completely dead and would have to be replaced. My flashlight terminals and contacts had corroded, hence I now carry spare flashlights and batteries. Also, as a result of the VOR problems I encountered, both Felts Field VOR approaches were taken out of service for nearly six months. Few of us had known of the problem of heavy snow covering a VOR site, though most of our area's VORs are in heavy-snow territory.

A small equipment failure—the flashlight—nearly made that flight my last. Momentary lapses of priorities probably have caused many accidents. I obviously made other errors in judgment and execution. Adding unexpected distractions nearly proved deadly.

The decision to sneak through the flight with one alternator was the foundation of all that followed. One point among many to be gained from this and the previous account is the lulling attitude that flying regularly with less than a whole airplane can develop in a pilot, leading him to believe that he's made it before and therefore will again, that equipment problems are an acceptable fact of life, and that he can keep playing the odds and expect to beat them. Such daring is tantamount to equipmental scud running.

What to Dump and What to Keep

If the low-voltage light comes on, do not assume that you have lost the alternator or voltage regulator, but rather that a protective device against overvoltage may be operating. Turn off the alternator switch; the low-voltage light should then go out, if over voltage was the problem. Similarly, don't assume a dead alternator if a zero-left ammeter is showing any charge, though a lower than normal indication for the load you are putting on it (depending on which and how many devices you are using) may indicate trouble on the boil. For a third shot at the trouble, try to reset the alternate field circuit breaker or any breaker that may be protecting a faulty device. If the alternator breaker feels hot, let it be. If a breaker resists resetting, don't force it. Circuit breakers are protective devices. They sometimes err, but when they are stubborn, they are only doing their job. When a breaker that serves two devices refuses to reset, turn off the devices and try resetting with each one individually on, then with both on, leading with one device and then with the other. Eliminating one delinquent device may be all that is needed.

If you are reduced to battery power, act quickly upon an already formed plan. Assuming that you are flying IFR, your first two priorities are to turn off everything that isn't absolutely necessary for flight to the nearest airport and to tell ATC what has happened and what you want to do. Continue to your destination only if it is the nearest feasible airport.

If you are IFR in VFR conditions, your best bet will be to

cancel IFR and head for an airport. If you are in cloud, seek a vector to the nearest VFR airport or to an airport with an ASR or, better, a PAR approach. An ILS is the next best choice, because its minimums will be lower than for nonprecision approaches. Before your departure and while en route, determine where the nearest VFR lies, in case you lose all communication with the ground (more about communications loss shortly).

Transmitting consumes a great amount of electrical power. Although you will soon turn off your transponder, you may want to squawk 7700 as you call ATC, to get their immediate attention. If you are assuming that you can conserve no more than just an hour of electrical power—do assume that, unless you *know* that you have a new and fully charged battery and that you caught the alternator or generator loss quickly—be sure to inform ATC. To be conservative, keep only one nav on, over which you can receive transmissions. Tell ATC that you will remain silent until you reach or near either the IAF or a point the controller will designate. Thus all radios, save one nav, plus DME, internal and external lights, and the transponder will go off. Remember that you must save power for electrically driven flaps and the landing gear, although loss of these items is survivable.

You should have the appropriate Sectional at hand, but if you don't, you will need to get it out and unfolded. You may have to dive into your approach plate book; you may have to set up a way for your flashlight to illuminate the panel without your having to hold it. It could therefore pay to let the autopilot fly straight and level briefly as you set things up. An autopilot set for straight-and-level flight *in nonturbulent air* drains little power; any other mode will cost you. Get all your cockpit reorganization done promptly and then hand-fly. However, if the battery's endurance is in doubt, kill the autopilot right away. If there is heavy doubt, turn off all the electronics and dead reckon by heading, clock, and pilotage (if you have the ground) until a navaid or ATC vector becomes necessary.

In a total blackout, head immediately for where you can safely descend. Again, know your position, where the nearest VFR is, and how to dead reckon to the closest practicable airport. If you are reasonably near flat land or a large body of water, head that way if IFR conditions are pervasive.

If you lose the electronics, you can lose your fuel quantity indication. This can be frightening at first, but since gas gauges are not good guarantors anyway, it is smart to keep track of your fuel consumption (provided by the manufacturer and your own experience) by settings tables and the clock, all the way from start-up. At least every half hour or when you switch tanks, record the switch and the gauge indications, just in case. Pilots in crisis do forget where they last saw the needles. Fuel uncertainty is one big reason for an expedited landing. Should you run dry in cloud, maintaining a safe glide will be extremely difficult, especially if you must turn. Electrical failure could remove the turn coordinator, and the loss of the engine can kill the attitude indicator.

The Sounds of Silence

It doesn't take a total electrical failure to wipe out communications. In fact, com failure is not a rare event. Losing your radios VFR is, of course, a bother. You may even have to remember light gun signals.

IFR com loss is more serious but not necessarily catastrophic, if you know what to do, as set out in FAR 91.127—"IFR Operations: Two-Way Radio Communications Failure." If you do not abide by the rules, you can send high anxiety over traffic separation vibrating through the System.

Many pilots believe, if briefly, that they have a com failure when they are really suffering from impatience. The absence of an immediate response to a first or second call breeds assumption of the worst. Some callers leave the frequency too soon; others stop calling, instead of waiting reasonably or taking logical steps to make contact. Radios do go out, of course, and pilots are either given wrong frequencies or copy them wrong. Contact failure is more often procedural than mechanical, and there are remedies.

Jot down every frequency you are given, partly so you can return to the previous freq if the new guys, who may be sitting next to the old guys in the radar room, can't be raised. Using your en route and approach charts, have the published frequencies at hand to check against discrepancies. If they are talking on the new frequency but won't talk to you, listen for the presence of a problem that could be demanding the controller's full attention.

If you aren't receiving anything on a frequency, check your volume and squelch controls; make sure the audio switches are properly set. Has the earphone jack been accidentally kicked from its receptacle? Has an overzealous co-pilot flicked a switch or turned a knob? You might tune to Unicom—to see if you can receive any frequency—and then 121.5. Check the circuit breakers. Go from your headset to the speaker system or vice versa. If you are getting no results from your boom mike, try the hand mike. (A spare hand mike can be a blessing.) And remember that if two mikes are being used, they both will be silenced if even one jack is loose. Check also for a stuck keying button.

If you cannot hear, you cannot be sure if you have lost both audio and transmission or just one, so first try to contact ATC as if you can transmit. To indicate a communications emergency, squawk 7700 for one minute and then 7600, the communications-failure code, for 15. Turn up the reception on your nav, tuned to the VOR you are working, and tell ATC which VOR you are listening on. Be sure to pause long enough to let them answer. Keep squawking 7700–7600 as before, until contact is made. If your transmission is gone but you can receive, the controller may have you squawk ident or particular codes in answer to his questions about your condition. If you hear from no one, broadcast your intentions anyway.

As with total electrical failure IFR, losing communications IFR calls for a landing *as soon as practicable*. If you are in VFR conditions, land and call ATC from the airport to explain why you deviated from your clearance. If only partial com has been lost, tell ATC, if you can, that you are investigating the problem, will be silent for a bit to conserve power, and will recontact shortly, if you can. If a total electrical failure then occurs, ATC will know why your transponder suddenly stops squawking. While Center may not be able to track your primary radar return, terminal facilities can.

If you cannot get to VFR conditions, having lost your com but retained your nav, continue IFR you must. ATC expects that you will follow a specific procedure and hierarchy of options punctiliously, as they work to keep you separated from other aircraft. The procedures are based on the principle that you will do what both you and ATC can predict about your subsequent route. When communications are lost, follow *the most recent route for which you were cleared;* in other words, just keep going. However, if your clearance did not extend to your destination, fly the clearance to its limit, then fly *the route you were told to expect after the limit*. One reason for requesting an EFC (expect further clearance) time on receiving holding instructions is that if you lose communications during the hold, you and ATC will know when you will leave it. Similarly, if you are being vectored to a course or a fix, ask where you are being directed, so that you can go there if you lose your radios. If you were given no expected route, fly *the route you originally filed in your flight plan*. If the cleared and filed routes are not contiguous, make the best transition you can.

Do not make arbitrary changes if you are going to remain IFR. Fly the altitude you were last assigned. If you were told to expect an altitude change, go to that altitude at the time you would have been assigned the change.

Never fly below an MEA, even if your last assigned altitude lies below an approaching higher MEA. Climb to the new MEA.

The basic rule is to fly (1) the last assigned altitude, then (2) the expected altitude or (3) the minimum en route altitude, whichever is higher. When the MEA rises at a particular fix, begin the climb *upon reaching the fix*. If your climb performance is such that you cannot be sure of obstruction clearance, begin climbing shortly before reaching the fix. Such a circumstance is rare, but keep a good eye on the en route chart. A minimum crossing altitude (MCA) may be stipulated at a fix to provide adequate clearance of sharply rising terrain. On the chart, the MCA will be indicated by a flag, and the requisite altitude will be listed. *You must cross the fix at that altitude*.

As you approach your destination airport, trust that ATC will clear the airspace covering all the approaches for at least 30 minutes after your ETA, which is your liftoff time plus the estimated time en route filed in your flight plan. While you may shoot any approach you choose, you may not begin before your ETA, and you must start at the appropriate IAF. If you arrive at the IAF before your ETA, hold at the fix; if you must descend from your en route altitude to the IAF, do so in a holding pattern on the fix. Use common sense in descending, observing the MSAs as you plan the approach. If there is no published holding pattern for the IAF, hold on the approach course and on the procedure turn side—that is, use the airspace that is normally protected. Help ATC to anticipate your actions by conforming to the procedures with as little individual innovation as possible.

Fly the approach and missed approach procedures as if you had full communications. From the missed approach, go to your filed alternate by the most expeditious route. ATC will expect you to do so.

While these procedures may not cover *every* contingency, they are based upon the necessity of the pilot-System partnership working according to shared assumptions—the fewer the surprises, the safer the work. ATC's foremost concern is to keep blind traffic separated. Should you be in a tricky situation and in doubt, do what will keep you out of others' way. That isn't always easy to ascertain, but set procedures provide the best tools for a start, along with knowledge and common sense.

Systems failures can be survived, if the pilot uses to the utmost what remains available, maintaining a clear mind and sound priorities.

The Defense That Dares Not Rest

We have come a long way through crises that have killed, injured, and terrified pilots and passengers. As we have seen, some crises can verge on being acts of God or gremlins, but the overwhelming majority become mortal threats because the pilot's defense in some way fails. If not every crisis can be prevented, most can, or at least can be survived, but it takes effort, knowledge, and, above all, judgment.

Among all systems failures, a pilot's lack of judgment is the worst. A truly tragic condition is good judgment that wants to work but is thwarted by what we choose to call . . .

The Dirty Harry Syndrome

As you have no doubt seen, Dirty Harry Callahan is a cinematic San Francisco cop (played by Clint Eastwood) who crashes automobiles through store fronts at will, commits small massacres with a large-caliber handgun, self-righteously breaks the professional rules by which he is charged to maintain public order, and with a hard eye and a cold heart, dares his enemies to attack him. "Go on," he taunts them "make my day," anticipating the move that will justify his blowing them away. And when Harry has wasted his foes, he is apt to moralize on their gall: "A man's just gotta know his limitations."

The saving presence of stuntmen, cameramen, special effects men, and guardian-angel scriptwriters enables Harry to survive his hectic days. In *our* world, Harry, who gets to have no limitations and who personifies pure impulse and instinct untempered by good judgment, would be fast-tracked to a prison, or an asylum, or a cemetery. His hide may be tough, but his judgment is weak.

Good judgment is the foundation of safe flying, yet a little touch of Harry lurks in the human weakness we all share. Pilots get into trouble when they are guided by impulse and instinct rather than by adequate thought and prudence. Researchers from the FAA and Embry-Riddle Aeronautical University have analyzed judgment and instinct and have identified five mind-sets that are good judgment's worst adversaries:

• *Antiauthoritarianism.* Resentment of established rules and procedures that prevent a person from doing things his own way. The antiauthoritarian thinker rejects good advice (for example, "VFR not recommended"), no matter how well-founded it may be.

• *Impulsivity.* The reflexive habit of doing the first thing that comes to mind when a decision is to be made. Impulsivity precludes an evaluation of alternatives (such as, fly the missed approach, don't bust minimums) and analyzing the implications of a decision or act.

• *Invulnerability.* The self-deception that one is immune from a harmful occurrence. The "invulnerable" pilot believes that accidents happen only to other people and is therefore prone to take risks and push them ever further. ("I've made it with low fuel before, why not this time?")

• *Macho.* This hazardous thought pattern is closely associated with overconfidence but is manifested by an urge to engage in overly difficult actions to impress other people. ("You're not fretting about a li'l ol' thunderbumper, are you?" or "Short? You think this field is short for a night landing? Just *watch!*")

• *External control.* A mind-set in which a person feels that he can do little, if anything, to control what happens to him. The completion of a safe flight is attributed to good luck ("Cheated fate again!''); an accident or incident, to bad luck (''Just wasn't my day''). Such a person tends to depend on other people to make decisions and to take action for him (for example, the magical controller and his miraculous vectors).

Dirty Harry probably would put these patterns on his list of ''Things to Reinforce Today.'' We pilots, in contrast, are responsible for clearing such patterns out of our thinking.

Making a first error in judgment is like falling down a step. Unchecked, the momentum of making one and then another and another bad decision is like that of rolling down a staircase to the inevitable crunch. As the many accounts in this book illustrate, aircraft accidents are usually caused not by a single error of judgment but by an accelerating progression of them. Just as fatigue, illness, or booze can tunnel our vision, so can poor judgment push critical realities from our minds.

Researchers have made the important discovery that judgment is not purely innate but can be *learned*. It has been said that our mistakes are stored tools for future use, like stones on which to hone our skills. Avoiding the many cockpit crises we have described, through such storing and honing, has been the object of this book.

INDEX